Retrieving Bones

Stories and Poems of the Korean War

Edited and with an Introduction by
W. D. Ehrhart and
Philip K. Jason

Rutgers University Press
New Brunswick, New Jersey, and London

Library of Congress Cataloging-in-Publication Data

Retrieving bones: Stories and poems of the Korean War / edited by W. D. Ehrhart
and Philip K. Jason.
     p.   cm.
Includes bibliographical references.
    ISBN 0-8135-2638-8 (cloth : alk. paper). — ISBN 0-8135-2639-6
(paper : alk. paper)
    1. Korean War, 1950–1953—Literary collections.   2. American literature—
20th century.   3. War stories, American.   4. War poetry, American.
I. Ehrhart, W. D. (William Daniel), 1948–   . II. Jason, Philip K., 1941–
PS509.K67R48   1999
810.8'0358—dc21   98-52668
                                                  CIP

British Cataloging-in-Publication data for this book is available from the
British Library

Manufactured in the United States of America

Contents

Ode for the American Dead in Asia*

1.

God love you now, if no one else will ever,
Corpse in the paddy, or dead on a high hill
In the fine and ruinous summer of a war
You never wanted. All your false flags were
Of bravery and ignorance, like grade school maps:
Colors of countries you would never see—
Until that weekend in eternity
When, laughing, well armed, perfectly ready to kill
The world and your brother, the safe commanders sent
You into your future. Oh, dead on a hill,
Dead in a paddy, leeched and tumbled to
A tomb of footnotes. We mourn a changeling: you:
Handselled to poverty and drummed to war
By distinguished masters whom you never knew.

2.

The bee that spins his metal from the sun,
The shy mole drifting like a miner ghost
Through midnight earth—all happy creatures run
As strict as trains on rails the circuits of
Blind instinct. Happy in your summer follies,
You mined a culture that was mined for war:
The state to mold you, church to bless, and always
The elders to confirm you in your ignorance.
No scholar put your thinking cap on nor
Warned that in dead seas fishes died in schools
Before inventing legs to walk the land.
The rulers stuck a tennis racket in your hand,
An Ark against the flood. In time of change
Courage is not enough: the blind mole dies,
And you on your hill, who did not know the rules.

---

*Originally titled "Ode for the American Dead in Korea," then retitled in the early 1970s during the
Vietnam War.

3.

Wet in the windy counties of the dawn
The lone crow skirls his draggled passage home:
And God (whose sparrows fall aslant his gaze,
Like grace or confetti) blinks and he is gone,
And you are gone. Your scarecrow valor grows
And rusts like early lilac while the rose
Blooms in Dakota and the stock exchange
Flowers. Roses, rents, all things conspire
To crown your death with wreaths of living fire.
And the public mourners come: the politic tear
Is cast in the Forum. But, in another year,
We will mourn you, whose fossil courage fills
The limestone histories: brave: ignorant: amazed:
Dead in the rice paddies, dead on the nameless hills.

Thomas McGrath

Maps

EAST ASIA

USSR

CHINA

SEA
OF
JAPAN

JAPAN

38TH°N PARALLEL

KOREA

YELLOW
SEA

PACIFIC OCEAN

EAST CHINA
SEA

RYUKYU
ISLANDS

TAIWAN

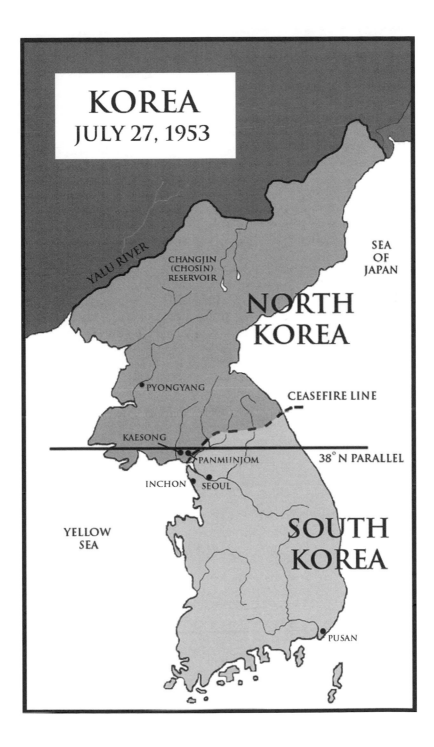

KOREA
JULY 27, 1953

YALU RIVER

CHANGJIN
(CHOSIN)
RESERVOIR

SEA
OF
JAPAN

NORTH
KOREA

PYONGYANG

CEASEFIRE LINE

KAESONG

PANMUNJOM

38° N PARALLEL

INCHON   SEOUL

YELLOW
SEA

SOUTH
KOREA

PUSAN

Introduction

Historical and Literary Contexts

On June 25th, 1950, North Korean troops crossed the 38th parallel, the demarcation line between Kim Il Sung's communist North Korea and the non-communist south (Republic of Korea, or ROK) established by the Allied victors at the end of World War II. It was a full-scale assault, the object of which was the reunification of the Korean peninsula by force of arms. Whether the attack was entirely unprovoked or not is a matter of debate; certainly US-backed autocrat Syngman Rhee had made no secret of his desire to conquer the north by military force. In any case, the attack caught both South Koreans and Americans completely off-guard and disastrously unprepared. The North Korean army reached and took Seoul, Rhee's capital, in just a few days, and by September, subjected to defeat after defeat, US/ROK forces held on by their fingernails to a tiny perimeter around the southernmost port city of Pusan.

But the North Koreans had exhausted themselves and could not penetrate what came to be known as the Pusan Perimeter, and soon the sheer weight and volume of American industrial might combined with the rapid mobilization of draftees and reservists allowed US/ROK forces to drive the North Koreans out of South Korea. But they did not stop at that. By November, US/ROK forces held most of North Korea as well, and were approaching the Yalu River, the boundary between North Korea and newly communist China, in spite of Chinese warnings to keep away.

The Chinese meant what they said, however, and as the harsh Korean winter was just beginning to settle in, tens and scores of thousands of Chinese "volunteers" smashed into the approaching US/ROK forces, sending them for a second time in six months into headlong retreat that did not stop until Seoul had been lost again. But by then communist supply lines were once more stretched thin and US/ROK forces, with shorter supply lines and vast amounts of materiel, were able to push the communist armies out of Seoul and back to the 38th parallel where the fighting had begun almost a year earlier. Along this line, for another two years and more while truce negotiations dragged on and on and on, a war of attrition was waged, rivaling in ferocity and futility if not in size the trench warfare along the Western Front during the Great War.

By the time the truce was finally signed on July 27th, 1953, somewhere over a million Americans had fought in Korea, with peak strength reaching 440,000 in the spring of 1953. Fifty-four thousand Americans died there, and twice that many were wounded.[1] By way of comparison, the Korean War lasted twice as long as American engagement in World War I and only seven months less than American engagement in World War II. Almost as many soldiers died in Korea as would die later in Vietnam (54,000 to 58,000), though the Korean War lasted only one-third as long. To call what happened in Korea a "police action" or a "conflict" was and is to play semantic games at the expense of reality. It was a war.

In legal theory, it was a war fought under the United Nations flag, and more than a dozen countries sent military forces to Korea, ranging from 60,000 British troops to a single platoon from Luxembourg. In truth, however, a US-initiated resolution to fight in Korea passed the UN Security Council only because the Soviet Union was boycotting council sessions at the time. The "UN police action" was in reality an armed extension of US foreign policy, directed and controlled by the US government and its military, and fought largely by American and, in even greater numbers, South Korean forces.

There were many reasons for the lack of US/ROK preparation and for the nearly disastrous consequences. Having helped to establish a client state in South Korea, US leaders were largely focused on the growing Cold War with the Soviet Union, the main battleground of which in the 1940s and 1950s seemed to be Europe. America's citizens wanted life to be "normal" after the long ordeals of the Great Depression and World War II. No one wanted to take rumors of impending war between the two Koreas seriously. Indeed, in a speech in January 1950, Dean Acheson, President Harry

S. Truman's secretary of state, did not include South Korea among the nations of Asia the United States considered vital to its national interests.

Only when North Korea invaded South Korea did US policymakers decide that this apparent extension of the Cold War turned hot would have to be challenged. But the closest available US forces in Japan and the Philippines were essentially peacetime occupation forces: a constabulary in military uniform. Moreover, because the US feared its own client Syngman Rhee might invade North Korea if he felt strong enough to do so, the training and equipment of the ROK army at the outset of the fighting were no better than that of US forces in Asia. Militarily, neither South Korea nor the United States was ready for what occurred in June 1950.

Moreover, US civilian and military leaders had difficulty determining how to respond to the Korean situation or what to choose as appropriate and obtainable goals. The Supreme Commander in Asia, the by-then-legendary General Douglas MacArthur, complicated matters with his daring and brilliantly successful landing at Inchon in September 1950. This action, which cut off North Korean forces besieging the Pusan Perimeter far to the south and forced a hasty North Korean withdrawal, suddenly made total defeat of North Korea seem possible. MacArthur's confidence in an early and complete victory and his own unwillingness in November 1950 to accept the new reality of Chinese intervention nearly spelled disaster and defeat for a second time in the first six months of the war.

At the outset, the stated objective of the US was to restore the security of South Korea, to push the invader back above the 38th parallel. However, after the resounding success of the Inchon landing, the mission clearly changed to that of defeating communism on the Korean peninsula and reuniting the country under Syngman Rhee. Once China entered the war, US policymakers soon realized they would have to settle for the original, more modest goal.

In the minds of many, little was accomplished at great cost. Though South Korea ended up with a modest net gain in territory, the line of demarcation at the war's outbreak, the famous 38th parallel, was essentially the line of demarcation at its conclusion. Though the containment of North Korea was achieved and South Korea has prospered in the decades that have followed the conclusion of open hostilities, the North Korean threat to South Korean security has remained potent. Large numbers of US forces (up to 40,000) have been stationed in South Korea continuously for nearly half a century to help guard against the threat of another North Korean invasion. From the perspective of how the Vietnam War ended—the total defeat of the US client state and reunification of all of Vietnam under a communist regime—the resolution in Korea now looks somewhat more positive than it once did. Nevertheless, it was only a return to the uneasy status quo that had prevailed at the outset.

The Korean War was the superhot flashpoint in the ironically named Cold War waged otherwise on political and economic fronts between the United States and its allies and clients and the Union of Soviet Socialist Republics and its allies and clients, between capitalism and communism. It both shaped and was shaped by the Cold War in significant ways, most notably by being America's first "limited" war. While some US strategists in and out of the military—MacArthur among them—were sure that attacks against China itself would bring the war to a hasty conclusion, most feared that expanding the war beyond the Korean peninsula risked either an unwinnable land war with China or direct Soviet intervention. The latter possibility raised the spectre of World War III and an exchange of nuclear weapons (the USSR having exploded an atom bomb in 1949). Truman finally relieved MacArthur of command at least in part because MacArthur simply could not accept fighting a limited war. Even though his firing caused a major public outcry, most Americans were not ready for another war on a grand scale only five years after the end of World War II.

Indeed, the build-up of troops and supplies in Korea was carried out reluctantly. Policymakers and planners perceived Korea as a deliberate communist diversion from the real battlegrounds between the US and the USSR in Europe and Japan (a perception dependent upon communism as a monolithic movement directed from Moscow, which history has subsequently proven to be largely incorrect). At the same time, ordinary Americans and their elected representatives did not want to take seriously either the commitment to South Korea or the threat to US forces already on hand.

The first Americans called up to fight in Korea were mostly reservists who had served in World War II and who had begun to build families and careers. Their reluctance to be called upon again is and was understandable, but it took about a year before properly trained younger recruits reached Korea in significant numbers. Meanwhile, when General Matthew Ridgway took command of the 8th Army in Korea in December 1950 after the death in a jeep accident of the former commander, Walton Walker, he found a dispirited fighting force in the midst of its second major retreat. His soldiers were victims of betrayal on many levels: unsure objectives, insufficient numbers and training, equipment shortages, inappropriate clothing, and ignorance of the enemy's guerrilla tactics could all be attributed to errors in leadership, if not outright indifference.

Moreover, relations between US and ROK troops were always uneasy and often hostile. Language and cultural barriers were never successfully bridged. Most attempts to integrate ROK draftees into US units failed dismally. ROK draftees often seemed to Americans to be less than committed soldiers while the insensitivity of many American soldiers to Koreans (calling them "gooks," for instance, or the routine propositioning of women and girls) created deep resentment among our allies. Because Americans couldn't tell the difference between North and South Koreans either by language or by appearance, enemy infiltration was especially demoralizing, as it would be more than a decade later in Vietnam, and led to Americans tending to distrust any and all Koreans they encountered and treating them accordingly.

All of these things will sound familiar to anyone who fought in or has studied the Vietnam War, and in fact there are many parallels between the two wars, among them the US decision not to use nuclear weapons for fear that the Soviets would feel compelled to respond in kind; US support for regimes that were, while noncommunist, nevertheless autocratic, unrepresentative, and unpopular; the existence of "sanctuary" territory for communist forces (in China during the Korean War, in Cambodia during the Vietnam War); individual troop rotation (in Korea based on a point system, in Vietnam based solely on time in country); and the awkward situation of simultaneously fighting and negotiating. Helicopters, flak jackets, and night vision devices were used in Korea long before becoming "unique" to Vietnam, and many Vietnam War veterans might be surprised to hear that the word "gook" predates their war as well. (It may even predate the Korean War.)

In fact, the Americans in Korea were learning—or should have been learning—lessons they would have to relearn in Vietnam. Air supremacy was necessary, for instance, but it was not sufficient to sever supply lines, especially when enemy troops were not dependent on roads, moved at night, and individually carried much of what they needed for sustenance and combat. Climate and terrain were as much adversaries as enemy forces. Equipment and training that had served adequately in the past were not appropriate in the circumstances. Unreliable maps were worse than no maps at all. Language and cultural barriers made teamwork with client forces extremely difficult (some would say impossible). An enemy's commitment and perseverance could far exceed its observable resources. And long periods of inactivity or low activity (while truces were being negotiated) were detrimental to morale and discipline.

US commanders were also learning in Korea—or once again, should have learned—that it made a difference to soldiers to know one's fellow citizens supported them. Though there was no antiwar movement like the one that arose in opposition to the Vietnam War, public support for the Korean War, initially very strong, dwindled away as US casualties mounted and the war dragged on with no victory in sight. The American economy in the early 1950s was strong, and most Americans were able to get on with their lives as though there were no war. These circumstances left soldiers in Korea to wonder if anyone beyond their families and friends and a few politicians even knew a war was going on.

They had good reason to wonder. According to Robert J. Donovan, network evening news programs were only fifteen minutes long during the Korean War years, and the brief segments on Korea consisted of newsreel footage, often of poor quality, with the more gruesome scenes of battle usually edited out. The long delay between the events depicted and their appearance on TV news programs, caused by the need to process film and fly it from Korea to the US, further reduced any sense of immediacy. There was also nothing like the regular nationwide news shows that we have become used to until NBC developed "Today" in 1952. The only regular reporting of the war on television, an NBC Sunday afternoon show called "Battle Report," relied on information supplied largely by administration officials. Radio coverage, filled with obscure Korean place names, brought home only the foreignness of the enterprise. Though there was excellent daily newspaper coverage, US citizens were moving quickly to other parts of the paper.

A year after the commencement of hostilities—a year that saw the front lines shifting almost constantly and often precipitously—a fairly stable front was finally achieved, US/ROK and North Korean/Chinese forces thereafter maintaining largely defensive positions and probing for advantage through two more years of tediously slow negotiations. Though there was considerable bloodshed in those two years, the fighting covered a narrow territorial range. The air war grew in magnitude and intensity, but with no visible impact on the ground. Often, great numbers of lives were lost in battles to take and retake and retake yet again this hill or that one. (S.L.A. Marshall's *Pork Chop Hill* is the definitive and masterful narrative of such operations.) Yet clearly there was stalemate: neither side could budge the other without risking complete exhaustion and/or uncontrollable escalation. When the truce was finally signed in the summer of 1953 (there has never been a peace treaty), it had the flavor of anticlimax. Servicemen returned to a country that had little interest in, understanding of, or appreciation for what they had been through.

Thus, literary responses to the Korean War did not find an eager readership, and certainly not a sustained level of interest. Although dozens of novels were written and published, only Pat Frank's *Hold Back the Night* (1951), James Michener's *The Bridges of Toko-Ri* (1953), and Richard Hooker's *M*A*S*H* (1968) maintained themselves in print for any length of time, and none of these ever acquired the stature or readership of such classic World War II novels as Norman Mailer's *The Naked and the Dead* (1948), James Jones's *From Here to Eternity* (1951), or Joseph Heller's *Catch-22* (1961). For every novel of the Korean War published through the 1950s and 1960s, there were many more published about World War II.

The reasons are undoubtedly many and complex. World War II was perceived as a grand and global crusade to save the world itself, to save civilization, and it ended in clearcut victory with the United States of America bestriding the world, unchallenged in its military and economic supremacy. That was something to read about. Who wanted to read about a backwater war that possessed neither grand scale nor apparent nobility and that ended not with a bang but a whimper? Who wanted to remember, let alone deal with, the ambiguities and uncertainties of limited war? Who wanted to be reminded that the most powerful nation on earth had been frustrated (and nearly defeated not once but twice) by a bunch of unsophisticated Asian peasants in sneakers? The Korean War did not capture the American popular imagination.

Similarly, the literary output from the Vietnam War, which began in the late 1960s and gained momentum in the 1970s, overwhelmed the relative trickle of imaginative representations dealing with the Korean War. For though the Vietnam War also lacked nobility (presidential candidate Ronald Reagan's famous 1980 quote notwithstanding), was similarly ambiguous and uncertain, and ended badly (much worse than the Korean War from the point of view of most Americans), it too captured the American popular imagination just as powerfully as did World War II.

Again, the reasons why are undoubtedly many and complex, but World War II and the Vietnam War each touched the very fabric of the society, altered an entire generation, and changed both the perception and self-perception of the nation on the world stage in ways that the Korean War simply did not.

Literarily, books like Michael Herr's *Dispatches* (1977) and Tim O'Brien's *Going After Cacciato* (1978) and *The Things They Carried* (1990) have achieved a stature equal to those of Jones, Mailer, and Heller. Indeed, the critical and commercial success of Vietnam War publications produced a second wave of Korean War novels in the 1980s and 1990s (the first having come in the 1950s and 1960s). Already by the late 1960s, novels of the Korean War were being influenced by that monumental cultural juggernaut known as "the Vietnam Experience," and the Korean War was losing whatever distinctiveness it possessed as a coherent pattern of memory and symbolization. (Consider, for instance, that the movie and television series based on Hooker's novel *M*A*S*H* were from the very start perceived by most viewers to be "really" about the Vietnam War, not the Korean War.) The Korean War, which was situated first in the shadow of World War II, lived on (barely) in the shadow of the Vietnam War, though perhaps it should have been the other way around.

Certainly for those who fought there, for those who maintained the military establishment, and for those who reported the war, Korea had its distinction. The scale of the war was sufficient to justify its recognition as a major episode in US history. Yet students today know almost nothing about it. It is read as a footnote or as a prelude to engagements that have much deeper and more intense cultural penetration. Though the pages of popular magazines such as *Collier's* and the *Saturday Evening Post* regularly published illustrated feature articles about the war as well as many short stories, more highbrow publications dealt with it primarily on the plain of political debate and denied it the life-pulse of narrative representation. One can leaf through the university-based journals of the 1950s and find only the scantiest traces of a Korean War. Editors and publishers mostly kept Korea cold by making the heat of lived experience, whether related as memoir or fiction or poetry, unavailable.

Though a number of presses did chance to bring novels to the marketplace, few publishers or specialists in contemporary literature found shorter literary reflections of the Korean War to be suitable materials for anthology representation. A few stories made it into general anthologies from time to time, but the only gathering of short fiction devoted entirely to the Korean War is Albert B. Tibbets's *Courage in Korea: Stories of the Korean War* (1962). Tibbets collects ten stories, but represents only six authors. He presents four pieces by William Chamberlain, two by Emile C. Schurmacher, and one each by W. Douglas Lansford, John Godey, Francis Chase, Jr., and Jacland Marmur. Schurmacher's pieces had first appeared in the men's magazines *Saga* and *Stag*. Those by Chamberlain, Lansford, Chase, and Marmur appeared in the *Saturday Evening Post*. Godey's appeared in *Collier's*. Thus, of the ten stories, seven were first seen by the readers of a single, though enormously influential, weekly magazine. This balance, or imbalance, is in part a reflection of the periodical marketplace for Korean War literature during the 1950s.

However, Tibbets's selection policy is further influenced by his title theme: courage. In an introductory essay, "'No Farther,' Said the Young Men," Tibbets presents the characters in these stories as stand-ins for the young men who stood by the promises of the United States and the United Nations to save South Korea from communist aggression. He chooses stories that portray their "hardship and suffering . . . as they made their gallant, unyielding stand in that distant land" (xiv). Thus, *Courage in Korea* is quite self-consciously a flag-waving collection. It provides a narrow view drawn from a narrow sampling.

In his more wide-ranging *American Heroes All* (1966), Tibbets represents the Korean War only once with yet another William Chamberlain/*Saturday Evening Post* story.

In between the two war anthologies by Tibbets came what is perhaps the most successful anthology of American war literature of its era: F. Van Wyck Mason's *American Men at Arms* (1964). Unlike Tibbets, Mason represents the fictional realm of combat experience primarily by excerpting novels. His

Korean War section presents passages from Glen Ross's *The Last Campaign*, Quentin Reynolds's *Known But to God*, Ernest Frankel's *Band of Brothers*, Michener's *The Bridges of Toko-Ri*, Curt Anders's *The Price of Courage*, and Thomas Anderson's *Your Own Beloved Sons*. Mason also offers a passage from Rod Serling's play, *The Rack*. Only two short narratives are presented that were written to be complete in themselves: "A Plethora of Sergeants" from John Sack's collection of vignettes *From Here to Shimbashi*, and Jacland Marmur's story "The Bloodstained Beach" (the one title that overlaps with Tibbets's selections). One benefit of Mason's approach is that his selections have, on the whole, greater literary merit than those of Tibbets. However, it seems clear that his guiding purpose is to give little tastes of novels rather than to seek out worthy short fiction.

Later short story collections tend to erase the Korean War. In putting together *Soldiers and Civilians: Americans at War and at Home* (1986), Tom Jenks selects nothing to represent either the experience of those who served in Korea or the stateside lives influenced by that war. Paul Fussell's *The Norton Book of Modern War* (1991) includes neither fiction nor poetry about Korea, but only nonfiction pieces by Marguerite Higgins and Jean Larteguy. Critics and historians of war literature have been similarly neglectful. Peter Aichinger, in *The American Soldier in Fiction, 1880–1963* (1975), provides a four-page chapter that covers only three titles. Jeffrey Walsh's *American War Literature 1914 to Vietnam* (1982) has no discussion of Korean War literature at all. A fleeting reference to *M*A*S*H* places it as a Vietnam War novel. Only Arne Axelsson's *Restrained Response: American Novels of the Cold War and Korea, 1945–1962* (1990) gives significant attention to Korean War fiction—though no attention to short stories. With scant attention by anthologists and critics, it's no wonder that the prevailing view is that few, if any, writers had their imaginations sparked by the war in Korea.

The prevailing view is wrong. If there is not a great wealth of literature from the Korean War comparable to the bodies produced from either World War II or the Vietnam War, there is nevertheless significant work in multiple genres worth retrieving, examining, and retaining. We have opted here to emphasize those works of merit that can be presented whole and complete in an anthology format, that is to say: short stories and poems. (The few apparent exceptions to this guideline will be explained forthwith.) These, as it happens, are also the forms that have most suffered from neglect. An annotated reading list elsewhere in this book, developed primarily by Colonel James R. Kerin, Jr., of the English Department at the US Military Academy, will point to many of the more significant longer literary works.

It is perhaps surprising how few of the writers who published short stories about the war actually served in it, especially when compared to the novelists and poets. Much of the short fiction of the Korean War was written by people with some military experience—perhaps in World War II, perhaps in Korea before or after the years of fighting, perhaps stateside during the war—whose imaginations, military experiences, and passionate attention to the story-telling potential of the war led them to fashion these narratives. Many, like William Chamberlain, were already professional writers who found in the nonfiction accounts and eyewitness testimonies more than enough material for whatever readership they could engage during and shortly after the years of fighting in Korea. Of those authors of short fiction who did serve in Korea, the interested reader might elsewhere make the acquaintance of Richard Blum (*The Late Lt. Dessin and Other Stories*, 1967), Salvatore La Puma (*Teaching Angels to Fly*, 1992), and John Schultz (*The Tongues of Men*, 1969). Though we did not include any of their stories for a variety of reasons (set in Japan rather than Korea, set in Korea but post-July 1953, or simply too long for our anthology format), we commend each of these writers to your attention.

The Writers and Their Works

Meanwhile, we offer the following assortment of tales. We have tried to arrange them more or less in chronological order based on the internal action of each story.

"Rice" by **Henry Steiner** comes at the opening of this collection to represent the situation in South Korea before the outbreak of the war—or, to put it another way, after the end of World War II. The US ran a full-scale military government in Korea for three years (1945–1948), reshaping institutions formed under half a century of Japanese colonial rule and unwittingly preparing for the police state that was to follow.

Henry Malcolm Steiner was born in San Francisco in 1923. After receiving a degree in engineering from Stanford in 1945, he began what became a most distinguished career as a practicing engineer and (after earning his Stanford PhD in 1965) an engineering professor. Since 1976 he has been professor of engineering administration at George Washington University. His various contracts, consultancies, and academic appointments have taken him to Mexico, Central and South America, and Saudi Arabia. As a young man, Steiner also wrote fiction before turning his attention exclusively to engineering, publishing stories in *Prairie Schooner*, *Epoch*, and *The Mexican Quarterly Review* among others. Before all that, however, at the outset of his career, he spent 1946–1947 in Korea as an engineering field supervisor under Military Government auspices.[2]

In "Rice," Steiner captures the struggling but submerged Korean national character in his portraiture of Japanese, Chinese, and "friendly" American influences. Mr. Han is suspicious of the claim that his fellow Koreans will benefit from the new government's pricing policy. To him, it is no better than the outright theft characteristic of Japan's imperialist regime, and he curses at Mr. Song—the unfortunate go-between—in Japanese to make his point. Song, perhaps ousted from his university position in the wake of institutional upheavals, is a misplaced person, an awkward lackey for Military Government policies. The Americans, Captain Frazer and Sergeant Biancoli, are functionaries in a system they only somewhat understand among a people they do not understand at all. "Rice," then, is a story of compromised attempts to bring stability to an unstable situation. It is also a story of contrasting sensibilities thrown together in a situation that makes full understanding and communication hopeless.

Like Steiner, **Vern Sneider** also worked in South Korea during the time of US Military Government control. Born as Vernon Sneider near Monroe, Michigan, in 1916, he received his AB in philosophy from Notre Dame University in 1940, and a year later began eighteen months of army service in the Aleutian Islands. In 1945, he was sent to the Military Government School at Princeton and subsequently assigned to an occupation team that landed on Okinawa in April, soon after the US wrested control of the island from Japan. Sneider served there as commander of Tobaru Village, which after several years he transformed into the setting for his famous novel *Teahouse of the August Moon* (1951), later successfully adapted as a stage play and a movie. Sneider next served as a US civilian administrator in Korea. He was in charge of reopening welfare and education programs in Kyonggi province, which includes Seoul. Many of the stories collected in *A Long Way* *from Home* (1956) are drawn from his observations while stationed in Korea between the end of World War II and the outbreak of the Korean War.

The title story, which we include here, reveals Sneider's deep sympathy for the Korean people and his sensitivity to the impact of contrasting cultures so well displayed in his popular novel. Beyond the issue of contrast is that of cultural imperialism. Kim's own identity is threatened by his fondness for and dependence on the American military establishment which is at once his country's savior, protector, and exploiter. On a cultural level, this American establishment is no less of a challenge than an enemy's invading army. Sneider seems aware of the danger even as his light, sentimental touch undercuts its true seriousness.

Sneider's other books are *A Pail of Oysters* (1953, set on Formosa), *The King from Ashtabula* (1960, set in a small Pacific island nation), and *West of North Star* (1972). After a long career as a short story and television writer, Sneider died in 1981.

Best known as an awardwinning, bestselling detective novelist for his Dave Robicheaux books, **James Lee Burke** spent a long apprenticeship during which he won critical acclaim without developing a steady readership. Born in 1936 in Texas, Burke grew up in Houston as well as in New Iberia, Louisiana (home of his famous detective). He attended the University of Southwestern Louisiana for two years, then transferred in 1957 to the University of Missouri where he completed a BA in 1959 and an MA in 1960.

By the 1980s he was teaching American literature and creative writing at Wichita State University. Several early novels were followed by a story collection, *The Convict* (1985), which included the Korean War tale that had previously appeared in *Cimarron Review*. One of his most widely acclaimed novels of this period is *The Lost Get-Back Boogie* (1986), which features a Korean War veteran. Soon after, Burke published *The Neon Rain* (1987), initiating the detective series that has brought him fortune as well as fame. Though he never served in the military, Burke gives an authentic Vietnam War background to detective Robicheaux and a Korean War background to Robicheaux's superior in the New Iberia Sheriff's Department.

By setting "We Build Churches, Inc." in November of 1950, Burke can allow his narrator to register the surprise of confronting Chinese troops following the near-defeat of North Korea that brought US/ROK forces almost to the Yalu River (ROK units and several US recon units actually reached the Yalu briefly). The "potato masher" thrown by the North Koreans is a cylindrical concussion grenade mounted on a wooden handle. This "stick grenade" or "chicom hand grenade" (for Chinese Communist) was later used by Viet Cong and North Vietnamese Army soldiers.

Just as convincing as these details of chronology and weaponry are the portraits of Doc (the narrator), Jace Bradford, and Willard Posey. Bradford's story of his Puritan church-building heritage and its connection with the accumulation of real estate has an eerie association with the concept of American do-gooder imperialism. The confusion that comes with the Chinese attack is handled with economy and precision, as is the ensuing slaughter. So, too, is the transmutation of Bradford's story and the reference to the cloud formation that looks like Jesus Christ (this part of Burke's story has a basis in newspaper accounts and a published photograph) into Doc's search for redemptive action and faith while a POW. More "literary" than many of the other stories selected for this collection, "We Build Churches, Inc." is also most fully a work of the creative imagination, though Burke surely knows firsthand the odd mixture of goodheartedness and racism in a character like Willard Posey.

In his short life, **Eugene Burdick** produced several major commercial successes, some of which have continuing effects in American popular and political culture. Born in 1918 in Sheldon, Iowa, he earned a BA from Stanford University in 1942. Upon graduation, he entered the navy, serving twenty-six months in the Pacific as a gunnery officer. Burdick left the service in 1946 as a lieutenant commander. The same year, he published a story in *Harper's* that was selected for the *Prize Stories of 1947: The O. Henry Awards*. A Rhodes Scholar, he completed his PhD in 1950 and went on to build his career as a political theorist at the University of California, Berkeley, an association he maintained until his death in 1965.

Burdick mixed his love of political science with his aspirations as a writer. His novel *The Ninth Wave* (1956) proved that there was an audience for fiction based on political issues and thought. Two years later, his collaboration with William J. Lederer produced *The Ugly American*, a book that galvanized cold war political positions. In the following years, Burdick wrote or co-wrote several more novels: *Fail-Safe* (1962), *The 480* (1964), *Sarkhan* (1965), and *Nina's Book* (1965). *The Blue of Capricorn* (1961) is a collection of fiction and nonfiction narratives set in the South Pacific. Burdick also contributed to professional journals and fashioned scripts for film and television.

The posthumous collection *A Role in Manila: Fifteen Tales of War, Postwar, Peace, and Adventure* (1966) brought together much of Burdick's early short fiction. "Cold Day, Cold Fear," which first appeared in *Collier's* in 1951, shows several sides of Burdick: the cold warrior, the entertainer, and also the compassionate humanist. Like many narratives of the Korean War (most notable in this regard is James Brady's memoir *The Coldest War*), Burdick's story attends to the extreme weather conditions. The cold becomes more than a literal reality; it gains metaphorical power. Burdick is also concerned with representing a strained, hesitant comradeship between the American soldier and the South Korean who has been assigned to his company. The closing references to napalm and to a helicopter rescue remind us not only that these icons of the Vietnam War had been used in the Korean War (indeed, they had been employed, though on a much smaller scale, in World War II) but also that they appeared in Korean War literature before there was ever such a thing as Vietnam War literature.

William Chamberlain, born Edwin William Chamberlain in 1903 in Challis, Idaho, attended the University of Idaho for two years before entering the US Military Academy with the class of 1927. During his West Point years, he showed his literary inclinations by working on the cadet magazine. Upon graduation, Chamberlain began a twenty-year career that included service in the G3 Division of the War Department General Staff during World War II. He retired as a brigadier general in 1946.

Soon after retirement from the service, Chamberlain began a successful career as a short story writer and novelist. His specialties were western, combat, and cold war narratives. Typical Chamberlain titles are *Trumpets of Company K* (1954), *Combat General* (1963), *Red January* (1964), and *China Strike* (1967). The summer 1966 issue of *Assembly*, the US Military Academy alumni magazine, announced that "Bill Chamberlain died in El Paso, where he had moved from the Washington area several years ago, continuing his work as an active professional writer. He had some 60 short stories and several novels to his credit. Interment was in the Arlington National Cemetery." During the 1950s, Chamberlain's stories were a regular feature in the *Saturday Evening Post.*

One such story is "The Trapped Battalion," a work that provides the officer's perspective and the problems of command so familiar to Chamberlain. Like many stories of Korea, it also poses a problem of isolation. Being cut off or hemmed in by the enemy, by terrain, by hostile weather conditions, or by some combination of these is not unusual in warfare, but the circumstances of the first year of fighting in Korea produced such situations with distressing frequency. In his portraits of Major Lang and his subordinates, Chamberlain is able to present a range of American types and a range of attitudes about the war. The sentimental chord struck with Pat Delevan and her group of war orphans is also typical Chamberlain and typical *Saturday Evening Post*. The successful bridge-building and river crossing, the cooperative efforts of tough guys who are also good-hearted—these features and others blend to provide the entertaining, authentically detailed, and inspirational flavor found in so many of Chamberlain's stories of World War II and Korea.

Writing mostly in Spanish, **Rolando Hinojosa** is not well known among English-speaking readers, but in the Spanish-speaking community in the US, throughout Latin America, and even in Europe, he has been widely published and widely read ever since winning the Premio Casa de las Americas in 1976 with his second novel, *Klail City y sus alrededores*. He is the only writer in this collection represented by both prose and poetry.

Hinojosa was born in 1929 in the Rio Grande Valley of Texas to a Mexican-American father and an Anglo-American mother. His Hispanic ancestors settled on the north bank of the Rio Grande in the 1740s; his Anglo grandfather arrived from Illinois in the 1880s when Hinojosa's mother was a young child. The tension and conflict between Hispanic and Anglo cultures, and the struggle of the valley's Mexican-Americans to preserve and perpetuate their Chicano identity, lies at the heart of most of Hinojosa's writing. Like William Faulkner and Yoknapatawpha County, Hinojosa has created a fictional world—Klail City, Belken County, Texas—and peopled it with a cast of characters who appear and reappear throughout his work, including *The Useless Servants* and *Korean Love Songs*, the books from which we have respectively taken his prose and poetry selections. These two books, by the way, were both written originally in English, which is unusual for Hinojosa, but as he has said, the army experience wasn't lived in Spanish, so it was easier to write about it in English.

Hinojosa enlisted in the army in 1946, serving two years. He then began college, but was called back into the army in 1949 and sent to Korea in early July 1950, just nine days after the North Korean invasion. He served as a tank crewman with a reconnaissance unit, sustaining two minor wounds. After his release from the army, he went on to earn BA, MA, and PhD degrees. In addition to his career as a writer, he has also had a successful career as a university professor and administrator, and currently teaches at the University of Texas in Austin.

As we mentioned earlier, though we determined at the outset not to select writing excerpted from larger works, we've made a few exceptions. Hinojosa's "Hoengsong" is one of them. We did this because *The Useless Servants* (1993) is written in the form of a diary with each diary entry a self-contained unit. "Hoengsong" reads almost as if it had been written as a story, even coming complete with its own title, and we enjoyed it enough, and felt it too important, not to include it.

"Lost Soldier" by **Stanford Whitmore** appeared in *Accent* in 1953 and a year later was included in *Prize Stories of 1954: The O. Henry Awards*. Born in Sioux City, Iowa, in 1925, Whitmore was raised on Chicago's South Side. He served a three-year hitch as a divebomber aircrewman in the Marine Corps (1943–1946). After working in a steel mill, he entered the University of Illinois at Navy Pier in Chicago. Transferring to Stanford University in 1948, he studied with Wallace Stegner and received his AB in 1950.[3]

Whitmore began his writing career with several short stories and an impressive first novel about a jazz pianist, *Solo* (1955). By the 1960s, however, he had turned to writing for movies and television. His first feature film, *War Hunt* (1962), shares with "Lost Soldier" the Korean War setting. Among Whitmore's ten or so other screenplays (some of which were for television movies) are *Your Cheatin' Heart* (1964), *Glory Boy* (1971), *Baby Blue Marine* (1976), *The Dark* (1979), and *Supercarrier* (1988). He also wrote for such television series as *The Wild, Wild West* and *The Fugitive.*

"Lost Soldier" is based on an actual event that was reported during the Korean War. It is in the tradition of "counterparts" stories, as the two isolated figures, temporarily lost to their commands and to their larger selves, wait like two matched dots in the snow. It explores vulnerability, isolation, innocence, shared identity, and the difference between the mindless, chaotic killing of the battlefield and the coldly calculating premeditation of something akin to murder.

"Sailors at Their Mourning: A Memory" by **John Deck** has as its core Deck's own experience as a crewman on an anti-submarine patrol aircraft. Born in 1931 in Compton, California, Deck joined the navy in 1950 shortly after his graduation from Compton High School. He served from 1950 to 1954, then went on to earn BA and MA degrees from California State University at San Francisco. His stories have appeared in *Paris Review, Esquire*, and the *Best American Short Stories* annual. "Sailors at Their Mourning: A Memory" appeared in Deck's collection *Greased Samba and Other Stories* (1970). It followed Deck's novel, *One Morning, for Pleasure* (1968) and was followed in turn by *Rancho Paradise* (1972), a nonfiction account of retirement living in a mobile home community on the edge of the California desert.

Over the last two decades, Deck's literary efforts have been supplemented—and to a great extent supplanted—by various teaching and writing jobs. Most recently he worked as a technical writer for a computer firm. In retirement, he has returned to fiction writing in what he calls "a second and far more demanding apprenticeship." Deck hopes to revisit "those tours of duty in Japan and Korea," which remain "vivid, naggingly persistent."

"Sailors at Their Mourning: A Memory" is a reminder of the extent to which occupied Japan was a staging area for US participation in the Korean War. It also reminds us (along with many of the poems of Keith Wilson) of the important, though largely unheralded, contribution of naval forces—including naval aviation—to the war effort. But primarily, of course, it is a story of mourning. The theme of warriors' grief, which goes back at least to Homer's *Iliad*, is not often the central concern in contemporary war literature, and it is rarely treated with such precision and dignity as Deck brings to bear. The sailors' grief is here complicated by the psychology of betrayal ("They give 'em planes that ain't worth a damn. . .") and by a sense—accurate or not—of diminished capacities of US fighting forces. This last motif pivots on the conflict between the career serviceman and the short-term enlistee and between the already legendary moral status of World War II in which the older sailors served and the questionable moral status of the Korean War, in spite of the chaplain's calming platitudes about "a cause which had the support of God."

We discovered "Graves" by **Mark Power** in James Laughlin's prestigious and adventurous *New Directions in Prose and Poetry* (no. 18, 1964). The story grows out of a novel-in-progress that Power abandoned. During his two years of active army duty, Power served in Korea for about sixteen months from 1957 to 1959 as a radio operator for an artillery unit that kept an atomic cannon pointed north. His immediate superiors, noncommisioned officers who had served during the war, often recounted the story of the stern, puritanical officer who had a nervous breakdown and entered a long period of denial after killing someone he had initially attempted to rescue.

Stylistically complex and ambiguous with regard to time markers, Power's fashioning of these rumored happenings in "Graves" employs stream-of-consciousness techniques in an attempt to approximate the unsteady state of the spiritually wounded Captain Graves, a man who reaches his limit in Korea after valiant service in World War II.

Among the centers of interest in "Graves" are the attitudes towards both Koreans and women: a mad magnification of the racist and misogynistic impulses that are often part of the warrior ethos. "Graves" shares with other stories in this collection a concern with the isolated or alienated figure. And, of course, the extreme cold is a register both of tangible and intangible conditions.

After his military service, Power entered art school. Finding that his true artistic strengths and interests lay in the visual arts, he has built a highly successful career as a photographer, art educator, and journalist on photography and other visual arts. Since 1971, Power has taught at the Corcoran School of Art in Washington, DC. His photographic work is represented in many permanent collections, and his reviews and critical essays have appeared widely in newspapers and magazines.

Donald R. Depew was born in Washington, DC, in 1927 and raised in the Pittsburgh area. He earned a BA from Princeton University in 1949. In September 1950, he joined the Quartermaster Corps, and from January to September 1952 he served in Korea as a sergeant in the Plans and Operations Division of the Quartermaster Base Depot. His responsibilities included overseeing the work of "indigenous" typists like the young women in his story. In his subsequent civilian life, Depew has worked as a writer for government and corporations, as a freelance business writer and photographer, and as a forensic photographer.

"Indigenous Girls" is one of those headquarters or, to use the Vietnam War phrase, REMF stories (for "rear echelon" followed by an obscene phrase we can't use here) that no anthology of war fiction should do without. The charm of the story is in Depew's portrayal of the strenuous attempts to overcome the language barrier, the mixed success, and the sweet awkwardness of cultural and gender accommodations. Along the way, Depew sheds light on economic conditions in wartime Korea and explores the shifting line between subservient, demeaning dependence and sincere, innocent gratitude. Again, cultural difference—or indifference—comes into focus as Miss Pok's gift of indigenous strawberries leads to an unintended but crushing insult. The war against North Korea and Communist China seems far away, though it frames this tiny drama in the war for dignity and respect that was waged within an alliance of unequals.

At the time "Indigenous Girls" was published in *Harper's Monthly* in March 1953, Depew told the editors that he was amazed at how the South Koreans "kept their courage, their determination, their devotion to their families . . . and in the case of those who had had little contact with the Americans, their modesty." Though he had been told quasi-officially "that the South Koreans were a pack of liars and thieves," he found that no Korean ever stole from him and "many gave me gifts when I left."

Robert O. Bowen was born in 1920 in Bridgeport, Connecticut. He served in the navy from 1937 to 1945, including three years as a prisoner of war of the Japanese in the Philippines. Bowen eventually attended the University of Alabama, earning a BA in 1948 and an MA in 1950. By the early 1950s, Bowen had established himself as a fiction writer with three novels published by the prestigious Knopf imprint: *The Weight of the Cross* (1951), *Bamboo* (1953), and *Sidestreet* (1954). "A Matter of Price," which first appeared in *Prairie Schooner* (1954) and then in *Best American Short Stories* (1955), is from this most active time in Bowen's career as a fiction writer. During this period, Bowen taught writing at Cornell and worked on the Cornell literary journal, *Epoch*.

Beginning in 1960, Bowen was an editor and author for the Colonial Press in Northport, Alabama. His *Marlow the Master and Other Stories* as well as a college style manual and a book about communism come from this period and this press. Bowen also wrote reference works on Alaska, where he enjoyed mountaineering. One of his best known books is *The New Professors*, a collection of essays published by Holt in 1960. Since settling in Alaska in 1963, Bowen has been a public relations and management consultant and has run an employment agency. He remains involved in the Anchorage business and cultural communities, and he is especially active in POW and other veterans' organizations.

"A Matter of Price" is one of numerous tales of the Korean War that remind us that many who served there had already seen service in World War II. Moreover, through the lens of Captain Carson's memory, Bowen records two levels of contrast between the earlier war and the later: "The Korean thing had not been a war that he could take pride in or find order in. . . . A real war forced order, was fought for a purpose; this marred it in anything it touched." The particulars ("They killed gooks and they helped gooks") parallel those features often incorrectly heralded as unique aspects of the American war in Vietnam. For Carson, the difference between World War II and the Korean War includes a difference in legitimacy of purpose, and from this vantage point one can understand the contrast he has experienced between being a soldier who killed the enemy in Europe and being a man who has come to enjoy killing in Korea. The pleasure, in part, is a response to the extremes of deprivation he has suffered in Korea; but in part, too, the pleasure indicates that what he views as a corrupt enterprise has corrupted him personally. There is pain in Carson's soul as well as in his body, and his decision to forego the lobotomy that would diminish his awareness of pain is also a moral decision to deal with the consequences of his actions. The story, Bowen writes, is based on the experiences of a friend.

James Drought was born in Aurora, Illinois in 1931. Though his military service (1952–1954 as an army paratrooper) overlapped with the Korean War, he remained stateside at Fort Bragg, North Carolina, where he wrote press releases and speeches for the Office of Public Relations. Some of what he observed regarding the racial integration of the army is a concern of his 1963 novel, *Mover: A Modern Tragedy*. After his time in uniform, Drought held several editorial positions. His own ambitions as a writer, however, did not make a dent with commercial publishers. Determined to reach an audience, he founded Skylight Press and began publishing his own works. These include *Mover, The Secret: An Oratorical Novel* (1963), *The Enemy* (1964), *Drugoth* (1965), and *Superstar for President* (1978). Many of Drought's works found mass market reprints on the heels of their small press appearances. His best-known work is *The Gypsy Moths* (1964), which was adapted for a successful film in 1969. He died in 1983.

Our selection from Drought's *The Secret* is another exception to not excerpting from longer works. In this case we did so because the chapter is self-contained (the only one in the novel that deals directly and exclusively with the Korean War); it vividly encapsulates a tour of duty and anticipates the antiwar sensibility that developed later in the 1960s, a sensibility spearheaded by alternative magazines and presses. It also suggests that problems encountered in the Vietnam War were not unique to that war, as we've already pointed out.

While the sensibilities, conventions, and perspectives of many of the stories in this anthology would seem familiar to the World War II generation of readers, Drought's story uncannily looks forward to and anticipates the attitude and tenor of much of the Vietnam War literature that would only begin to emerge five years after *The Secret* was first published. The contempt for authority, the bitterness, the caustic flippancy all stand in stark contrast to the tone of stories like "The Trapped Battalion." Similar attitudes, however, can be found in many of the poems included here. Consider, for instance, William Childress's "Combat Iambic," Reg Saner's "They Said," or Keith Wilson's "Commentary." Like Drought, the poets seem to anticipate an unglorious future rather than harking back to the glorious past.

There are a number of contrasts between the short fiction and the poetry of the Korean War. While stories do appear in various periodicals during and just after the war, poetry is rarely in evidence in these same publications, even those that regularly published poetry. Two slim poetry pamphlets appeared during the war. *Hell's Music: A Verse Narrative of the Korean War* (1950), by Paal Ramberg and Jerome Miller, holds only historical interest. *Korean Lullaby* (undated, but probably 1951 or 1952), by *Spartacus* author Howard Fast, contains three poems. The first and third, "Korean Lullaby" and "A Song of Peace," are undistinguished, manipulative rhymed verse. The middle poem, "Korean Litany," a sequence in which seven soldiers speak from beyond the grave, is far more engaging though equally polemical. World War II veteran Thomas McGrath's poem, which we have used here as a kind of foreword or preface to the entire anthology, appears in his 1955 book *Figures of the Double World*. A poem of Edith Sitwell's, "The War Orphans," appears in the November 1957 *Atlantic Monthly*. Most poems about the Korean War don't begin to appear until the 1960s, and are written by veterans of the fighting. Why so few of the stories have come from writers who were veterans of the Korean War while so many of the poems have is hard to say. We can only note the difference.

What is not different, however, is the lack of attention that has been paid to the poetry that has been written. As with the fiction, the poetry languishes in the shadow of the wars which come before and after it. The World War II poems of John Ciardi, James Dickey, Alan Dugan, Richard Eberhart, Anthony Hecht, Richard Hugo, Randall Jarrell, William Meredith, Howard Nemerov, Louis Simpson, and W. D. Snodgrass have all been anthologized, for instance, as have the Vietnam War poems of John Balaban, D. F. Brown, *Retrieving Bones* co-editor Ehrhart, Bryan Alec Floyd, Yusef Komunyakaa, Gerald McCarthy, Marilyn McMahon, Walter McDonald, Basil Paquet, Dale Ritterbusch, and Bruce Weigl.[4]

Korean War poems, however, are hard to come by and seldom anthologized. We found McGrath's poem in *The Voice That Is Great Within Us* (1970), and William Childress's "Korea Bound, 1952" first appeared in *Harper's* in 1965 and was anthologized in *America Forever New* in 1968. But these are exceptions. The first and only anthology we could locate devoted entirely to Korean War poetry, *The Hermit Kingdom: Poems of the Korean War*— which includes James Magner, Jr., William Wantling, and Keith Wilson among a number of other far less capable poets—did not appear until 1995. As we've already mentioned, Fussell includes no Korean War poetry in his 1991 *Norton Book of Modern War*, nor does Carolyn Forché include any in *Against Forgetting: Twentieth Century Poetry of Witness* (1993), though both include poems from other wars.[5] Not until the fall–winter 1997 issue of *War, Literature & the Arts* appeared (called *I Remember: Soldier-Poets of the Korean War*, ed. W. D. Ehrhart,) had any serious attention been paid to the poetry.

We include a selection of that poetry here. Because the poems do not lend themselves to the same internal chronological ordering we used for the stories, and trying to arrange them by chronological order of publication also presents difficulties, we offer them simply by alphabetical order according to the poets.

William Childress, born in 1933 in Hugo, Oklahoma, grew up in a family of sharecroppers and migrant cottonpickers. He joined the army in 1951 at age eighteen and was sent to Korea the following year, where he served as a demolitions expert and secret courier. He subsequently earned a BA from

Fresno State and an MFA from the University of Iowa. Over the years, Childress has worked as a college teacher, juvenile counselor, writer-editor, speechwriter, and freelance writer and photojournalist. Recently retired, from 1983 until 1997 he wrote a column called "Out of the Ozarks" for the St. Louis *Post-Dispatch*.

Childress's two books of poetry appeared within a year of each other— *Burning the Years* in 1971, *Lobo* in 1972—and his most active years as a poet came between 1960 and 1970. A 1986 reprint combining both books, *Burning the Years and Lobo: Poems 1962–1975*, includes fewer than half a dozen poems not in either of the earlier two.

Childress takes his subject matter from a wide variety of sources: the natural world and its inhabitants, the agricultural west and southwest of his childhood, the unnatural worlds of urban poverty and button-down America, and the whimsy of his own imagination. But war is the subject of a number of his poems, not just the Korean War, as the poems in this selection demonstrate, but also World War II and the Vietnam War. His poem "The Long March," beginning as it does in Korea but ending up in Vietnam, may well be the most striking poem in this anthology.

Indeed, while those who fought the Korean War were closer in age and temperament to the veterans of World War II, the Vietnam War seems to have been a catalyst for many of these poets, releasing pent-up feelings that had perhaps been held in check by the personal and cultural stoicism bequeathed to them by their generational older brothers and by the restraints forced on public utterance by the atmosphere created in the 1950s by Senator Joseph McCarthy and the House Un-American Activities Committee.

While Childress, for example, did write several of his best Korean War poems prior to the vast American air and ground commitment in Vietnam ("The Soldiers" in 1961 and "Shell Shock" in 1962), his poems become more pointed, more cynical, and more bitter as the Sixties—and the Vietnam War—advance. And while Childress can say, with what sounds very much like pride, resentment, and envy all at once, "Korean veterans did not come home and start throwing tantrums like many Viet vets did. We simply faded back into civilian life—no monuments, and not even a doughnut wagon to meet the [troop ship] I came home on," his poems suggest that the price of simply fading back into civilian life was very dear indeed.

Rolando Hinojosa you have already met. We include in the poetry section selections from his 1978 *Korean Love Songs*, a collection of thirty-eight sequential poems, along with one additional poem, "Native Son Home from Asia."[6] The narrator of the poems in *Korean Love Songs*, Rafe Buenrostro, is a recurrent character in many of Hinojosa's books, and it is from his fictional diary that Hinojosa's prose selection, "Hoengsong," is taken. One could count these poems from *Korean Love Songs*, perhaps, as a third exception to our "no excerpts" approach since the poems in the sequence are all interrelated and form something of a narrative-in-verse, but each poem is nevertheless its own entity with its own title, and we simply haven't space for all thirty-eight poems in any case.

Born in 1928, **James Magner, Jr.**, grew up in New York City, Long Island, and New Rochelle, and joined the army in 1948. Like Hinojosa, he ended up in Korea during the first year of the war, that terrible year that saw the front move violently and swiftly from the 38th Parallel south to Pusan, then north to the Yalu River, then south again to below Seoul, then north once more to where it all started. Magner, however, was not around to see the line stabilized again at the 38th Parallel. While fighting as an infantry sergeant, he was badly wounded by machinegun fire in February 1951 and evacuated out of Korea. Discharged from the army, he entered a Catholic monastery of the Passionist Order, where he remained for five years. Thereafter, Magner earned a BA in philosophy from Duquesne University, and MA and PhD degrees in English from the University of Pittsburgh. In 1962, he began teaching in the English department at John Carroll University in Cleveland, Ohio, where he has been ever since.

Magner's poetry reflects his deeply religious concerns and his lifelong desire to bridge the gulf between human imperfection and divine perfection and to understand the mysteries and contradictions of creation. Only a handful of the poems in his ten books deal directly with the Korean War, but those that do make clear that for Magner, to forget is to render utterly meaningless the suffering, the sorrow, and the irreplaceable losses.

The poetry of **Reg Saner** generally reflects a man most at home when out of doors and fully engaged with the natural world around him: hiking, mountain climbing, skiing, camping under the stars. Much of his writing is inspired by the American West with its mountains and deserts and high plains stretching away to horizons distant enough to make a man reflect humbly upon the universe and his place in it. Not one of the poems in his four books even uses the word "Korea," and if you didn't already know Saner had fought in Korea, you would not likely ever suspect it from reading his books. "I have not really tried to write about Korea," Saner has said. "I wanted to forget."

Reg Saner was born in 1929 in Jacksonville, Illinois. After graduating from St. Norbert College in 1950, he entered the army as an officer and served in Korea in 1952 and 1953, spending six months as an infantry platoon leader and earning a Bronze Star. After the war, he earned MA and PhD degrees from the University of Illinois, taking a position in 1962 with the English department at the University of Colorado in Boulder, where he still teaches.

Of the selections we've made, only "Re-Runs" appears in one of Saner's books (*Red Letters*, 1989). "They Said" is taken from *Demilitarized Zones: Veterans After Vietnam* (1976); that the editors of this anthology found a Korean War veteran's poem as applicable to the Vietnam War as it is to his own war is yet another manifestation of the parallels between the two wars. "Flag Memoir" appears in a 1991 issue of *Ontario Review*. Note how the "torn head" in "Re-Runs" reappears much more explicitly and graphically in "Flag Memoir." Saner may have wanted to forget the Korean War, but the images in "Flag Memoir" are anything but forgettable.

In a letter to W. D. Ehrhart, Len Fulton, who in 1966 published *The Source* by **William Wantling**, describes Wantling as "a superbly unruly poet (and person)." If anything, that's an understatement. In the foreword to *The Source*, Wantling is quoted as saying, "When I was in Korea, they gave me my first shot of morphine. It killed the pain. It was beautiful. Five years later I was in San Quentin on narcotics." By 1974, not yet forty-one, he was dead.

Born in what is now East Peoria, Illinois, in 1933, Wantling enlisted in the Marines soon after graduating from East Peoria High School, arriving in Korea in November 1952. In the winter of 1953, he was seriously wounded, including burns on the leg, spending ten days in a coma and another eight weeks in the hospital before eventually recovering. Discharged with the rank of sergeant in 1955, he spent the next three years in southern California living mostly as a street hustler and petty criminal until he was convicted in 1958 of forgery and narcotics.

In prison, Wantling discovered poetry and the poet in himself, and as early as 1959, he began publishing poems in *Wormwood Review*. After five and a half years, Wantling was released from San Quentin and returned to

Illinois, eventually earning BA and MA degrees from Illinois State University. But Wantling never escaped his dependency on drugs and alcohol, in spite of repeated visits to hospitals and psychiatric clinics. He lived at fever pitch, consuming prodigious amounts of whatever drugs he could get his hands on. The official cause of his death was heart failure, but it's probably more accurate to say that he died of hard living.

Wantling's poetry conveys a strong sense of the poet—at least this poet—as outsider and rebel. Even in his heyday, he published almost entirely in the smallest of the small presses and journals. Like Childress and Wilson, he has poems that deal with both Hiroshima ("It's Cold for August") and the Vietnam War ("Your Children's Dead Eyes"), but beyond that and the fact of his being a Korean War veteran, his poems bear little resemblance in style or subject to any of the other poets included here. They are frenetic and boisterous, full of restless energy. Wantling wrote only a handful of poems about the Korean War, but they suggest that what he saw and did in Korea when he was still only a teenager changed his life forever, and not for the better.

Keith Wilson, born in 1927 in Clovis, New Mexico, went to Korea for the first time in 1950 as an ensign fresh out of the US Naval Academy. He returned from his third tour in Korean waters in 1953. "I expected nothing from war," he has said. "I was a professional. I didn't, however, expect to be lied to and betrayed. I was very proud of the UN flag at our mast head when we went in to launch attacks. When I found out that Korea was all a very dirty and murderous joke, I was silenced for many years."

Wilson, who had intended a career in the navy, instead got out and returned to his native New Mexico, earning an MA degree from the University of New Mexico before commencing a career in academia. He is currently professor emeritus at New Mexico State University, where he taught for many years. He has also had a prolific career as a poet and writer, publishing over two dozen books and chapbooks since 1967. A great deal of his work is rooted deeply in the American Southwest, especially New Mexico, and he has a particular interest in and affinity for Native American and Spanish-American cultures.

But Wilson's experiences in the Korean War provide the foundation for one of his most important books, *Graves Registry*. "I started writing *Graves Registry* in the winter of 1966 in anger that our government was again fighting an undeclared war in a situation that I, from my experiences in Korea, knew we could never win," he says. Until then, he'd written nothing at all about his experiences in the Korean War: "I had buried it inside. It took the pressure of rage and fear for the young men [of the Vietnam generation] that made me write it and it poured out, page after page."

First published by Grove Press in 1969 as *Graves Registry & Other Poems*, it contained the Korean War poems along with poems about the Southwest. In 1992, Clark City Press published an updated edition called simply *Graves Registry* and containing the original Korean War poems; additional poems from his 1972 *Midwatch*, including a number that deal explicitly with the Vietnam War; and some fifty newer poems. Taken altogether, they weave the literary and the political into a single tableau that moves across time and geography, but our selections here, of course, are necessarily limited to poems dealing with Korea, most of which are grouped together at the beginning of the book.

Wilson's poems are not about the big battalions and the pitched battles, but about coastal operations and guerilla raids, shattered villages, and shattered ideals. They are peopled by Americans, yes, but also by Koreans and Japanese, refugees and cripples, and by warriors, yes, but also and more so by the defenseless and the innocent who always become the wreckage of war. They are Wilson's explanation of how he began his life expecting to be a warrior and ended up being a teacher instead.

In his memoir, *The Coldest War*, James Brady writes: "Korea gave us a brief shelf of history books, no great war novel or film, not a single memorable song, a wonderful combat journal by Martin Russ called *The Last Parallel*". Thus, even authoritative writers who "were there" foster the misconception that there is little of value to recover from this period of our history. They are writing from vague impressions rather than examining the facts. They are looking at the "nots" and paying little or no attention to the "whats." If greatness has not been attained (and we are not so sure it hasn't), there are nevertheless scores of well-crafted, readable, and important novels about the Korean War.[7] There are dozens of films, many of them quite fine. There are more than enough affecting stories and poems to fill several volumes. There are enough memoirs and histories to fill several shelves.

Yet the shelves of bookstores—even stores specializing in secondhand books—treat the Korean War as an appendage of the wars that straddle it, marked, as they usually are, "World War II and Korea" or "Korea and Vietnam," if the word "Korea" appears at all. Look for the shelf marked "Korean War History" or "Korean War Literature." You will be hard pressed to find it, and this in spite of the fact that many of the novels at least were popular book club selections in their day.

The low level of public response to the war, as we have already suggested, has complex sources. But it has had several clear consequences: the neglect of a literary heritage possessing power, beauty, and humanity; and the kind of amnesia that leads to ignorance, misunderstanding, and repeated mistakes. As this anthology demonstrates, there is very much a body of work that can be called Korean War literature, and it can teach us a great deal about an important experience in American history that shaped the nature of the Cold War that shaped the world we live in today. If we continue to neglect this literature, we do so at our own peril. It is time and long past time to open our minds and broaden our vision in ways that only literature can help us to do.

Notes to Introduction

1. Earl Tilford of the Center for Strategic Studies at Carlisle Army Barracks estimates that a million US service personnel fought in Korea between 1950 and 1953. Paul Edwards of the Center for the Study of the Korean War estimates 1.2 million. Edwards puts US casualties at 103,284 wounded in action; 34,600 killed in action; 11,029 nonbattle deaths; and 5,178 missing in action. Harry Summers, Jr., in the *Korean War Almanac*, lists casualties as 103,284 WIA; 33,629 KIA; and 20,617 other deaths.

2. Vita dated June 1997 provided to PKJ in May 1998. Biographical information on many of the writers represented here is scarce. For Robert O. Bowen, Eugene Burdick, James Lee Burke, William Childress, James Drought, Reg Saner, and Vern Sneider we have drawn upon one or more volumes of the *Contemporary Authors* series. Vern Sneider is also profiled in the 1956 *Current Biography*. The jackets of several of James Magner, Jr.'s books provide biographical details. For some of these authors, we have gathered information through correspondence and interviews to supplement and even supplant material in print or to compensate for its absence: Robert O. Bowen, William Childress, John Deck, Donald R. Depew, Rolando Hinojosa, James Magner, Jr., Mark Power, Reg Saner, Henry Steiner, Stanford Whitmore, and Keith Wilson. Unless otherwise stated, comments and information attributed to these authors are from such sources. In the case of William Wantling, we have relied primarily on John Pyros's *William Wantling: A Biography & Selected Works*, (Peoria, Ill.: Spoon River Poetry Press, 1981) and Kevin E. Jones's unpublished doctoral dissertation *Finding Jewels in the Awkward Mud: A Reconsideration of William Wantling and His Poetry*, (Illinois State University, 1994). For Rolando Hinojosa, we depend in part on José David Saldívar's *The Rolando Hinojosa Reader* (Houston: Arte Público, 1985). Material on William Chamberlain is derived, in part, from US Army and US Military Academy records and publications researched by Colonel James R. Kerin, Jr.

3. The reader might enjoy this coincidence: of the twelve fiction writers represented here, three of them—Whitmore, Steiner, and Burdick—studied writing at Stanford University under Wallace Stegner.

4. Readers should know that World War II veterans James Dickey and William Meredith also served in the Korean War. While it is difficult to determine if any of Dickey's poems derive from that experience, it is clear that two of Meredith's do. These are "The Old Ones," collected in *The

Open Sea and Other Poems (New York: Knopf, 1961), and "A Korean Woman Seated by a Wall," collected first in *Earth Walk: New & Selected Poems* (New York: Knopf, 1970) and again in *Effort at Speech: New and Selected Poems* (Evanston, Ill.: Northwestern University Press, 1997).

5. Forché does include one poet, Etheridge Knight, whom she identifies as a Korean War veteran, but none of the poems she includes is about the Korean War. Indeed, a careful perusal of Knight's poetry reveals only one mention of the Korean War, in a poem called "At a VA Hospital in the Middle of the United States of America: An Act in a Play," and the reference is generic only, coming in the midst of stock references to World War I, World War II, and the Vietnam War. During a telephone conversation with W. D. Ehrhart on 8 June 1997, Jean Anaporte-Easton, who is editing a collection of Knight's letters and correspondence, suggested that Knight, while a veteran of the Korean War era, might not ever have served in Korea. Copies of Knight's military records, obtained by Thomas C. Johnson, a graduate student at Butler University, were subsequently made available to W. D. Ehrhart on 27 October 1997. While the original records were partially destroyed by fire, and are therefore incomplete and difficult to read, careful inspection gives no indication of any kind that Knight served in Korea and strongly suggests otherwise.

6. Joey or Pepe Vielma is both a character in *Korean Love Songs* and the subject of "Native Son Home from Asia" (*Maize* 1, no. 3, 1978). A careful reader will notice that in the former, Vielma's unit is identified as the 219th Field Artillery Battalion while in the latter it is Company D, 160th Regiment, 40th Division. In an e-mail to W. D. Ehrhart dated 25 February 1997, Hinojosa explained that the former unit was a literary creation of his own while the latter was his brother's outfit in World War II and "I wanted to remember him in my work." How Vielma can die as a member of one outfit in one poem but a member of another outfit in another poem, Hinojosa left unexplained.

7. Many of these are briefly discussed in Philip K. Jason's "Vietnam War Themes in Korean War Fiction," *South Atlantic Review* 61, no. 1 (winter 1996): 109–121.

Works Cited

Aichinger, Peter. *The American Soldier in Fiction, 1880–1963: A History of Attitudes Toward Warfare and the Military Establishment*. Ames: Iowa State University Press, 1975.

Axelsson, Arne. *Restrained Response: American Novels of the Cold War and Korea, 1945–1962*. New York: Greenwood, 1990.

Brady, James. *The Coldest War: A Memoir of Korea*. New York: Orion Books, 1990.

Donovan, Robert J. *Nemesis: Truman and Johnson in the Coils of War in Asia*. New York: St. Martin's Press, 1984.

Edwards, Paul M., ed. *The Hermit Kingdom: Poems of the Korean War*. Dubuque, Iowa: Kendall/Hunt, 1995.

Ehrhart, W. D. "Soldier-Poets of the Korean War." *War, Literature & the Arts*, 9, no. 2 (fall–winter 1997): 1–47. Introduces Ehrhart's special issue of this journal titled *I Remember: Soldier-Poets of the Korean War*.

Fast, Howard. *Korean Lullaby*. New York: American Peace Crusade, [c. 1951–1952].

Forché, Carolyn, ed. *Against Forgetting: Twentieth Century Poetry of Witness*. New York: Norton, 1993.

Fussell, Paul, ed. *The Norton Book of Modern War*. New York: Norton, 1991.

Jenks, Tom, ed. *Soldiers and Civilians: Americans at War and at Home*. New York: Bantam, 1986.

Mason, F. Van Wyck, ed. *American Men at Arms*. Boston: Little, Brown, 1964.

Ramberg, Paal, and Jerome Miller. *Hell's Music: A Verse Narrative of the Korean War*. New London, Minn.: Green Spires Press, 1950.

Tibbets, Albert B., ed. *Courage in Korea: Stories of the Korean War*. Boston: Little, Brown, 1962.
———. *American Heroes All*. Boston: Little, Brown, 1966.

Walsh, Jeffrey. *American War Literature 1914 to Vietnam*. New York: St. Martin's Press, 1982.

Retrieving Bones

Stories

Henry Steiner

~ Rice

It was a day that should have started softly, mounting into noon and after-noon, and then sloping away into the smoky autumn evening. Instead it was bright and hard like the preceding spring when the rice was green and the bitter Korean winter of 1946–47 just past.

In the jeep, Captain Frazer turned around to Mr. Song and said, "It's just like spring."

Mr. Song, sitting in the back seat, smiled diffidently and answered, "Yes."

Frazer waited. When Mr. Song remained silent, Frazer looked at Sergeant Biancoli who, saying nothing, drove with his eyes fixed on the road. On his face was an expression of brooding discontent, and Frazer stared at him curiously, indifferently, as he might have inspected an animal in a zoo.

He turned again to Mr. Song and asked, "You came down from Seoul yesterday?"

Mr. Song said "Yes" again and smiled again, but the smile was jerked out of existence by a violent shock. He clawed desperately for a handhold as he went up off the seat with his arms outstretched like wings and almost fell between the two Americans in the front seats.

Sergeant Biancoli muttered, "Hang on, for Chrissakes."

Mr. Song's hat had fallen off. As he tried to regain his seat, he stepped on the brim and ground the floor dirt into the soft felt. Picking it up and brushing at it ineffectually, he placed it askew on his head and caught hold of the seat back just in time to prevent another flight.

"This is your first job with the Americans, isn't it?" Frazer asked.

"No," Mr. Song answered. "When I was a boy I interpreted for an American missionary." He did not tell them that the present job was his last defense against gradual starvation, nor that he had invested all his remaining funds in what he thought were suitable clothes for the new work. He bounced again and felt a sharp edge cut into one of the new shoes where it was tucked under the Captain's seat. Pulling it out with a grimace, he looked sadly at the long scratch on the toe and the polish covered with dust.

"Well, this is a tough one to start you out on," Frazer said seriously. "God knows, rice collection is always a headache, but the old man we're going to see this morning is a hard customer. Did you hear about it in the village last night?"

"No, I did not," Mr. Song murmured. He had come in on the bus with a charcoal burner on the back and all the windows broken, with his paper suitcase in his hand, with his new suit and new shoes and new hat. He had come all the way from Seoul, away from the University and the old life, broken now like the bridges on the road where the bus had to go down in the dry stream bed and waddle up the other side with everyone pushing and the chickens squawking, and Mr. Song still sitting inside looking dignified as befitted a scholar and University professor.

When he had met Frazer, Mr. Song had spread out his ceremonial manners in front of him like an ancient and fragile tapestry. And it had seemed that Frazer had not even known what Mr. Song was doing. Perhaps the formal words sounded silly in English, but Mr. Underwood, the missionary, would have bowed and said them in return. Of course, Mr. Song had reflected, it was too much to expect that all Americans would be like old Mr. Underwood.

After the brief, impersonal instructions, Mr. Song had found an inexpensive hotel. There in a narrow, cold little room with sliding paper doors and no furniture except the sleeping mat, he had spent the night. His sleep was troubled by dreams of the old life at the University with the new young students, and then somehow of childhood.

Frazer said, "You'll have to find out those things. It's up to you to get the information on what's going on in these places. The old man we're going to see this morning—his name is Han—has hidden his rice crop. Every farmer does that, of course, but not even your police could find out where it is. He wouldn't tell them."

Frazer waited a moment. Then he sighed and said, "I suppose you know it's not usual for Koreans to refuse their police anything."

He waited again, but another bump came and Mr. Song's hat fell off for the second time.

"Well, old Han wouldn't tell them," Frazer continued, "and they didn't do anything but threaten him. I think they must be afraid to touch him. He's the head of a clan. There's also the effect of those riots at Kwanju a few weeks ago over the farmers your police tortured. I suppose you heard about that up in Seoul."

Mr. Song nodded, but at the same time he thought, *They are not my police.*

He had heard a little about it. Some students had held a meeting in protest over the police atrocities against the farmers, but the students were so few. All of them put together were only a fraction of the body that had once attended. No one had any money any more, or clothes, or time to go to the University and listen to the quiet voice of Mr. Song explaining the subjunctive in the English language, and how it might be used to translate Li Po. Everyone spent his hours in attempting to sell what he had gathered over a lifetime, and watching the treasures disappear like winter snow and the rice they bought disappear also. Suddenly Mr. Song thought that everything was disappearing, that even he might—especially he might—disappear.

"Well, I'm glad to hear you've heard of something," Frazer said sarcastically.

Mr. Song kept his face expressionless, except for the discomfort which he was not able to conceal.

Frazer spoke over his shoulder. "The old man has got to sell us the rice at the legal price: one hundred and seventy-five won—providing he'll tell us where it is."

Mr. Song said, "One hundred and seventy-five won." He knew that in Seoul the retail price was now almost one thousand won, except in the government sales where the amount one could purchase was rationed, but the rice was only one-fifth as much. "Mr. Han will not want to sell," he said.

"You can bet he won't want to sell," Frazer said wryly. "None of them want to sell at the legal price."

Mr. Song's head bounced up and down in what began as a nod.

"I want to be sure, Mr. Song, you understand the necessity for what we're doing so you'll be able to speak convincingly to Mr. Han. You know what would happen in the city if the government didn't buy and sell at a price people can pay?"

"The city people would starve to death," Mr. Song said like a child reciting a lesson.

"That's right," Frazer continued gravely. "They would starve. But many farmers don't care and don't want to know. I've seen violence before during rice collection."

"I understand," Mr. Song said. "I agree that it is necessary to have rice at a low price."

"You clearly understand there may be trouble? Someone may get hurt? I tell you so you'll be warned."

"I understand," Mr. Song said thinking, *This is a difficult service he performs. He is very serious.*

"I hope you do. I certainly hope you do." Frazer stared at Mr. Song's eyes until Mr. Song looked away in embarrassment.

They stopped in front of the house and the truck with the laborers pulled up behind them. While waiting for the dust to pass away they looked at the four pillars of the house and the Chinese characters written on them, at the white clothed men lounging on the porch who smoked and watched them. Somewhere inside a child began to cry and they listened to that until it was cut off in mid-breath. It left them hanging there in what was now like silence. Gradually it was filled with bird sounds and the wind-rustle in the trees. All of them waited in the little draw off the river like a hostile audience watching an empty stage.

"Well, let's get going," Frazer said and got out. Mr. Song followed him, and finally Biancoli pulled himself abruptly out of the jeep and leaned on the hood on the side away from the house.

"Find out who Han is, Mr. Song, and let's talk to him and get out of here," Frazer said, suddenly impatient.

Mr. Song approached the porch, feeling the eyes on his hat and suit and shoes, wishing that he too wore the traditional white. It occurred to him that this was all foolishness: the ominous atmosphere, and the hostility between the Koreans and the collection party so strong that it was like a bridge under his feet. *I should be back in my chambers translating, or in the classroom teaching,* he thought angrily. But he kept on walking until he was close in front of the porch. After the preliminary words of politeness—Seoul politeness, Capital politeness—he asked for Mr. Han.

An old man rose, and without speaking to Mr. Song, descended with dignity from the porch, walked past him and stopped in front of Frazer. Mr. Song bowed his head at the insult and turned back to stand behind Frazer.

"Tell him we'll give him the legal price of one hundred and seventy-five won for his rice," Frazer said curtly.

Before Mr. Song could say a word, the old man shook his head.

"Wait until you hear the question before you answer it," Frazer said clearly into the old man's unchanging face and unwavering eyes. Mr. Song told him the legal price.

The old man still did not look at him.

"Tell him he must sell to us at that price. Tell him we must fill our quotas," Frazer insisted.

The old man shook his head again.

"Tell him he's got to listen to the question before he answers it," Frazer added patiently.

"You must sell to the government, Mr. Han," Mr. Song said quietly in Korean. "That is the law."

Abruptly the old man recognized Mr. Song's existence. He spoke in a high, rapid voice and in the dialect of the region. "I do not have to sell to anyone. It is my rice, from my land. I will ask what I please for it. The price you offer is far too low."

"Well, what's he say, Mr. Song?" Frazer asked.

"He says he will not sell."

"Tell him if he doesn't sell, we'll confiscate the rice."

Mr. Song said placatingly in Korean, "The people in the cities are starving. They cannot pay the high prices on the open market. That is why the government sets this low price and makes out a quota."

"The government of thieves! Let those in the cities come back to the land if they wish to eat." Mr. Han's eyes, the color of yellow river-water, became bright and wet with emotion. "Let them depend on the rain as I do and starve when it does not come. Let the river sweep away all they have. For years I have worked the land for the Japanese and saw them take my rice away. Now I have the land and the rice. The government wants to take it away again. It is the same as the Japanese."

"What does he say?" Frazer asked.

"One moment please, Captain Frazer." And then in Korean to the old man, "But this is not for the Japanese. This is for your own people. The Americans are helping us."

"Yes, I know. They will sell the rice to the robbers for five times what they give me. Then the robbers will sell it to the people for ten times. What do these foreigners know!" The speech came shooting out of the old man's mouth.

"You are right," Mr. Song said, "some of the rice may go to thieves, there to be sold again, but is it no comfort to know that you are behaving justly, that you are helping others who would starve without you? At least you will gain merit in the eyes of God no matter what sins others may commit."

The old man ignored him again.

Mr. Song turned to Frazer and said, "He says no."

"You mean you talked that much and all he said was no? You interpreters are all alike. Now. Tell him if he doesn't tell us where it is, we'll send the military police and take him to jail. Not Koreans this time—American police."

When Mr. Song had translated that, the old man said earnestly, almost despairingly, "What can a man do?" And then with force, "Tell him he will never find it. I did not tell the police. I will not tell him. Let him know I will let it rot where it is rather than tell him."

Mr. Song said, "He will not sell. This man is very angry. He feels he is being treated unjustly. I think he will fight soon."

On the porch a young man with a thin face rose to his feet.

"Let him fight," Frazer said. "Maybe he can beat the Korean police and the American Army all by himself. Biancoli!" Biancoli straightened up. "Search the house."

Biancoli said, "Yessir," and unbuttoned the holster flap of his .45. He began to walk toward the porch, toward the seated men, with the sun glinting on the insignia pinned to his fatigue cap.

"Do not enter my house!" the old man shouted at his back. "You have no right to enter my house!"

Mr. Song said, "He asks that you not enter his house."

Captain Frazer said nothing.

Mr. Song looked at him in surprise. "He asks that you not enter his house," Mr. Song repeated.

Frazer shook his head disgustedly. "I have no choice," he said slowly. "We've got to fill our quota. To do that we've got to find Mr. Han's rice, and we'll search since he won't tell us where it is. Try and explain that to him."

Mr. Song began, "Captain Frazer says—"

The old man shouted, "Do not enter my house." He looked once at Frazer's face and then, with his straw sandals scuffing the dust, he ran behind the house.

All the men on the porch were standing now. A murmur rose from them when Mr. Han ran. Biancoli hesitated.

For a moment Mr. Song thought the old man had hidden his face from the indignity about to come to his name. He gasped when the old man returned running with the scythe in his hand, yet for a bright instant Mr. Song was filled with the thought that something was going to happen and he would watch it.

The young man on the porch jumped down. With a shout he ran to intercept Han. While Biancoli fumbled for his gun, the old man, eyes glaring, leaning forward with the scythe clenched in his two hands, dust spurting from his feet, raced toward him.

Biancoli clawed the gun from its holster with rigid muscles and fear filling his face. From the house, a woman's voice cried out.

Biancoli got the gun out, pulled the hammer back, and fired when the old man was almost on top of him, the scythe upraised.

The sound was loud. For an instant afterward, even before it echoed up the valley, all became suspended: expressions, voices, wind, Biancoli with the pistol thrust out from his hip like a pointing finger, and the old man caught in mid-stride, eyes still glaring, scythe still upraised but without life, like a statue.

Then the instant collapsed. The old man's leading leg crumbled under him. He fell at Biancoli's feet, the scythe jabbing the dust and then it too falling over, soundlessly.

Biancoli swung around a little to face the young man running toward him, and Frazer yelled, "Don't shoot!"

The young man went down on his knees next to Mr. Han and began to turn him over. From the house came flying white skirts, swift rubber sandals and an old woman's face, contorted, tears already streaming from the eyes, mouth open. The white-clothed men tumbled off the porch and the laborers off the truck.

The son turned the old man on his back while Biancoli looked down on them, the pistol held limply on the end of his hanging arm

Frazer came up and bent over the old man. Looking up, he grated, "Did you have to shoot him in the chest?"

"I almost didn't make it at all, Captain," Biancoli's voice sounded full, as if he were about to weep. His face was mask-like with surprise, sorrow, and bewilderment.

The woman was on her knees beside the old man, her hands covering her face as she rocked back and forth.

To Mr. Song, bending over, staring into the old man's face, it was terrifying to see the eyes open and look into his, and the mouth open and the words breathe out, "Yu Bakka!" and then the eyes close again and the bearded mouth remain open with its yellow teeth.

Mr. Song looked at it for a moment before he realized that it was dead. Then he rose and turned to the son, who had also stood up, with the words of sorrow and regret on his lips. Before he could speak, the young face with its eyes glaring was thrust close against his to shout deafeningly, "Ka! Get out! Ka!" He pulled back shocked, and wiped his mouth with his hand.

The son turned to the laborers in their baggy army fatigues and shouted in each of their faces, "Ka! Ka! Ka!" They turned, shamefaced, and went back to the truck.

Before the son could reach him, Frazer returned to the jeep and yelled back, "Let's get out of here," with a slight waver in his voice.

Mr. Song, who had been standing, staring stunned with the back of his hand still to his face, turned and almost ran to the jeep, and Biancoli, with the old expression of brooding inwardness wiped away, came slowly around to the driver's side.

"Put that thing away!" Frazer ordered angrily.

Biancoli shoved the pistol back in its holster. "I almost didn't make it, Captain," Biancoli muttered thickly. "He was right on top of me. I couldn't do anything else." Biancoli waited until Mr. Song had climbed dazedly into the back seat again and then climbed in himself.

"Come on, let's get out of here! Get us moving, for Christ's sake!" Frazer said.

As they started to back out, Mr. Song suddenly awoke. Holding on to the roof supports, his knuckles white, he leaned over the side and yelled back to the son staring after them, to all the faces staring after them, "Do not ever tell them where the rice is! Never!" He leaned back in and sat down, not even bothering to wipe the spittle from the corners of his mouth, not answering when the Captain looked at him questioningly.

~

They were on their way back to Inchon when Captain Frazer turned around to Mr. Song and said, "What did he say to you just before he died?"

Mr. Song stared past him through the windshield. "He called me a thief," he said. "In Japanese."

Neither of the men in the front Seat said anything. Sergeant Biancoli stared at the road and Captain Frazer looked at Mr. Song.

After a while, Captain Frazer said, "Don't let it get you, Mr. Song. You had nothing to do with it." Then he added quietly, "It was the old man's fault. He shouldn't have tried to kill Biancoli."

Mr. Song said, "The old man is dead. No matter what you say, it is true that the old man is dead." He still stared past the Captain's head.

"Yes, the old man is dead. But remember I told you there might be trouble."

Mr. Song did not answer.

"I told you why we were doing this, didn't I?"

Mr. Song said, "Yes."

"Has anything changed now with the argument?"

"The old man is dead."

"Yes, he's dead. Of course he's dead. We all saw him dead!" Frazer glared at Mr. Song's blank, cold face. "That doesn't change the fact that what we did was right. Biancoli had to protect himself. We had to find the rice!" Then with an effort, Frazer said, "A man can't keep what he has while others starve—not any more."

Mr. Song thought, *The old man is dead. The brave, ignorant old man.*

"He did no good, you know," Frazer continued. "The police'll surely find the rice now. They'll question the wife or the son without fear, now that the old man . . ."

Surprise filtered into Mr. Song. "They will find the rice?" he said.

"The police aren't to blame for what happened, so they're free to do what they want," Frazer said bitterly. "Now let's all just forget about it."

They were almost to Inchon when Mr. Song said, "Please stop the automobile."

Frazer turned and examined him.

Mr. Song's face was calm. "Please stop the automobile," he said again.

When Biancoli had braked the jeep to a stop, Mr. Song got out.

"Wait a minute, Biancoli," Frazer said quickly. Then to Mr. Song: "I know how you feel. Think of the ten people who'll starve without Mr. Han's rice. Balance them against Mr. Han back there."

Mr. Song heard only a jumble of foreign words which he did not attempt to understand. Wooden-faced, he waited.

"What can I tell you to convince you? To kill a man is a terrible thing, but to kill ten, even though you don't see them die immediately, is much worse. You've seen them starve at Seoul station in the winter. So have I—"

Mr. Song, still not listening, thought, *Why does he argue with me like this?* He was drawn to a detached contemplation of the Western face with the blue eyes, the bitter expression, the twisting mouth, and the almost passionate jargon. Mr. Song was reminded of someone. Of course! Mr. Han had looked exactly like this when he had argued against taking the rice! Something like a chill overtook Mr. Song as Frazer defended himself. He listened.

In a moment, Mr. Song thought: *Who is right? They argue the same way, with the same face, and yet both would have killed. This man speaks to me as if I am his conscience.* Then Mr. Song remembered the yard and Mr. Han with the great stain on his chest and the blood creeping away in little branched vines from some vast root underneath him.

"Yu bakka!" Mr. Song said, in Japanese as it had been said to him. He spoke suddenly, throwing the words from him.

He saw Frazer's face deepen and recede into a mask of defeat. The face itself sighed at him, and Mr. Song almost said, "No, wait. I did not mean it. I would have said the same to Mr. Han had you not killed him." But he did not speak.

Frazer said in a voice drained of expression, "Let's go, Biancoli. It doesn't do any good to explain." He did not look again at Mr. Song, but turned his face away with the blue eyes dead in it.

The jeep sprang forward and Mr. Song was left with the dust sifting down on him. As the jeep grew smaller in his eyes, Mr. Song opened his mouth, his face alive with emotion, and almost shouted after them. Then he looked down at his dusty shoes with the long scratch on one of the toes.

The dust from the jeep blew away from the road and floated over the squares of the rice paddies—dry now that the harvest was in—to fall in minute rain on the brittle, clustered stalks. Mr. Song looked at the barren land, and felt himself an old man, felt the dust like the ashes of the dead on his head, and whispered to himself as the engine sounds died away, "I know nothing."

Vern Sneider

∽ A Long Way from Home

1

It was morning in Korea. The sun, rising out of the Sea of Japan, had not yet penetrated the mist rising from the paddy field and from the Naktong River. This morning, smoke from breakfast fires did not hang over the quiet Naktong villages, filling the air with the fine fragrance of burning pine. This morning, flames licked at the thatched roofs of the homes, the sharp smell of burnt cordite corroded the breeze, and all along the line the casualty-ridden American companies desperately dug in against the reinforced northern battalions.

Kim Won Il, standing in the mixed formation of Americans and Koreans, just behind the front southeast of Taegu, was afraid. He was in his nineteenth year—a shy, slender youth, dressed in new American fatigues, wearing a steel helmet and carrying a gun slung over his shoulder. Until a few weeks before, he had never been more than ten ri from his home village, near Suwon, had never even been more than ten ri from his father's small farm. Today he was a rifleman. He had been a rifleman for about fifteen hours.

He glanced uncertainly at the tall, husky American beside him, the one they said was his buddy. He was only vaguely familiar with this strange term "buddy," even though the studious interpreter, until recently a scholar at the University in Seoul, had explained it the preceding afternoon to the group gathered around him: "*Buddy* . . ." the interpreter pronounced the word clearly and distinctly in English, then went on in his own tongue, ". . . that is the

American army name for a very special friend. Each of you who has volunteered to serve with the Americans will be assigned one of these buddies. He will be beside you at all times. He will show you the ropes, as they call it. Do you understand?"

Kim didn't understand this thing called "the ropes," but though he wanted to ask questions, his own shyness kept him silent. For his countrymen around him, especially the youths from the cities who spoke the smart talk, those with the ready phrases on their lips, were nodding.

Glancing now at his buddy, Kim was filled with doubts. This husky American did not look like a very special friend. The American's eyes were filled with sleep. And irritability was plain on his face, Kim noted, as the man glared at the one before them with the paper in his hand, the one who most assuredly held great authority.

Perhaps he had been rash to volunteer on the preceding day, Kim told himself. Perhaps he had been foolish to listen to the gray-haired American with the silver eagle on his collar, who had come driving into Taegu. But it was the haggard look of the gray-haired man, and his own deep respect for age, that caused Kim to pause with the other homeless youths on the streets.

"Help is coming," the colonel had told them in Japanese. "It's on board ship at San Francisco and Seattle. It's only a matter of days before it arrives." But the colonel couldn't keep the worry from his face, nor could he keep his eyes from drifting to the north.

"In the meantime we need volunteers to fill the regiment," the colonel went on. "We need men to replace our casualties." And his eyes clouded as he saw the apathetic, half-starved faces before him.

Kim didn't understand such military talk. For a moment he stared blankly at the gray-haired one. Then, like the others, he slowly turned and started up the road.

The colonel stood helplessly as he saw the only replacements he knew drift away from him. Then anger swept him, flushing his face. "Wait!" he called, and like the others, Kim stared back.

"Men," he said, "those of you who join us will receive three meals a day." He reached into his pocket. "I will see that each of you receives a full package of cigarettes, just like this one." His hand was trembling. "And God help me, I'll see that you're trained. Maybe we have only a day or a few hours—

I don't know." His eyes drifted to the north, and his shoulders were slumped from weariness. "But I'll see that you're trained. If I can't get you trained, I'll disband you rather than throw you in raw."

But Kim hardly heard, or understood that. He was staring at the good cigarettes, and his lungs ached for the smoke from tobacco. Then there was the promise of food, and his belly was filled only with hunger.

Yet that was yesterday. Now in this strange formation there was not even one from his home village. There was not even one he knew, only a husky American beside him who didn't speak his tongue, nor he the American's.

The one of great authority was looking at his paper, and new doubts crept into Kim's mind. He had to remember a strange name, and he had to remember that English word "here." Slowly he repeated both, over and over.

For he wasn't even Kim Won Il any longer. The name his grandfather, the aged one, had so proudly bestowed on him was gone, had vanished, just as had his home village. "You see," the scholarly interpreter had told them, "no longer will you use your own names. The Americans are giving you new ones. I think it is hard for them to remember and pronounce the Korean words. Besides, they have bestowed a great honor on us. They call us the Irish of the Orient, because they say our temperament is that of the Irish on the other side of the world. So from now on, you will go by these Irish names they give you," he said.

Patrick Tobin, Kim repeated in his mind. Patrick Tobin, for truly he wanted to remember his own name.

Platoon Sergeant Emery looked at the list in his hand, then at the formation before him. Though he was only twenty-seven, the last few weeks had added years to the sergeant's age; his face was lined and he badly needed a shave. The familiar faces were growing fewer and fewer, he noticed. Pulaski was gone. They had left him dying on the banks of the Kum. Wilson, Taylor, Lehr—only God knew where they were, their places taken now by the bronze-skinned men with the Irish names, standing beside the dog-tired GI's. But roll call was roll call, and Sergeant Emery flicked his list: "Gobel."

"Yo," answered a sleepy American.

"William O'Dwyer."

"Here." A tall Korean nodded brightly.

"Sanders."

"Yeah."

"Bernard Shaw."

"Here."

And fright swept up in Kim Won Il, then, for his name had slipped from his mind. It was written on the band wrapped around his arm, but that did little good; he couldn't read the English letters. Helplessly he looked to his buddy. But his buddy, his very special friend, paid no attention. His buddy was grumbling in the strange tongue of the Americans, "Come on, let's get it over."

"Mason."

"Yo," the husky American beside Kim replied.

"Patrick Tobin."

Silence fell on the formation. Kim saw the heads of his countrymen turn, saw them look inquisitively at one another as the voice of the one of authority boomed out, "Mason, do you have Patrick Tobin?"

"How the hell do I know?"

"Well, look at his arm band!"

Kim felt his arm being grabbed roughly. "Yeah," the husky American said. And Kim, catching a glimpse of his buddy's face, thought: Indeed, he is an irritable one. Then, hearing the snickering, Kim flushed in shame. Pak Yup Sung, who had come from Seoul, the capital . . . Pak, who could converse at such great length on any subject, was openly laughing at him for forgetting his name.

He heard the names being called, heard his countrymen answer, "Here." And his shame grew, and he looked down. But then there was a silence over the formation again. Heads turned, ready to laugh, as the one of authority repeated, "Desmond Fitzgerald." And Kim, too, glanced about inquiringly.

"Here," an American in the file ahead said, indicating a little Korean with a jerk of his thumb. Pak Yup Sung snickered. But Kim couldn't laugh at this other one who had forgotten his name. Though the back of this one called Desmond Fitzgerald was to him, Kim saw many things. The man was small and perhaps all of forty, but his hands weren't soft and smooth like the hands of those from the cities. They were rough hands, calloused by the handles of the plow, as were Kim's. He had a strong back, like that of one who was used to carrying great shocks of rice during the harvest. No, Kim couldn't laugh at this one, who surely came from the villages, too.

Suddenly the formation began breaking up, and Kim glanced hesitantly at his buddy. "Look, Patrick, I'm going to hit the sack again," the American said in his strange tongue. "Get yourself some chow." Kim did not understand, and the American went on: "*Watakushi wa nemasu . . .* I sleep. *Wakari-masu-ka . . .* understand?"

Yes, Kim understood those words. They were in Japanese, and he knew that this was one of the soldiers who had come over from duty in Japan.

The American walked away from him, leaving Kim alone, doubtful. Some of his countrymen, their buddies with them, were forming a line. And though he could see that food was being given out, and though his stomach growled from hunger, still Kim hesitated.

"What should we do, my brother?" someone beside him asked in Korean. Turning, Kim saw the one called Desmond Fitzgerald.

"I do not know," he replied.

"Do you think we should line up?"

"I think we must have our buddies with us. The interpreter told us yesterday that they would show us what to do."

"Perhaps you are right." Desmond nodded. "But my buddy is going back to sleep."

"Mine, too," Kim said, looking at the back of the husky American who was heading toward what had once been a school. His hunger returned then, a sharp, gnawing pain in his belly. With the exception of the one American meal on the preceding evening, it had been many days since he tasted any food besides the bark from trees. Was this a special friend, he asked himself, who left you alone, without food, while he slept?

A roar from the one of authority caused Kim to look up. "All right, you lunkheads," Platoon Sergeant Emery shouted at the disappearing troops. "Get back here. Get these guys some chow." His orders were occasioned by the half dozen or so regimental staff officers prowling the area, tight-lipped men who had pored over the Intelligence overlays, men who had seen the red rectangles indicating the northern divisions massing just above Taegu and knew they were ready to drive. Men who realized the importance of the new-made Irish and who were there checking on their colonel's order that the Irish receive hot meals, and enough. "Come on, Mason."

Kim's buddy turned. "Jeez, Sarge, this is supposed to be a rest area."

"Rest area!" Sergeant Emery indicated the manned machine-gun positions and a ridge, a scant three miles distance. "What do you think is up in those hills? The USO? Now get back here!"

Kim saw his very special friend come toward him, his face twisted in anger. "Come on, Patrick," he said roughly, then pointed at the one of authority. "Son of a bitch."

Kim didn't understand the words, but the tone of voice told him that this was a phrase of scorn. Yet it was the one of authority who was seeing that he was fed.

He followed the American through the chow line, and as his buddy began to grumble, Kim grew frightened. "Jeez. S.O.S. When are you jokers going to learn to cook?" his buddy was saying, and Kim saw that his anger was directed toward the one with the food. He tried to control his fright. Suppose the one with the food grew angry with them? Suppose he refused to feed them?

"Hey, Patrick," his buddy said, pointing. "S.O.S."

Kim saw that the one with the food was growing angry. He wanted to hurry, to get away. But his buddy—like many others—sauntered along, grumbling at those behind the kettles. And Kim couldn't control his surprise when, in spite of this, their mess kits were heaped full and each was given a package of good American cigarettes.

He sat beside his buddy on a little hill. His buddy set down his own mess kit and shook his head. " *Warui* . . . bad."

Warui . . . bad. No, first-class, good, Kim thought. But he didn't want to say so and displease this American. He started to sip from the metal cup. But the cup was hot and burned his lips.

"You're doing it the hard way, Patrick." His buddy shook his head. "See, like this." The American took Kim's cup, tilted it, poured coffee out over the brim and handed it back. "Try it."

Hesitantly, Kim brought the cup to his lips, but now the metal had miraculously cooled and didn't burn at all. Yet the black liquid was bitter, causing him to screw up his face.

"Yeah, *warui* . . . bad." Mason nodded, emptying his own cup onto the ground. Then he arose. "I'm going to hit the sack."

"Hit the sack?" Kim repeated in English.

"Sleepu . . . *nemasu.*"

"Ah, *so-desu-ka* . . . is it so?" Furtively, Kim glanced at his buddy's mess kit, at the food that had hardly been touched. He could eat his own breakfast and this too—more even, if only his buddy would . . . But his buddy paid no attention. He walked over to a pit dug in the ground and threw his food away. This American was indeed a strange one, Kim thought. He didn't want the food himself, yet he would rather throw it onto the dirt than share it.

Down near the field kitchen, a cook called, "Seconds." But Kim, not understanding the language, bent to his own breakfast.

The one of great authority was coming down the line, was watching the groups sitting on the hummocks. Seeing that Kim was alone, the one of authority walked over, his anger evident. "Patrick," Sergeant Emery said, "where's Mason?"

"Mason?"

The sergeant nodded. "Buddy. *Doko* . . . where?"

Kim's stomach muscles tightened. He knew Mason was going to sleep, and he knew Mason hated this one before him. Suppose he told? What would his buddy do to him? He glanced uncertainly at the one of authority, who went on, "Did he hit the sack?"

The words had a familiar ring, and Kim knew this one suspected. Do not tell, his mind warned him. Yet wasn't this the one who made certain that he ate this morning? His so-called buddy hadn't cared about that. And he pointed. "Hit the sack . . . sleepu."

The sergeant wheeled away, and Kim caught a glimpse of his face, saw the rage written there, and began to tremble. He should never have talked, should never have told that this Mason had gone back to sleep. The one of authority strode rapidly toward the school, and Kim realized he had gotten his buddy into trouble.

He didn't know what to do. But looking around, he saw that other Americans had slipped away too. To one side sat Desmond Fitzgerald, all alone. Kim wanted to tell Desmond what he had done, wanted to ask Desmond's advice, but it was not the custom to come right out and speak your mind to those you had just met. Instead, he simply squatted on his heels and opened his cigarettes.

"Do you wish to smoke, my brother?" He offered the pack.

Desmond's flat face lit in a smile, and he bowed. "I thank you, but I have some." And he left unsaid what both understood: "You better save them. Perhaps you will need them later."

They squatted there smoking, two men from the villages to whom words did not readily come—one desperately wanting to ask advice, the other knowing that advice was wanted.

It was Pak Yup Sung, that one from Seoul, the capital, that one who could converse at such great length on any subject, who stopped before them. Pak had already learned to tilt his helmet at a jaunty angle, had already learned to let its strap flap back and forth freely, instead of fastening it tight under his chin. And Pak regarded them coldly. "Did you wash your eating equipment?" he asked.

They looked at him, a little frightened. "No my brother, we—"

"Well, you are supposed to."

"We did not know."

"Well, you better go right over there."

They rose to their feet, and Pak went on. "You are supposed to wash it after every meal. That is the regulation."

And because they were appreciative of such help, both bowed. "We thank you, my brother," Desmond said.

2

They fell in for training soon after chow, under the watchful eyes of the company officers, men who were determined to crowd basic training into one day, if necessary, in order to bring the crippled companies up to full strength. And as Kim took his place in ranks, he was afraid to look at his buddy. For he had seen the one of authority shouting at this Mason about going off to sleep, and surely, Kim told himself, his buddy would know that he had caused the trouble.

But Mason didn't so much as glance at Kim. Mason merely knew that he'd been told to "get the hell out of that sack." And now he was mad at authority in general.

They walked to the range at route step. Every available man was there, and in the movements and tone of the instructors there was the urgency that communicated itself to the men. The studious interpreter was sweating as he explained the process of zeroing in a rifle, but Kim hardly heard. His eyes kept stealing to the face of his buddy, who was now griping about the heat of the morning sun; and thinking his buddy's anger was directed at him, Kim looked to the ground. Later, when he lay down on the line, like the others, he did not remember a word of explanation, did not know what was expected of him, and he began to tremble. Then Sergeant Emery came along. "Mason," he said, "you're supposed to be coaching him."

Mason, lying on the ground beside Kim, looked up. "All right, Sarge, you know the language. Tell me what I'm supposed to say."

The studious interpreter was called then, and with the group gathered around him, Kim's nervousness increased. He tried to follow instructions, tried too hard and failed. Sergeant Emery shook his head. "Move over, Patrick, and I'll show you how it's done." Quickly, expertly, Emery adjusted the sights and slipped to one side.

The interpreter said, "The sergeant says you are to fire a round. He says to aim directly at the eye of the bull."

"Aim for the eye of the bull," the interpreter repeated, and Kim stared blankly, not understanding the phrase.

"Fire," the interpreter said.

Numbly, Kim pulled the trigger, and a cloud of dirt shot up some fifteen feet in front of him.

The colonel saw the shot, and he remembered the report of his S-2, the Intelligence officer: "They've started pushing across the Naktong, sir, but we don't know for certain if it's an all-out attack or just a crazy *banzai* charge."

The colonel dropped to his knees, then lay flat beside Kim.

"Aim first. Then squeeze the trigger slowly. Don't jerk," he said in Japanese.

The nearness of this great one, the half-dozen or so people standing over him, caused his hand to shake. He looked to his buddy for help, but his buddy, his very special friend, only stood there.

He tried, tried as hard as he could all that day on the range. But there was always someone standing over him. "Don't jerk the trigger. Don't cant the rifle." The phrases of instruction raced through his brain in a meaningless jumble. And though the help was offered with the best intentions, it only increased his nervousness. And Mason, who earlier in the day had said, "Boy, you should have stuck to your plowing," by evening looked at him solemnly and soberly.

As they marched back to quarters that evening, Mason, seeing Kim's face twisted in pain and nervous nausea, shook his head, and said, "By God, boy, we got to get you oriented."

That evening Kim sat alone in a room of the abandoned school, now serving as a barracks. "Hit the sack, Patrick," Mason told him. "I'll clean your rifle."

But he couldn't stretch out on the blankets spread on the floor. He sat cross-legged, watching the others. A few Americans, heads propped on arms, lay reading, while down at the end of the room Pak Yup Sung was busy talking to a group of his countrymen. "I do not think I missed placing more than two or three shots in the eye of the bull all day," Pak was telling them. Then he slapped his forehead in a new gesture he had picked up. "But that Patrick Tobin—all but two or three shots in the dirt."

The roar of laughter made Kim look quickly out the window. "And what of Desmond Fitzgerald?" someone asked.

"I wish we had more like him," Pak said. "On the side of the northerners."

Kim pretended not to hear the guffaws. He gazed steadily out of the window into the twilight. He had always liked the twilight best. Then his stomach was filled from the evening meal, and he would sit beside his father and grandfather on the veranda, smoking contentedly.

His lips curled in a smile as memory carried him from the squad room. Often he and his father and grandfather would walk down to where the crossroad entered the town. He would squat on his heels, like the rest, and respectfully listen to the talk of the elders.

"It will be a good harvest this year," he could hear his grandfather say, and the solemn faces of their neighbors would nod in agreement as they looked toward the paddies, descending in terrace after terrace down the golden hillsides. And each man would tell of his expected yield to his neighbors.

The fathers would laugh, but often, too, they would grow quiet in the evening when a band of the people-of-the-road came down through the valley from the north. Their faces were always the same, lean, hungry faces. "My brothers," they would say, "do you have work we can do?" Their faces would light hopefully. "Any kind of work at all?"

There was never work for them, yet tea was always offered, and they would squat on their heels, sipping its refreshing warmth. "You are lucky, my brothers," they would say, shaking their heads. "You are very lucky the Americans and not the others occupied this part of the country."

Kim and his neighbors had seen but few Americans in the years of the occupation—only those who had driven through their village on the way to some bigger, more important place. But they knew the Americans had brought their own food with them and did not strip the land like the others. They knew the Americans had made it possible for them to purchase the holdings of the former Japanese landlords. And they saw, with their own eyes, that the people-of-the-road always went in the same direction— always south, never north. Thus they would nod in agreement.

The longing for his village caused Kim to bite his lips. The memory of his grandfather's words caused an aching in his heart. "Soon, my son," the old one said, "we must find you a wife, for truly you are coming of age. I will speak to Lee Il Sung about his youngest daughter."

It was as if Kim himself had chosen. Long had he thought of this youngest daughter of Lee Il Sung. And while never had either dared show the least signs of familiarity, still the flush of her cheek when he passed, the eyes that stealthily drifted toward him when the elders were not looking, and the quivering in his chest that came then . . . Yes, it was as if he himself had chosen.

But that was then, long weeks ago. That was before, and this was now. Now his home village no longer existed. The thatched roofs that had once sparkled in the evening sun were charred and black. Never again would his father and grandfather sit smoking with their friends. And the youngest daughter of Lee Il Sung? Who in this world knew what had happened to her?

The voice of Pak Yup Sung, telling a long and somewhat intimate story of his friendship with a dancing girl of Seoul, reached Kim. Seeing the bare room, its floors covered with the olive-colored blankets, Kim knew he didn't belong here. He looked about slowly. It was best to leave, to slip off with the homeless ones like himself. To go back where each was so concerned, so worried over his own safety, that one could drift into obscurity and not have a crowd of people standing over him offering advice.

He thought of the good American food and the good American cigarettes. Those were hard to leave, but there was always the bark of the trees. A plan began forming in his mind. Most of the Americans, he noticed, had tried to slip out of sight of the one of authority all during the day, had tried to go to sleep. Now, with the coming of darkness, he was certain they would fall into immediate slumber. Then he would simply creep from this room into the night. The Americans, he felt, would never miss him, would never need him. He was unaware that at this moment up at headquarters the regiment was receiving orders to be prepared to move out at a moment's notice. And that the worried, gray-haired colonel was silently begging Providence for another day, or two, or three.

3

Kim's buddy, Mason, came in then, carrying the cleaned rifles. "Hey, Patrick, no hit the sack?" Mason asked.

Kim shook his head. "No sleepu."

"Oh, sick? *Byoki?*"

"*Byoki*, no."

"Good." Mason leaned the rifles against the wall, then picked up a Red Cross pad. "Write letter now."

"Write letter?" Kim questioned.

Mason's gestures explained the phrase.

"Oh." Kim nodded.

"Yeah, to my girl friend. See—" Mason pulled a billfold from his pocket—"here she is."

Kim eyed the picture of the girl with the long, dark hair. "*Okusan?*"

"*Okusan.*" Mason scratched his head. "Oh, wifu . . . no, no. *Koibito* . . . girl friend. *Itsuka* wifu . . . someday wife."

"*Wakarimasu* . . . I understand." Kim looked to his buddy who was holding the picture in his hand, who was studying it closely. And there, in the twilight, he noticed that this American, too, seemed lonely.

The American shook his head. "Ya damn right, Patrick. *Itsuka* wifu. *Itsuka* housu in Hoboken."

"Housu in Hoboken?" Kim questioned.

"Housu means *uchi.*"

"Oh." Kim nodded. "*Uchi.*"

"Ya damn right. I'm gonna build a housu, Patrick. Have kids . . . *kodomo. Itsuka* . . . someday."

"Good. Good."

The American grinned at him. "Yep, Patrick, housu in Hoboken." Then he bent over his pad and wet the pencil with his tongue. Kim watched him spell out the strange letters. Other Americans were doing the same. Kim wished that he could write a letter to tell the trouble in his heart. But there was no place to send such a letter. There was no one left any more.

Darkness began to fall, blankets were hung over the windows, and candles were lighted. In all this world, there are few places as lonely as a squad room when night closes in. The melancholy of the room, his sense of not belonging, came strong to Kim. Yes, he would have to slip away. Surely all would soon be asleep. He need wait only a little while. He lay back on his blankets and put an arm over his eyes. It would only be a little while longer.

The door was thrown open, and Kim looked up. The one of great authority came in, out of breath, his face lined with excitement. And Kim grew alarmed. Had there been a sudden attack? Had the northerners broken through and reached here? He saw the Americans put down their pencils, saw them gather around the one of authority. His buddy's voice rose above the group. "Jeez, where is it?"

"Down the road. They just moved in this afternoon, and they got cases of it."

"Yeow!" A shrill shriek cut the air, freezing Kim's blood. Indeed there must have been an attack.

The Americans gathered around Platoon Sergeant Emery, excitement in their voices. "Now look," Sergeant Emery explained. "We're alerted, but I can cover with the Old Man if a couple of you slip out. Mason, you and Thompson and Wilson take off. That Quartermaster outfit has it stored in the second tent, just off the road."

"Good deal," Mason said. "Hey, wait a minute, I got an idea. Look, the three of us won't be able to carry much. How about taking Patrick and a couple others along?"

"What for?"

"Well, you know those Korean pants they wore when they came in, those baggy things that tie around the ankles? See, if we take them along, we can shove all the beer cans down into the pants. Jeez, it's just like having barracks bags along."

It was a nervous Kim who slipped out of his American fatigues and into his tattered Korean clothing. Though the Americans kept slapping him on the back and saying, "*Biru*," he didn't know what to make of it. He saw that little Desmond Fitzgerald, too, had changed into his Korean clothes.

"Do we go to meet the northerners, my brother?" Desmond whispered anxiously. "If so, shouldn't they let us carry our rifles? Pak Yup Sung warned me that I must carry my rifle at all times because of the guerrillas."

Kim was unable to answer. No, they were not going to meet the northerners, he felt, for he was certain he and Desmond were about to be punished in some way for having failed so miserably in the day's training. They moved out into the darkness, three Americans with their three buddies. The Americans held their guns in their hands. They talked in whispers to their own outposts and were passed through very quickly. Kim wondered if he shouldn't run. He eyed Desmond, who seemed to have the same thoughts. Perhaps when a good opportunity presented itself, he could . . .

"Hey, Patrick," Mason whispered and took him by the arm. "This way." Mason put a finger to his lips. "Don't worry about our positions. They know who we are. They're passing the word down the line, and they won't shoot. But the bastards said they wouldn't let us back into the area unless we forked over two cans of beer for each man on post. That's that damn C Company for you."

Not understanding the English, Kim looked uncertainly at his buddy. They dropped off the road into the paddy fields, and the Americans, with their own positions at their back, grew most careful.

Kim noted they moved only when the breeze rustled the stocks of rice. At other times they lay dead still. No word was spoken and the six of them inched forward on their bellies, always waiting for the breeze to cover their movements.

They reached a paddy ridge and stopped. The moon was an old, dying moon, yet by its faint light Kim could see the tents dark against the sky. Maybe this was an attack, after all. He glanced at his buddy. Mason was carefully scanning the ground. After a few minutes he aimed his rifle toward an object, propped it so it wouldn't fall, then slipped to one side, motioning to Kim.

Kim knew he must move only when the breeze blew; when it did, he inched toward the gun, puzzled. Maybe his buddy wanted him to fire. He reached for the trigger, but his buddy stopped him, pointing to the sights of the rifle, then to Kim's eye. He understood then. His buddy wanted him to look. Glancing down the barrel, he saw the helmet, saw the man low against the ground, apparently lying in a hole, and he nodded.

One by one all crawled forward to glance through the sights. The position of the rifle was changed, each looked again, and in a matter of minutes Mason indicated the Quartermaster outposts guarding this side of the tents. Then they moved forward, between the outposts, silent men, crawling on their bellies. He didn't know how far they crawled, but their progress was slow and tortuous, and he felt he had been crawling, all his life. When they finally came up by the tent his face was dripping with sweat and his short jacket was wet.

Two Americans remained outside in the shadows, and Mason led the three Koreans in. Kim could barely hear his buddy move. He couldn't see in the darkness and uncertainty closed over him. Then he felt a can thrust in his hand. "*Pantsu* . . . pants, Patrick," Mason whispered.

He didn't understand, and the can was thrust between his cloth belt and his body. As can after can was shoved against his stomach, he caught on and carefully, silently lowered them into the legs of his trousers. He explained to Desmond and the other Korean what must be done.

But new doubts crept into his mind. He had no idea where they were, but surely it must be behind the northerners' lines. The cans pressed tightly against his legs. The weight of them was pulling down his trousers. He tightened the band at his waist, tightened the bands at his ankles, so the cans wouldn't drop out. But how would they ever slip back? He couldn't crawl like this. The metal striking on metal would make an awful noise and the bullets from the guns, out there in the night, would surely find him.

"Buddy." He took Mason's arm and indicated his fears by gesture.

"O.K., O.K.," Mason reassured him. "Wait here."

The three of them were loaded down, and cautiously Mason led them outside. "Put up your hands, Patrick," Mason whispered.

"*Nani* . . . what?"

Mason showed him. Desmond Fitzgerald and the other also put up their hands, and the Americans brought up their guns. Then Kim felt the rifle shoved in his back, and Mason's voice was loud. "All right, keep walking, you son of a bitches, straight ahead."

It seemed to Kim that a thousand cries rang out in the night. "Halt! Who goes there?"

"American patrol with prisoners," Mason yelled.

"Advance to be recognized."

Mason feigned ignorance. "How the hell do we know where you're at? Come and recognize us."

A deadly silence closed over the area, and Kim felt his heart pounding against his ribs. What kind of a trap was this? In a moment, a flashlight cut the blackness, played over them, and a voice sang out, "Corporal of the Guard . . . Post Number Four." And it was a puzzled corporal who sent for his officer.

The lieutenant was short and chesty. His fatigues were new and crinkly and his hand was on his pistol as he regarded the group in the beam of the flashlight—the three Koreans with hands high overhead, and the three grim Americans with rifles in the Koreans' backs.

"We're an Intelligence patrol, sir," Mason explained. "They sent us out to grab prisoners, and we got these three. In coming back we wandered into your area. I kinda got twisted in my bearings."

The lieutenant looked at the sky. Polaris, the north star, was there shining bright; and having just completed a course in map reading, he was skeptical. It didn't make sense to him. "If you are on patrol why are you moving northwest toward the front, instead of southeast, away from it?" he asked.

Mason regarded him. "Oh, we weren't behind their lines, sir. You see, we're in reserve, so they sent us out to round up these jokers who slipped in." He regarded the lieutenant again. "Didn't they tell you there were guerrillas in the area, sir?"

The lieutenant knew there were guerrillas in the area; he knew they were everywhere. Still it angered him to have an enlisted man tell him. "Why the hell do you think I have outposts out if I didn't know there were guerrillas around?" he demanded.

"Oh, do you have them out, sir?" Mason asked innocently. "Golly, I didn't know that. We must have walked right through them without knowing it."

The lieutenant flushed in the darkness. It would never do to have the colonel hear of this. Quickly he played his flashlight over the new-made Irish.

"What have they got stuffed inside their pants there?"

Mason looked at the bulging beer cans, then at the figure of the young lieutenant. "Grenades, sir. They came in here to really blow hell out of the place. If I were you, sir, I'd tighten up on my security. Conceal the outposts better."

"All right, soldier," the lieutenant flashed. "I'll take care of the security of this outfit."

But Mason was enjoying this, not having such an opportunity very often. "I'm sorry, sir. I didn't mean to tell you what to do." His face grew solemn. "Only I'd hate to see a bunch of guys blown to hell, because some—someone messes up the detail. A couple of these jokers, standing where we are now, could really give this outfit the business."

For a moment the lieutenant was tempted to put him under arrest, was tempted to charge him with disrespect toward an officer. But looking at the tents, he realized the truth of Mason's words, and he was facing six men who had come into the middle of his camp without being seen. "All right, soldier," he said, "just get out of here and leave this place to me. Sergeant, take them out to the road."

When they were once again in the darkness, the Americans brought down their rifles. But Kim still held his hands in the air, as did Desmond and the other. Mason made them put down their hands, handed Kim his rifle, then quickly opened cans of beer. Realizing what had happened, a smile crossed Kim's face, and Desmond Fitzgerald also grinned.

4

Indeed these Americans confused Kim. All day they had tried to sleep, but now that evening was here, now that they had a chance to sleep, the thought of it seemed far from their minds. The beer was passed out in the squad room; even the one of authority joined in. And Kim, a newly opened can clutched tight, watched them spread a blanket, watched them bring out some ivory cubes.

"High dice rolls first," Mason said and expertly tossed boxcars.

"What is this, my brother?" Desmond Fitzgerald asked.

Kim shook his head. "I do not know. Let us watch."

They crowded in with the group. And while the faces of the Americans grew solemn, the faces of their Korean buddies were filled with curiosity. Kim saw his buddy place some money in the middle, pick up the cubes, then thrust them forward. "Blow on 'em, Patrick."

"*Nani* . . . what? "

His buddy's gestures told him what to do. And Mason broke into a stream of very rapid talk which Kim did not understand at all. But he heard, "Housu in Hoboken."

The dice were tossed out. They struck the wall and bounded back. "Seven," Mason yelled. "Seven it is. Let it ride."

Thoughtfully, Kim took a sip of beer. From the faces of the other Americans, he knew his buddy had won. More money was put out and Mason thrust the dice at Kim again. "Blow on 'em, Pat."

This time Kim knew what to do.

"Seven." The dice clicked against the wall. "Seven it is. It rides."

"I see how it works," Kim whispered to Desmond. "You get the number seven up and you win the money."

"Ah, is it so?" Desmond took a swallow from his can.

"Patrick, blow on 'em." Again his buddy broke into the stream of rapid talk. Anxiously Kim leaned forward. He counted the numbers: "One . . . two . . . three . . . four. Four." In alarm, he looked at his buddy who, he was convinced, had lost.

But his buddy didn't seem concerned. "Little Joe, Patrick. I think we'll take two to one on that."

"I'm with him," Sergeant Emery said. He began to count out money, and the bills were stacked high.

"There must be more to the game," Desmond whispered. "Perhaps when you roll four, you get another chance."

Kim blew on the proffered dice and edged forward. Mason shook them deliberately, perhaps too deliberately, for as his arm came down a hand shot out stopping the dice. "Damn it, Mason. None of that." The speaker, Kim saw, was one of the Americans who had gone with them to get the beer.

"What the hell do you mean?"

"You know what I mean."

A tenseness fell over the group. The two Americans glared at each other.

"All right, wise guy," Mason said heatedly. "All right." He held out the dice. "Pat, roll 'em."

When Kim understood what was wanted of him, he grew tense. "Come on, Pat. Show this meat-head," Mason said, glaring at the other American. And Kim found himself at the head of the group. For a moment he didn't know what to do. But realizing there must be some pattern to this, he held out the dice. "Blow on 'em, buddy."

Mason blew, and Kim jiggled the dice in such a manner that even those who watched most closely were satisfied. His buddy had always talked at this moment, and Kim knew some phrase was demanded of him. "Housu in Hoboken," he breathed to himself, seven . . . then his buddy would win.

The dice bounced crazily and spun. "Seven," Kim whispered hopefully to himself. Then the fright crowded up in his chest. "Four." He had failed.

He wasn't exactly sure of what happened at that moment. His buddy was slapping him on the back, and the one of authority was shouting, "You made it, Patrick. You made it, you old son of a bitch."

"Made it?"

"We win. Hey, give Patrick another brew." Someone gave Kim another can. He took a swallow of beer, felt the dice being pressed into his hand. "Roll 'em again."

Slowly, he threw them out. "Five." Now he didn't know what to do and glanced at his buddy, who was considering. "Patrick, I think we'll take three to two on that."

Kim nodded. "Take three to two. Blow on 'em, buddy. Housu in Hoboken."

When he awoke in the morning a flash of pain seemed to split his head in two. Never before in his whole life had he been so thirsty. The one of authority was standing over him, was shaking him, and Kim looked up hopefully. "Sleepu?"

"Sleepu, hell. Get out of that sack, Patrick."

Kim looked again, just to make sure. Was this the same one who kept pounding him on the back last night and shouting: "Jeez, boy, thirteen straight passes!" Was this the one who had helped him take off his boots when the dizziness closed in? "Sleepu, no?" he questioned.

"Hit the deck!" The roar made Kim forget his aching head, and he sat up, though every muscle in his body cried out in protest.

"Mason!" the one of authority yelled, but Kim's buddy didn't stir. He lay flat on his back in all his clothing, with no cover over him, with his boots still on.

"O.K., Mason." Kim saw the one of authority draw back his foot and sharply kick the sole of Mason's boot.

Kim could hardly believe. Hadn't these two stood arm in arm last night, like lifelong friends, singing? Now one was kicking the other. The one of authority walked among the sleeping figures, kicking here, shaking there; all the time his gruff voice was shattering the quiet of the morning. What kind of an organization was this, Kim wondered. Sometimes they were the best of friends. Sometimes they were the worst enemies.

But his tortured brain would not permit much thinking, and like a man half dead he arose.

They fell into formation.

"Gobel."

"Yo."

Kim was not afraid of roll call this morning. He knew his name now.

"Sanders."

"Yeah."

"Bernard Shaw."

"Here."

"Mason."

A silence hung over the group. Pak Yup Sung turned, ready to laugh at his countryman who had forgotten his name. And Kim stared curiously at this Pak, this one who could converse at such great length on any subject. For last night Pak had never been able to win more than twice in a row.

"Mason!"

Quickly, Kim glanced at his friend. "Buddy, buddy," he whispered. But his friend paid no attention. He stood there weaving.

"Mason!"

Kim looked about desperately, then threw back his head and called at the top of his voice, "Yo."

After the formation broke up, Kim took his buddy, who surely needed help, by the arm. "Hit the sack," he said.

Mason shook his head. "No."

"No?" What was this, Kim wondered.

"*Kohi* . . . coffee."

"Oh, chow?" Together they went down through the line, with Kim doing the guiding. But this morning the sight of food nauseated Kim, made him gag. Like Mason, he too took only coffee and cigarettes. For a moment as the memory of the coffee's bitterness came, he didn't know if he wanted even this. Pouring some out, cooling the brim of the cup, he brought it to his lips. He took a swallow, hesitated. But his thirsty body demanded more. He brought the cup to his lips again.

As his head began to clear, he looked around at the groups sitting on the ground. Last night, he remembered, he had intended to leave. But this morning . . . well, this morning he wasn't sure that he wanted to run away.

A benevolent Providence granted them a few days' grace. And it wasn't until one night, five days later, that the doubts again crept into Kim's mind. On that night he lay in the lines and looked out at the hills rising dark and ominous to the north. All day those hills had been alive. When the angry whine of the rifles on them kicked dirt up around his position, Kim had looked for reassurance. Seeing his special buddy, seeing his many buddies around him, a feeling of security had come over him, and he fired back.

But tonight the lines were especially quiet, and Intelligence was worried, worried over the strange lull. And when Intelligence is worried, the patrols move forward to probe and search. And Kim was afraid. Where once he wanted to run from this group, to get away from it, now he didn't want to leave it. He wanted to lie there, knowing Mason was on one side of him, knowing the others were there, too, each helping and guarding the other.

Yet tonight he was selected as one of the group who would move forward into the land where there was no friendship. And he lay in the foxhole, his forehead wet with perspiration.

"Pat," he heard Mason whisper.

"Yes. Time?"

"Time no."

"Oh."

There was a long silence. "Hey, Pat, I'm coming over." He heard a soft movement, and in a moment Mason dropped in beside him. "What are you doing, buddy?"

Kim shook his head. "Doing nothing."

They squatted there and the moon was gone from the heavens. Only the shape of the American was visible; Kim could not see his face, yet he knew that face was troubled. For even though you have been on a thousand patrols, it is the waiting, the uncertainty of what the darkness holds that makes a thousand thoughts run through your mind. They squatted for a long time, and no word was spoken. Then Kim was able to make out that his buddy was peering at a picture in the darkness.

"*Koibito* . . . girl friend?" he asked.

"Yeah."

Kim smiled. "Nice. Someday *housu* in Hoboken."

"Yeah. Someday. Maybe." There was a dejection in Mason's voice that caused Kim to look into the night.

"You . . . *koibito,* Pat?" Mason asked.

The thought of Lee Il Sung's youngest daughter came. She who always blushed when he walked by, she whose eyes always stole to him when the elders were not looking. "Once," he answered.

"Once?"

"Yes. Now no. Where . . . don't know."

Mason was silent for a moment. "Housu no, Pat?"

"Housu no." In explanation Kim threw up his hands, indicating the burst of artillery. "Boom."

"They did it?" Mason pointed north. "They . . . boom?"

Kim bit his lip and his silence gave the answer.

"It was us, eh, Pat?" Mason's voice was low. "Damn, I'm sorry, boy."

The memory of his father and his grandfather came to Kim. They rested now out on the land that grew the good rice.

"Son of a bitch, I'm sorry, Pat."

It was the sincerity in the voice that made Kim say: "*Shikata-ga-nai . . . shikata-ga-nai* . . . it can't be helped."

"Yeah, *shikata-ga-nai,*" Mason replied. "But it's a sorry damn world, Pat."

The one of authority was crawling among the foxholes. "Time to move out," he whispered, and Kim moved beside his buddy, there in the darkness. There were six that formed in the group—three Americans and three men with the new Irish names, going out to probe the enemy positions. Going out to search for information so that others, higher up, could piece together the report of many patrols and arrive at conclusions regarding enemy strength, disposition and possible intention.

Little Desmond Fitzgerald was there, his face solemn as he moved down-slope beside Kim into the rice paddies. There was a corporal in charge, and slowly, cautiously they moved as he directed, away from the rifles which protected each other, until there were only six of them in the night.

They crawled in the dark of the moon. A faint rustling reached Kim, and he lay dead still. The others, too, heard and froze. They lay there for minutes, each man barely breathing, afraid that the sound of his breath would give him away. The northerners also had patrols out, Kim realized. The northerners were also searching, and the two patrols had nearly come face to face. But apparently the northerners had the same orders as they—to avoid all combat, not to fight except to protect themselves. For they, too, were seeking information, not battle.

And there in the night they began to circle—two groups of men, aware of each other's presence, enemies; yet each group began crawling hundreds of yards out of its way, crawling until their clothing was soaked with sweat to avoid each other. Yet each group was using its radio, was sending back information to its own lines. And the alerted positions began checking their machine guns and rifles, began watching the slopes before them for the slightest signs of any movement.

Kim looked to the dark ridges, then crawled over beside Mason, whispering, "Buddy, no . . . no!" His gestures told the American that surely the northerners had reported their presence.

"I know, Pat," Mason whispered back. "But we go. It can't be helped . . . *shikata-ga-nai.*"

5

It was a mistake to push up those ridges. It was foolish. Kim knew it. The northerners were waiting for them. "Buddy, no," the words flashed through his mind. Yet the group started forward. For a moment Kim hesitated, then, wiping the sweat from his forehead with the back of his hand, he followed.

But death was crawling with them in the darkness. The night wind died abruptly, allowing a faint sound to drift up-slope. And a frightened, youthful conscript from the northern provinces pulled the trigger of a captured American machine gun as his officers had ordered. Then, in his newness, he began swinging it wildly back and forth.

The bullets sprayed into them. A ricochet went swinging crazily into the darkness. And Kim hugged the ground as the youth froze on the trigger, firing until the last round was gone from the belt. Run, Kim's mind warned, move down-slope. He pushed himself up and the faint moan reached him, freezing him. Down-slope was the cover of the paddy ridges, safety from the guns of the northerners. They would never see him nor hear him if he slipped back down. But just ahead one of his group was hit. His face twisted in anguish.

Down-slope, get away—the words rushed through his mind. But, the moan came again, and he moved forward. He reached a sprawled figure, and as he touched it, it moved. "Buddy?" he whispered anxiously to the dark form.

"It is I, my brother," came the low voice of Desmond Fitzgerald.

"Are you wounded?"

"No."

"One moans. Is it your buddy?"

"He is dead."

From uphill came a mumbled curse in Korean as the machine-gun crew tried frantically to reload. Kim had seen such guns during his few days of training. He understood what it meant when the cover assembly was slammed down and the bolt drawn back, and he knew that in a moment the bullets would spray into them again. For the briefest instant he considered hugging the ground. But someone was moaning helplessly. Then the memory of another night came flooding back, the memory of that night when he had stood with an American rifle in his back and his trousers weighed down with cans of beer. Boldly, he rose to his knees. "My brothers," he called, "hold your fire. It is friends going out on patrol."

The youthful conscripts around the machine gun eyed each other uncertainly in the darkness. Then one called, "If you are going out on patrol, why do you approach us from the front?"

"You are confused," Kim answered quickly. "We were not approaching. We were circling to avoid the Americans that we just reported. No one told us you were there."

"How many of you are there?"

Kim understood the northerners were checking on them, understood that they knew the strength of their own patrol and that this could be a trap. He hesitated, then spoke quickly. "I do not know now that you have fired into us. Keep your gun silent while I search here. I'll call back to you.

"Search," came the reply.

"Help me, my brother," Kim whispered to Desmond, taking advantage of the uncertain truce. And the two of them crept forward. He found Mason then, sprawled face down on the bare hillside. "Buddy, buddy," he whispered, and a silent nod was his only reply.

"The other two are gone," Desmond, beside him, said. "There's only you and I remaining."

"And my buddy remains, too," Kim replied quickly. "We must get him back to the hospital they showed us." Then he called to the machine gunners. "There are two of us and our wounded officer left. We will continue with the patrol and take him along." The anger surged up in him. "Now hold your fire, fools, or I will report you."

Indecision swept over the gunners, and Kim called out again, "Do you hear, or must I report your foolishness?"

"Go," a voice answered quickly. "And keep your tongue still."

Kim whispered to Desmond, "My brother, will you carry him? I don't trust those fools. They might fire on us again."

And down-slope they went with little Desmond Fitzgerald bending under the weight of the husky American, just as he had once bent under the weight of the great sheaves of golden grain during the harvest. While behind them Kim Won Il, now Patrick Tobin, walked straight and erect, his own body a human shield against the machine gun.

They squatted on their heels in the tent of the Battalion Aid Station, two silent men from the villages of Korea. And the scholarly interpreter did his best to make them understand. "The Mr. Doctor says you must report back to your unit. If you just came back from patrol, surely the Military Intelligence is eagerly awaiting your report."

Kim looked at this one who had been a student at the University. And while Kim had great respect for the educated, still, he now regarded this one as he would any village dolt. Couldn't this one, with all his education, understand. "Buddy," he said, indicating the stretcher flat on the ground beneath the hissing lights. "Buddy!" He wasn't going back.

The young interpreter was at a loss and turned to the American doctor, on one knee beside Mason. "They will not go, Mr. Doctor. I explained to them a hundred times, yet they will not listen."

The doctor eyed the two men with the Irish names and knew that no authority on earth could move them from that shelter. He adjusted the small bottle of plasma, then bent. "Soldier," he said quietly to Mason, "tell them to go back. Intelligence has to know where that machine gun is located."

Kim saw his buddy's eyes open, and in spite of the great pain those eyes were angry. "Why the hell should I, Doc?" The voice was weak. "So they can get their guts blown out?"

"No, soldier," the doctor went on. "So Intelligence can have mortar fire put on that machine gun. So they can save someone else from having their guts blown out. Tell them, soldier. They'll listen to you."

Mason's eyes closed and for a long while he was silent, then, "Pat."

"*Hai* . . . yes." Kim moved beside the stretcher.

"Pat, you and Desmond go."

Kim shook his head. "No, buddy."

"I go, Pat."

"Oh?"

"Yeah, to America. Housu in Hoboken, Pat. Huh, Doc?" The doctor nodded. "That's right, soldier. Back to Hoboken."

"See, Pat. I go. You go, too."

Kim hesitated, but he saw a certain look on the doctor's face. And he knew then. He knew just as surely as the doctor and Mason himself. "Housu in Hoboken. Good. Good." He managed a smile.

"Yeah. Good, Pat. Someday you housu in Seoul, maybe."

"*Hai* . . . housu in Seoul." There was something in the doctor's eyes, as he glanced at Mason, that made Kim rise. "I go, buddy."

Mason looked up at him. "Desmond . . . where?"

"Here, buddy." Kim took Desmond's arm and brought him forward.

"Desmond," Mason went on. "You carry me back. Thanks. You, Pat, thanks." Mason's face twisted in pain. "Thanks. Pat, you and Desmond . . . a couple of good son of a bitches."

The studious interpreter's mouth flew open at these words that had never been listed in any dictionary or thesaurus, these words so despicable that they were only spoken in the gutter. Then his eyes widened in amazement because his two countrymen were bowing, were speaking in Japanese, in the honorific. "*Arigato gozaimasu* . . . we thank you very much."

Kim and Desmond walked from the tent and neither spoke, for the words were locked within them. But a thousand thoughts were running through

Kim's mind, thoughts of his father and grandfather, buried now on the land that grew the good rice. Thoughts of the youngest daughter of Lee Il Sung and the thatched roofs of his home village going up in flame. His lips twisted uncontrollably, and he looked to the back of Desmond Fitzgerald, the coarse fatigue clothing caked with American blood that had seeped through. And his thoughts were of a house in Hoboken that would never exist.

Anger and despair welled up in him, until he couldn't hold them back, and his voice came in English. "Sorry damn world," he said harshly. And little Desmond Fitzgerald beside him nodded.

A star shell lighted the dark ridges. And as its flickering light fell on the tent of the Battalion Aid Station, death came in the Korean night.

6

They came out of the line the next night. And Sergeant Emery, standing before his platoon in the early morning, absently unfolded the list in his hand. The familiar faces were growing fewer and fewer, he noted. Mason was gone. William O'Dwyer and Wilson, too, their places taken by fresh-faced recruits, some just over from across the Pacific, and some from the people-of-the-road.

He flicked the list. But some of the old gang remained. "Gobel."

"Yo."

"Shamus O'Reilly."

Silence hung over the formation, and Kim looked to see this one who had forgotten his name. He was a tall youth, barely eighteen. And Kim, seeing the newness of his fatigues, seeing his hand tremble, couldn't help but feel sorry for this one because Pak Yup Sung was already snickering.

There was a new one beside Kim, too, whose helmet bore no sign of mud. He was even smaller than Kim though he was an American. And Kim could see that he was a quiet one.

"Black."

"Here." An American replacement answered quickly.

"Desmond Fitzgerald."

"Yo."

"Taylor."

When the American beside him answered, Kim repeated the name "Taylor" to himself. So that was it. That was the name of his new buddy. He stiffened. This one wasn't his buddy, even though the one of authority had said so. Mason was his buddy.

"Dismissed," Sergeant Emery called. And Kim turned. He didn't want food this morning. He wanted to sleep, for when you sleep you don't think. And when you don't think the gloominess is shoved from your mind. He started for the abandoned warehouse, now serving as a barracks, then stopped and glanced back.

The new American, the small one, was standing with mess kit in hand, uncertainty written on his face. Well, let him eat if he wishes, Kim thought; he can find the kitchen. But looking again, Kim saw that this small one was indeed uneasy with strangers. Even before Sergeant Emery boomed, "All right, you lunkheads. Get these guys some chow," he was walking over.

"*Tabemasho* . . . let us eat," he said in Japanese, and the new one regarded him, not understanding.

So he didn't even understand that language. Kim shook his head. By God, boy, he thought, we certainly got to get you oriented. Then he pointed and said, "Chow."

They lined up before the kettles, and Pak Yup Sung, that one from Seoul, the capital, that one who could converse at such great length on any subject, came sauntering along, fully conscious of the new recruits. Fully conscious that they were eyeing his cocked helmet and thinking that indeed here was a veteran of great experience.

He regarded the long line, then came up to Kim and the small American. "I will slip in here," he announced.

Instinctively, the small American started to make room for him, and Kim's eyes flashed. "No you won't, my brother. You will take your place at the end of the line like the rest."

The new recruits were looking and Pak threw out his chest. "The one of authority has asked me to hurry and eat. He needs me for training today. You see, there is already talk that they are going to make me a corporal."

"Bull," Kim said in English, and Pak flushed.

"My brother, do you doubt my word?"

Kim stared at him. "Yes."

"All right. Then I shall have to report you."

Kim searched for a reply, but little Desmond Fitzgerald was already speaking. "Pak," he said, "blow it out your barracks bag." And as the red-faced

Pak went down to take his place at the end of the line, Desmond announced to one and all: "Guardhouse lawyer," he announced firmly in English, Japanese and Korean.

They sat in the shade of the warehouse eating their breakfast, and Kim kept watching his new buddy. This American was about his own age, Kim decided, and he wondered about him. "Girl friend?" he asked slowly.

The new one shook his head. "No."

"Oh." Kim considered. "Bad."

"Bad," the American agreed.

Seeing his solemn face, Kim went on quickly. "Someday girl friend."

The American grinned. "Someday."

"Good," Kim said. "Go home. Go to America. Have housu. Maybe have housu in Hoboken."

"No, in Kalamazoo."

"Oh, Kalamazoo. Good." Then Kim shook his head. "Me girl friend neither."

"Someday girl friend," the American said.

Kim smiled. "*Hai*, someday." Yes, he would go back to his home village, and he would rebuild the house of his father. He would gather the thatch from the hills for its roof, and its sides would be of gleaming white mortar. And someday they would come back—Lee Il Sung and his youngest daughter, she who always blushed when their eyes met.

A shrill whistle cut the quiet of the morning, and Sergeant Emery boomed, "All right, you lunkheads. Let's go."

Slowly Kim rose. "Come, buddy. We shoot."

The American pointed to his mess kit. "Wash?"

"*Hai*. There." Together they walked toward the boiling water. And as Kim looked out at the assembling troops, he couldn't help but shake his head. The thought of Mason came then. Mason, now this new one, Sergeant Emery and the rest. He turned. "Damn good outfit, buddy," he announced. "Best bunch of son of a bitches in world."

James Lee Burke

⌐ We Build Churches, Inc.

Across the frozen rice fields the brown North Korean hills were streaked with ice and pocked with craters from our 105s. It was cold and bright, and the concertina wire we had strung around our perimeter was half-buried in the snow, looping in and out of the surface like an ugly snake that had been lopped into segments by a lawnmower. But we really weren't worried about a frontal attack in that third week of November in 1950. We had killed Communists by the thousands all the way across North Korea, bulldozing their bodies into trenches and packing the fill down with tanks, until they fled into the hills under a gray sky and hid like bandits. Then the winter swept down out of China across the Yalu, and the hills cracked clear and sharp, and our F-80s and B-25s bombed them twelve hours a day with napalm and phosphorous and incendiaries that generated so much heat in the soil that the barren slopes were still smoking the next morning.

Jason Bradford was seated with his back against the ditch, looking at a picture on the front page of *The Stars and Stripes*. He had a blanket pulled up to his chin, and his mittened hands stuck out from under the blanket. The mitten on his right hand was cut away around the trigger finger. During the night his patrol had run into a North Korean listening post and had lost one marine to a potato masher that the Koreans had got away before the sergeant stitched them all over the hole. Jace's eyes were red around the rims, and he kept fingering his cheek as though he had a toothache.

"Give me another hit of gin, Doc," he said. "I'm going to get warm if I have to let the stuff eat down to my toenails."

I took a bottle of codeine out of my pack and handed it to him.

"Cheers," he said, and drank from the bottle's lip, washing the codeine over his teeth and swallowing it with the pleasure a martini would give him. "Now, look at that picture. A picture like that is not an accident."

A reporter from *The Stars and Stripes* had been photographing an airborne squadron of B-25s, but when the picture was developed, the planes appeared only in the right-hand corner and the frame was filled with the head and shoulders of Jesus Christ.

"You see, I took a course in meteorology at Amherst, and those kinds of clouds don't make a formation like that," Jace said.

"That's what they call an optical delusion," the corporal sitting across from us said. He was a tall hillbilly boy from north Alabama named Willard Posey. He hated the Marine Corps for a different reason than the rest of us: the corps had sent him to Korea to fight for gooks, whom he considered inferior even to blacks.

"There's a preacher on a radio station in Memphis that sells them things," he said.

"Willard, my friend, the whole world is not like the hill country of north Alabama. You have to understand that one of these days," Jace said.

"I ain't got your education," Willard said, "but I know that feller in Memphis is a crook and that ain't no picture of Jesus. You reckon he'd be looking down on a country full of heathens that tie up men with wire and machine-gun them?"

A week earlier we had found the bodies of sixteen marines frozen in the snow by the side of a railway track. We guessed that they had been captured in the south and for some reason taken off a prisoner train and executed. The bailing wire was so tight on their wrists that we couldn't snip through it without tearing the bloated skin.

Jace fingered his cheek again, pushing ice crystals from his mitten into his beard as though his jaw had no feeling.

"You remember that bunch of gooks we took prisoner about two months ago?" he said. "The lieutenant sent them to the rear with the ROKs. Do you think those guys made it beyond the first hill?"

"That's monkeys killing monkeys. They been doing that to each other on this shit pile for hundreds of years. That don't have nothing to do with us."

"It has everything to do with the lieutenant, and with us, too, Willard," Jace said.

"You better lay off that gin," Willard said, and picked up his M-1 and walked farther down the ditch.

Jace took another drink out of the bottle and rested his head back in his helmet. He had turned down officer's school at Quantico, which his education and good looks and career as a college lacrosse player should have made a natural extension of his life.

"Willard is not educable," I said.

"Ah, but that's it. He has been taught."

"Don't make a mystery out of a simple man."

"You southerners hang together, don't you? When it comes down to that choice between reason and blathering with a mouthful of collard greens, there's something atavistic in you that makes you home in on the latter like a fly on a pig flop."

"What is it, Jace?"

"That kid last night."

"It was just bad luck."

"My ass. He was only on the line one day. He shouldn't have been put on patrol. I could hear him breathing in the dark behind me, the kind of breathing you hear when a guy's heart is coming out his mouth. He must have wanted to prove something, because he worked himself up right behind the point. When we walked into the gooks, a potato masher came flying out of the hole. He just stared at it and poked at it with his foot, like it was something he didn't want to touch but couldn't run away from at the same time."

In the rear someone was trying to start a cold engine in a tank. The starter ground away like Coke-bottle glass in the still air.

"I must have been looking at him, yelling at him, because I saw him light up like fire was painted on one side of him."

"Give me the codeine and go to sleep."

"No sleep today, Doc. We're going to be stringing mines. Somebody said the First Division captured some Chinese at a reservoir up the road."

"Chinese?"

"They probably grabbed some Korean mountain people who speak a dialect, and some dumbass translator didn't know how to classify them."

"You better sleep, anyway."

Jace turned his face at me and squinted in the sunlight. His helmet cut a diagonal shadow across his eyes and made his face look as though it were sewn together from mismatched parts.

"What you got to understand is that I'm a practical man," he said. "I have one foot solidly in this world. That's because I come from a family that never got lost in the next world. We knew how to hold on to a big chunk of this one and deal with it."

I didn't know what introspection was taking him through a maze inside of himself or even if introspection was the word for it. His voice had a wired edge to it, and fatigue was an explanation that only civilians used. I had seen craziness come in many forms since I had been in Korea, but it usually got men when they first went on the firing line or after an artillery barrage when they became hysterical and had to be sedated with morphine. But Jace had been on the line since Inchon and had had his ticket punched at every stop across North Korea.

"Let me explain it this way," he said. "The first Bradford in Massachusetts was a ship's carpenter, and the Puritans were building churches all over the place. But it takes a lot of time to build a church out of squared logs, especially when you got to stop and kill off all the Indians and press witches to death. The first Bradford, the carpenter, was a religious man, and he had an idea that would take care of the problem for everybody. He hired a bunch of guys like himself and built the church on contract. He paid the other guys out of his pocket, and all he asked from the community was a small piece of land set aside in his name. He built churches in Salem, Cambridge, Haverhill, anywhere he found Puritans and wood. This went on for thirty years, until some farmers figured out that he probably owned more land than anyone else in the commonwealth. So these manure slingers got together and had him tried as a witch, and they had some good evidence to use against him. He was as strong as a draft horse, and he could poke one finger in the end of a musket and hold it out at arm's length. So the manure slingers said he was in league with Old Nick, and they tried to make him confess by ordeal. They staked him out in a field and put an oak door over his body and then added one stone to it at a time. You see, the deal was that if a witch confessed, all his property went back into the public domain. They crushed his chest and snapped his ribs like sticks, but he never let a word of guilt pass his lips.

"His sons inherited his property and they figured a way to protect it against the manure slingers. They incorporated under the name We Build Churches, Inc. You can't try a corporation for witchery, can you? Those Puritans would deep fry the balls of an individual, but they knew a business company was sacred.

"And my family has been building churches ever since, and we still own some of the land that was given to the carpenter. There's a bank in Cambridge built right on top of where he used to keep a smithy.

"Does that make sense to you? Do you know what I mean now by having a vision of both worlds?"

One eye seemed pulled down on his cheek, as though he were aiming along the sights of his M-1.

I didn't want to answer. I simply wanted the codeine back and to talk with the lieutenant about rotating Jace early. As a corpsman I could do it by saying that I thought he had walking pneumonia.

I heard a truck with snow chains on crunching up the road through the frozen rice field behind us. One of the chains was broken and swinging under the fender.

"That looks like the foot warmers now," I said. "Give me the codeine so you don't blow your face off."

I walked down the ditch past Willard, who was standing against the embankment with his hands in his armpits, smoking a cigarette without taking it from his mouth. The lieutenant was farther on with his back turned to me and his face bent down over an engineer's compass placed on a mess kit that he had flattened into the snow for a level. He turned an angle on the compass gingerly with one finger and then drew the angle on his note pad.

"Could I speak with you a minute, Lieutenant?"

"Go ahead," he said, his blue eyes still preoccupied with the mine pattern we were going to lay. He was an Annapolis graduate and a good officer, but he was single-minded sometimes and irritated by what he considered a complaint.

"Bradford's been spitting up phlegm for two weeks. I think he might have pneumonia."

"What's his temperature?"

"He won't let me take it."

The lieutenant's eyes swept into mine.

"What kind of bullshit are you handing me, Doc?"

"I thought he ought to ride back with the mine truck to the aid station."

"What you thought is you'd slip me a candyass con. You've been a corpsman too long for that, Doc."

"I'm supposed to make my recommendation to you, Lieutenant."

"You'd better listen to me and never do something like this again."

"Yes sir."

I walked back down the ditch feeling stupid and humiliated. Up ahead, I saw that Jace had climbed over the embankment and was headed toward the truck. As I passed Willard he caught my sleeve and pulled me to him.

"Don't wrinkle my threads," I said.

"Stay cool and have a smoke. I want to tell you something." He lit a Camel from the one he was smoking and handed it to me. "I heard what you said to the lieutenant, and I also heard what Bradford told you about that kid that got blowed up last night. You done the right thing trying to get him out of here. He ain't seeing things good in his head, and that gets people knocked off."

"What do you mean?"

"That kid wasn't behind the point. He was in the rear all the time. Them three gooks was in a hole at the top of an arroyo, and we didn't see them till the potato masher come end over end at us. We all went flying down the hill with it rolling down after us, but the kid stood there like his feet was locked in ice. Bradford was the last one down. Maybe he could have knocked the kid back. Maybe any of us could. It ain't nobody's fault. But I wanted you to know it didn't happen the way Bradford said. I tell you what. I'm going to stay so close on his butt he'll think he's got piles. If he starts talking crazy again or if I think he's going to screw up, I'm telling the lieutenant the same thing you did."

"You're all right, Willard."

"Shit. I got thirteen days to rotation and I ain't getting knocked off because of a crazy man."

~

When the sun went down over the hills, a red light spilled across the land and we felt the temperature drop in minutes. The wind blew down out of the hills, and the snow that had fallen that morning was polished into a thin, frozen cake that you could punch your finger through. Beyond the concertina wire the depressions where the mines had been set looked like slick dimples on a piece of moonscape. My feet and ears ached in the cold as though they had been beaten with boards.

In the purple gloom of the ditch Jace was looking around the edges of his pack for something. When he couldn't find it, he flipped the pack over, then unsnapped the canvas flap and rooted in it with an increasing urgency.

"Who took my newspaper?" he said.

Willard and I looked at his anxious face without replying.

"I want to know who took it. It was tucked inside the strap."

"The Indian was trying to start a fire," Willard said.

"You lying son of a bitch."

"You say that to me again and I'm going to break every bone in your face."

"You just try it. I'm not one of your darkies on the plantation. You took it, didn't you? Say it. You had to destroy what didn't fit into that ignorant southern mind of yours?"

"What?"

"You heard me. You can't think past what you hear on a hillbilly radio station or a bunch of captured gooks that get marched off behind a hill."

"I saw the Indian with it," I said.

"You tend to your own business, Doc," Willard said.

In the distance we heard the popping of small arms like a string of firecrackers, followed by two long bursts from a BAR on our right flank.

"What's that asshole doing?" Willard said, his face wooden in the red twilight.

Then we saw the Chinese moving out of the hills toward us. They appeared on the crests in silhouette, like ants swarming to the top of a sinking log, and poured down the slopes and arroyos onto the rice field. They marched a mortar barrage ahead of them across the field, blowing up the mines we had set earlier and sending geysers of snow and yellow earth high into the air. We shrank into fetal positions in the bottom of the ditch, each man white-faced and alone in his terror, as the reverberations through the ground grew in intensity. Then when they had bracketed our line, they turned it on in earnest. The explosions were like locomotive engines blowing apart. The ditch danced with light, flame rippled along the strands of concertina wire, and a long round hit the gasoline dump behind us and blew a balloon of fire over us that scalded our skin.

When the barrage lifted, the snow in the craters around us was still hissing from the heat of the buried shrapnel, and the rice field and the horizon of the hills were covered with small, dark men in quilted uniforms. They came at us in waves and walked over their own dead while we killed them by the thousands. The long stretch of field was streaked with tracers, and occasionally one of our mines went off and blew men into the air like piles of rags. We packed snow on our .30-caliber machine guns and fired them until the rifling went and the barrels melted. When somebody down the line yelled that they were pushing civilians ahead of them, the firing never let up. If anything, the machine gunners kept the trigger frozen back against the guard to get at the men who carried those murderous burp guns with the fifty-round drum clips.

The bottom of the ditch was strewn with spent shell casings and empty ammunition boxes. Willard was next to me, firing his M-1 over the edge of the embankment, his unused clips set in a neat line in the snow. I heard a shell whang dead center into his helmet and ricochet inside. He pirouetted around in slow motion, his helmet rolled off his shoulder, and the blood ran in red strings from under his stocking cap. There was a surgical cut along the crown of the skull that exposed his brain. He slid down against the ditch wall with one leg folded under him, his jaw distended as though he were about to yawn.

"Get the wounded ready to move, Doc," the lieutenant said. "We're going to get artillery in forty-five minutes and pull."

"In forty-five minutes we're going to be spaghetti."

"They got a priority in another sector. Get those men ready to move."

Five minutes later the lieutenant got it through the throat, and the artillery never came. Before we were overrun, we put a flame thrower in their faces and cooked them alive at thirty yards. Their uniforms were burnt away, and their blackened bodies piled up in a stack like people caught in a fire exit. Farther down the ditch I saw Jace with his back propped against the embankment, his face white with concussion and his coat singed and blown open.

I hadn't heard a grenade in the roar of burp guns, but when I pulled back his jacket, I saw the blood welling through the half-dozen tears in his sweater. His eyes were crossed, and he kept opening his mouth as though he were trying to clear his ears. I laid him down on a stretcher and buckled only the leg strap and made a marine pick up the other end.

"There ain't no place to go," the marine said.

"Over the top. There's an ambulance behind the tank."

"Oh shit, they're in the ditch."

The flank had gone, and then suddenly they were everywhere. They held their burp guns sideways on their shoulder slings and shot the living and the dead alike. Marines with empty rifles huddled in the bottom of the ditch and held their hands out against the bullets that raked across their bodies. The very brave stood up with bayonets and entrenching tools and were cut down in seconds. For the first and only time in my life I ran from an enemy. I dropped the stretcher and ran toward the right flank, where I heard a BAR man still hammering away. But I didn't have far to go, because I saw one of the small dark men on the embankment above me, his Mongolian face pinched in the cold, his quilted uniform and tennis shoes caked with snow. He had just pulled back the spring on the magazine and reset the sling, and I knew that those brass-cased armor-piercing rounds manufactured in Czechoslovakia had finally found their home.

Luke the Gook. How do you do. Punch my transfer ticket neatly, sir. Please do not disturb the dogtags. They have a practical value for reasons that you do not understand. Later they must be untaped and inserted between the teeth because the boxes get mixed up in the baggage car, and I do have to get off at San Antone tonight. Oh sorry, I see you must be about your business.

But he was a bad shot. He depressed the barrel too low on the sling, and his angle of fire cut across my calves like shafts of ice and knocked me headlong on the body of the lieutenant as though a bad comic had kicked my legs out from under me. In the seconds that I waited for the next burst to rip through my back, I could hear the lieutenant's wristwatch ticking in my face.

But when the burp gun roared again, it was aimed at a more worthy target, the BAR man who stood erect in the ditch, the tripod flopping under the barrel, firing until the breech locked empty and he was cut down by a half-dozen Chinese.

I spent the next thirty-two months in three POW camps. I was in the Bean Camp, which had been used by the Japanese for British prisoners during W.W. II, Pak's Palace outside of Pyongyang, and Camp Five in No Name Valley just south of the Yalu. I learned how political lunatics could turn men into self-hating, loathsome creatures who would live with the guilt of Judas the rest of their lives. I spent six weeks in a filthy hole under a sewer grate, with an encrusted G.I. helmet for a honey bucket, until I became the eighth man of eleven from our shack to inform on an escape attempt. But sometimes when I lay in the bottom of the hole and looked up through the iron squares at the clouds turning across the sky, I thought of Jace and Willard and Puritans knocking their axes into wood. Then at some moment between vision and the crush of the dirt walls upon me, between drifting light and the weight of witches' stones upon my chest, I knew that I would plane and bevel wood and build churches. I would build one at my home in Yoakum, in Goliad and Gonzales and San Antonio, any place there were pine trees and cottonwoods and water oaks to be felled. Then I saw the sky reform as a photograph and the ice clouds turn soft and porous as a eucharist.

Eugene Burdick

~ Cold Day, Cold Fear

They lay head to head in the ditch. There were a few inches of water in the ditch. An edge of rime ice would form on the water and then be pulled away by the slight current. The water exactly covered Eli's right leg, his right arm and hand, and cut a precise line down his body. He could see his hand under the water . . . the blue skin was wrinkled, the thumbnail was dead white, the veins stood out purple. He tried to close his hand and nothing happened. He squeezed again hard and in the shimmering water he thought his fingers wavered and started to close, but then he had no more strength.

My God, Eli thought, the inside of my head feels like my hand looks. Fear is just like the cold, just exactly.

He looked up and saw Kee's head close to his. There were only the two of them in the ditch. Two out of thirty. He wished suddenly he could cry. He was only eighteen; that was young enough to cry. . . . He told himself to move before he froze.

With an infinitely delicate movement he heaved himself up. He curved his body into a bow of cold muscle and carefully brought his right eye to the edge of the ditch. They were still there. Twenty-five yards away in a grove of young trees were four trucks and fifteen Communist soldiers. They had bent the young trees down and woven them into an expert camouflage. Even from that close Eli could barely make out the soldiers sitting on the running boards of the trucks and smoking.

As Eli watched, a two-wheeled wagon drawn by a hairy pony came down the narrow road. It was loaded with howitzer shells cradled in hay. Following it was a Russian M-4 tank. The tank was incredibly quiet for something so huge and dangerous. Eli felt the hair rise on his neck. All he could hear was the tiny rippling crack of frozen earth under its treads and the cough of its exhaust. The tank's gun was pointed down and it nosed along like some deadly prehistoric beast prowling a ruined landscape.

Two miles away was the main highway along which the Communists were advancing. That road was solid with vehicles and troops. Every few minutes an American jet plane would come skimming into the valley at Eli's right, make a swooping climb and then start a run along the highway. The vehicles would stop, the men would scatter. The plane would launch its rockets and a few trucks would begin to burn. Most of the Communists would come back to the trucks, leaving a few sprawled figures on the snow. The uninjured trucks would push the burning trucks aside. Like a vast brown indestructible worm the column would start again down the highway.

High above the highway a slow-flying L-17 liaison plane was circling. This was the plane which directed the fire of the attacking jets. It flew in calm slow circles. Eli wished with a terrible intensity that he could signal the plane, ask it for help. He felt the tears of self-pity start into his eyes. I don't want to die, he was saying silently to himself.

It began to get dark slowly, the blackness gathering in the mouths of the valley and then sliding gradually out into the plain. Eli pushed himself a bit higher, started to swing his eyes to the left and then stopped.

Go ahead, he told himself. It's darker now. It won't be so bad.

He could see them plainly. In the early twilight they looked like carelessly piled logs. Except that some of the logs ended in fingers, or clenched fists, or a GI boot. The piled bodies were motionless, turning stiff with the cold and four hours of death.

Eli heard a stirring in the ditch. He looked down and saw that Kee was grinning up at him. Kee always grinned. Nothing ever seemed to bother him.

"Crum down, US private," Kee said.

Eli obediently slid back into the ditch.

Eight weeks ago when Kee had been one of the South Koreans incorporated into Eli's company he could not speak a word of English and even now there were only a few words he knew. For some reason he had attached himself to Eli and, although Eli had resented it at first, in a few days he had grown to like Kee and then to become dependent upon him. Kee was Korean and he knew how to live in Korea, even a Korea that was at war. He could look at a hill and tell if troops had passed over that day; he could cook rice with wood that made no smoke or fire; he could dry hay, arrange it in layers inside a jacket, very carefully, and the jacket would keep you warm on a freezing night.

Once he had shown Eli how to load a rifle in a field which had only an eighteen-inch fringe of rice seedlings for cover. You rolled over on your back and laid the gun flat on your belly; without looking down you ejected the cold clip, put in a new one, rolled over on your belly again and were ready to go. Little thing, but there were seven dead Americans in the field who had tried to reload by hunching up on their knees and jamming the clip in. Kee didn't learn these things, he just knew them. Kee had made the small decisions, then the larger ones, and finally Eli felt restless when Kee was not around.

"Wait, US private," Kee whispered. "Verra hard, but we wait. Wait long time maybe."

Eli felt his body relax quietly back into the icy water, felt it push into the soft layer of mud. It was like coming home. He began to think almost lazily of the past, and the fear he had felt for the last four hours began to soften somewhat.

The memories came like bubbles rising to the surface of his mind. Each held solid for a moment and then shattered.

There was a day in Santa Barbara before he came overseas. All the family was sitting in the back yard. At the end of the lawn oranges hung from wax-green trees. His father came out of the house and gave him a can of beer.

"Well, here's to the soldier," he said in an embarrassed voice.

It was the first drink his father and he had ever shared. After the beer they had had potato salad, sliced ham, salad eggs, a freezer of ice cream.

The bubble of memory burst, another came up.

It was the unloading at Pusan. They stood at the rail of the ship, looking at the dirty town, the hordes of men, the mountains of equipment. A sergeant yelled at them, desperate with haste and fatigue.

"All right, gentlemen, let's go. Down the gangplank like a line of fat-assed birds and onto those trucks. Hop, hop, hop. Come on, come on."

In five minutes they were off the ship and in the trucks and bouncing down a dusty road. The big friendly ship got smaller and then vanished in the dust.

Dozens of other memories flooded across his mind, but when he finally came to the events of this morning and this afternoon his mind slowed down and went carefully. It seemed improbable that so much had happened.

They had been captured that morning just north of Pyongyang. The Communists had come swirling up out of the snow, falling on them while they were still in their tents. They tried to fire, but the Communists were around them in waves and masses of yelling men. They were taken prisoner and loaded into trucks. They were thirty American and South Korean prisoners, and with fifteen guards they started for the rear.

Early that afternoon the trucks stopped in the grove of trees, well away from the main highway. The guards gave them a burlap bag of withered apples and the prisoners split them up . . . three apples to a man. The guards gathered around their lieutenant and began to argue in low voices. They argued for a few minutes before the lieutenant raised his voice sharply, shouted a few words, pointed down the highway and gesticulated. The others fell silent and nodded.

The Communists picked up their burp guns and fanned out around the knot of prisoners. They made a semicircle around their captives. The prisoners shuffled together, staring at the guards. Some of them stopped eating, but a few kept on munching the apples. For a second they waited, the two groups facing one another in the cold silence of the Korean plain. Even then Eli felt no fear, only a sort of hungry, tired curiosity. The lieutenant sucked hard at the cigarette, threw the butt away and then dropped his hand. The burp guns all started to fire at once.

Eli actually saw bullets hitting men in the front of the group. Tiny circular puffs of dust rose from their clothing. He saw one man take a few steps toward the guards and then his chest splashed with puffs of dust. The man spun in a circle, balanced erratically on one toe and started slowly to collapse. In mid-fall his eyes glazed and Eli knew he was dead.

It was in that second, in the time that the man's eyes glazed and turned dull white, that the fear came up in Eli. It came up out of his stomach like a green bitter wave, so strong that he could taste it. He could feel the thud of the bullets hitting the men in front of him. He turned and started to run.

Kee and three other men turned and ran with him. In a few seconds they were running at top speed across the frozen fields. Behind them they could hear the sounds of the burp guns. Once an American started to swear and his words trailed off in a strangle. Eli began to run even faster. He seemed to be running more swiftly and lightly than he believed possible. He came to a ditch and felt his body lift and sail easily over. He flew over a hedge, jumped another ditch.

I can run faster than the bullets, he thought. In his great fear he actually believed it. He could hear the stitching of the burp guns, the yells, the deadly noises, but they had nothing to do with him. He looked sideways and saw Kee's face, the eternal grin deepened to a grimace with the strain of running. By now they were almost a hundred yards away and Eli began to feel a wild exultation.

Suddenly, however, the bullets began to come very close, making ugly small whines in the cold air as they went by. He realized that the guards had finished with the rest and were firing at them now. The whines came closer and one of the men fell. Then another man was hit twice with a sound like melon being cracked. Bullets slammed into the ground, struck up small rocks, ricocheted off into the sky.

In a dull second Eli realized that the speed and lightness were only illusions. In reality he was moving slowly across the field. His heavy GI boots weighed him down, his breath burned a hot tube down his throat. It was like the nightmares he'd had when he was a boy; dreams of trying to escape from faceless horror. He seemed heavy and unwieldy, felt as if he were running through water with weighted, agonizing steps. The skin on his back crawled as it anticipated the bullets.

He saw another ditch; they bore down on it slowly and just as he was about to leap Kee crashed sideways into him and carried the two of them into the ditch. Above them the last American kept running for a few yards; then in a moment he caught the concentrated fire of all the guns. He fell in a long sprawl, white bits of undigested apple spluttering from his mouth. The bullets kicked up dust for a few more seconds and then the silence returned.

Kee spun on his hands and knees; keeping low he began to crawl down the ditch. Eli followed him. In a few yards they came to a ditch that cut across the one they were in, one branch leading back toward the trucks. Without hesitating, Kee took that turn. Eli reached out and grabbed his heels.

"Not to the trucks, Kee," he said. "Jesus, you're going the wrong way."

"Proper thing, surprise," Kee said calmly. "Verra proper."

He was right, Eli thought. The Communists would expect them to take the opposite turn of the ditch. He wriggled after Kee. Several times they went into other connecting ditches, but each time Kee took the one that led them closer to the trucks. Finally they were within twenty-five yards. Kee stopped and the two of them lay flat in the ditch, so close to the trucks that they could hear the men talking.

For the rest of the afternoon they had been waiting, lying in the icy water, waiting for the Communists to move away. . . .

The exertion of looking out over the ditch had warmed Eli slightly. He could move the fingers of his hand now and for several moments he opened and closed them. The dead-white skin darkened as the blood flowed sluggishly through the veins.

The exercise had also loosened the grip of the cold, paralyzing fear. It was still there in his stomach, tightening to a clutching pain whenever he thought of the apples and the burp guns, but it seemed to ease whenever he moved.

"Kee," he said.

The Korean looked up at him, smiling.

"How old are you?"

Kee's face wrinkled in puzzlement for a moment.

Eli repeated the question.

Kee held up his fingers once, then all the fingers on one hand and a thumb. He was sixteen years old.

"Look, Kee, listen hard," Eli said. "Were you scared this afternoon? Scared? Understand? Scared?"

Kee stared at him and then the smile weakened on his face and suddenly it was no longer there and the face was different; childlike and naked. Then the smile sprang back. But Eli had his answer. Kee had been scared. He was scared now. Maybe he was scared all the time. The smile didn't mean anything. It was like a nervous twitch. Kee had no control over it.

Eli reached out and patted Kee on the shoulder. It was a quick protective pat, almost paternal.

Eli rolled over on his back; he felt the icy water flow over the cloth, soak greedily through and settle on his skin. He looked up at the sky. The L-17 was still there. He was thinking that he was two years older than Kee. Two whole years. The cold edges of his fear started to crumble like the rime ice dissipated by the slowly moving stream. His mind began to work.

Five minutes passed and Eli turned again toward Kee.

"Look, Kee, it's my baby now," he said. "You've carried the ball so far, but if I ever want to get back to Santa Barbara and you want to get to Kwanti I'd better get hot." Kee could understand none of it for Eli was talking fast and low, but Eli went on. "This is a high-powered affair, Kee, and you've done fine. Now just relax and let me give it a try."

Eli pulled himself to his knees, crouching low. He began to work his hands savagely, opening and closing them and rubbing them together. Hot flashes of pain jerked up the frozen muscles but he stayed at it. When his hands were limber he began to spread handfuls of the stiff cold mud over his clothes and on his face. The mud smelled—that rotten odor of Korea; the odor of fertilizer, of sour vegetation, of coldness. Kee helped him. Finally he was completely covered.

With a gentle push he brought his body out of the ditch. He was now in full view of the Communists, but in the gathering twilight and covered with mud he hoped that he could not be seen. He made himself move evenly and without jerks. He could feel small stones, burrs, and grass stubble. With a slow, excruciating wiggle he moved toward the pile of bodies. He moved like a piece of slowly shifting earth. It took him an eternity.

When he reached the first body he was only ten yards from the trucks. He searched it. The fear came flickering back but with a careful, deliberate act of mind he ignored it. Once there was a disturbance in the grove; the saplings parted and a head pushed out. Eli stiffened into absolute rigidity, feeling a growl rise in his throat. But the Communist was only staring up at the L-17. On the third body he found the flashlight he had been looking for. Clutching it, he turned and crawled back. Small, mud-covered hands reached out as from the bowels of the earth. Kee helped him slide back into the ditch.

He removed his jacket, tore off the sleeve and arranged the cuff around the flashlight. The rest of the sleeve stretched out in a long tube beyond the flashlight. It was an adaptation of the deflector on cannons which makes the flash invisible to anyone not directly in front of the muzzle. Now he could aim the flashlight without the Communists seeing it. Lying on his back, he searched the sky for the L-17. For one frozen moment he thought it had gone. Then he saw it. He aimed the sleeve with his left hand and with his right he began to blink out HELP in Morse code.

For a long time the little plane circled without a change in its pattern. Then almost imperceptibly it was nearer. Its form was clear above him and he could see how fragile the plane was. Suddenly a light began to blink.

WHO ARE YOU? the light asked.

Eli's finger shook on the flashlight button.

AMERICAN, he answered.

The plane wavered in the air, circled lower. Then it pulled back as if suspicious and struggled for more altitude. In the grove the Communists began to move around excitedly. Eli could hear their questioning voices.

Eli knew he had to convince the pilot of the plane that he was an American, that it was not a trap. But how? His mind went blank. He couldn't even think of his own name.

Suddenly the plane veered back and the tiny light began to blink again.

WHO LOVES LIL ABNER? the plane blinked.

For a moment Eli could not make sense of the words. His fingers trembled and the trembling spread from his fingers to his arms. Then the answer came to him easily; his hands tightened and he blinked back two words:

DAISY MAE.

ROGER, the plane said. WHAT DO YOU WANT?

BOMB GROVE TWENTY-FIVE YARDS WEST, Eli sent.

NAPALM. DANGEROUS FOR YOU.

BOMB AWAY.

The plane did not bother to reply. It banked and gained altitude. It made a wide, slow circle. Nothing happened for a long time. Then Eli could feel the tempo of the sound in the valley change. The long smooth arc of the jets was suddenly broken. The L-17 was directing them down the secondary road that ran beside the ditch.

Eli could see the first one coming. Its nose grew from a shiny speck to a huge glistening knob. Its engines seemed to suck in all the air in the valley, condensing it into a howling power that wailed out behind the plane. The plane did not fire. It was examining the grove. Two more jets followed; each held its fire.

Then the first jet came back. This time it seemed to be going slower. A half-mile away the innocent-looking black tubes under its wings shot forward, a red flame showing at the back of each one. For an instant the rockets seemed to hang in the air. Eli was conscious of a high whinnying noise. Then the earth shook. In the grove a row of trees collapsed in a red shattering flash; two trucks reared up, held together for an instant, and then split into fragments. A human figure turned over in the air like a tossed doll and fell back. The blast rolled over the ditch and Eli ducked down. Kee was lying with his arms shielding his face.

Eli heard new sounds and looked out again. A faulty rocket had failed to detonate and it went jarring down the road at incredible speed, striking sparks from stones, and finally tore itself into shreds.

Eli saw the guards piling into the two remaining trucks. The trucks started up and began to work toward the road. But the grove had been torn open and their movements were seen from the sky. A jet came powering down the valley. A hundred yards away it released one of the big napalm bombs from its wings.

Eli felt his stomach contract as the bomb slanted down and landed just in front of the two trucks. A tongue of flame lashed out and seared into the grove. Behind it rose a wave of fire which hung for a moment and then whooshed forward, engulfing the grove and the truck and the Communists. A blast of heat struck Eli and Kee. They flung themselves down, thankful now for the water and the mud. A few blobs of napalm flew over their heads and hissed out in the ditch.

Eli sat up. The whole landscape was bright; savage. Three times Eli saw men run out of the lake of fire, pawing at sightless eyes, screaming silent screams in the roar of the burning. Each time they collapsed at the edge of the fire.

The jets were high in the sky, circling watchfully. The fire in the grove died rapidly; finally only the tires and seats of the trucks were burning. Everything else had been charred black. Eli and Kee climbed out of the ditch and stood in the road.

A helicopter came down the valley. Its ugly beetle shape hung in the air, occasionally shifting sideways as the L-17 directed it. It came down directly over the grove. The wind from its rotors revived parts of the fire; a few trees burst into flames again, a truck flared up fitfully, black cinders swirled around Kee and Eli. The helicopter slid away from the grove and hovered a few feet off the ground, waiting. Eli and Kee climbed aboard.

The pilot of the helicopter was a young Marine lieutenant whose eyes were bloodshot with fatigue. He looked sideways at them as he lifted the plane straight into the sky.

"Hard day, huh?" he said.

"Yep, a long hard day," Eli said.

He turned to Kee, who had lived with fear for many years, and in the pale green light from the instrument panel he smiled and shook Kee's hand. Kee was not even startled. He shook hands calmly, the expression of his face unchanging, the grin fixed. Then the two of them leaned back in the corners of the cabin and fell asleep.

William Chamberlain

∼ The Trapped Battalion

The major's name was Steve Lang and he was young for the gold oak leaves which he wore. A scant five years before he had still been a cadet at the gray school on the Hudson. His mother, back in Shreveport, Louisiana, had a picture of him as he had been then. Straight and poised and beautiful in his tight-fitting gray uniform with the gleaming brass bell buttons.

Now he wore trousers—stuffed into combat boots—which were torn and frayed at the knees, and a combat jacket, one sleeve of which had been ripped half away, and a helmet dented by a Red Chinese bullet which had come too close.

Dark stubble covered his cheeks, and his mouth had grown into a hard line, and his eyes shadowed the weariness which had become almost too heavy to bear.

He had just brought his battalion—what there was left of it—down to the river here, and now they sought a crossing so that they could continue their running back; for one ragged battalion cannot stop two divisions already flushed with victory. They had found that out three days ago above the parallel. Before that, everything had been all right. The outfit had been sweeping north, cleaning out everything in front of it, and then the Chinese had hit—coming down from the Yalu like a horde of yellow locusts.

After that, everything had been a nightmare. Only, Steve Lang thought as he squatted in the snow with his back to the broken wall of a Korean house, you could awaken from nightmares. You could force your eyes open and know the sudden, familiar comfort of a warm bed and walls securely around you and the even, ordered sounds which you knew went with living. The tick of the clock in the hall and the muted clink of a radiator and the even breathing of your dog at the foot of the bed. The comfort of friendly darkness which was not filled with creeping men in padded coats; not filled with the sound of bugles yammering in the night and the crazy laughter of gunfire closing around you from all sides.

But you didn't awaken here. You kept on and on, and the nightmare grew more real and more terrifying endless minute by endless minute and endless hour by endless hour.

Steve Lang shrugged the thought impatiently away and brought his mind abruptly back to the business at hand. The business of getting the outfit across the river that lay before them—a river running darkly between the lowering hills with their snow-covered scrub. The business of taking care of the two-hundred-odd Korean refugees who squatted apathetically about the ruined village and waited with a terrible faith for Lang to do something for them. The business of tending the battalion's wounded, which filled three trucks. The business of fighting off the vanguard of the Chinese divisions which would come soon.

Lieutenant Haycross, one of the dozen officers left to the battalion now, shuffled his feet in the snow and moved his mittened hand nervously up and down the stock of his carbine. Lieutenant Haycross had never voted, but his face was the face of an old man. Tinged with gray and with his eyes set back too deeply above the thin planes of his cheeks.

"Sir," he was saying, "Sergeant Moon and I went two miles along the river in both directions. There's no way to get across with the trucks. No way at all."

Lang considered this without speaking. There was a faint trace of panic in the lieutenant's voice, he thought. He'd have to do something about that, because panic could be like a forest fire, once it started to spread. If the battalion was to get out, there must be no panic now. He must nip it in the bud. He smiled a little grimly in the dying afternoon. That was an easy thing to say, he thought; a heck of a lot harder thing to do with men who were hungry and tired and licked.

He got to his feet, unconsciously whipping his shoulders back in the gesture that West Point had taught him, and his eyes were cold and gray as he looked at Lieutenant Haycross.

"Get your chin up, lieutenant," he said, his voice carrying a lash. "All right, there's no bridge. What of it? We'll build a bridge."

Lieutenant Haycross stared back as though he thought that Lang had suddenly gone crazy, but automatically his body stiffened a little and his chin came up.

"Yes, sir," he said. "I don't know—I guess that it's just that the starch has sort of run out of all of us, sir."

"Why?" Lang asked.

Silly question, he thought; but then, war was the ultimate in silliness anyway. The thing that he had to do was plain. The battalion had its tail between its legs; the only way that he could take it on now was with the whip. Make these tired, beaten men fear him more than they feared the Gooks, for this was a green outfit with none of the steadying assurance which comes with battle experience.

Lieutenant Haycross blinked stupidly. "Sir, I guess that it's just that we're tired and—"

Lang stopped him. "Let it go. I want to see the officers and the senior noncoms here in fifteen minutes. Round them up, Haycross."

"Yes, sir," Haycross said, his voice a little more assured now. "Jim Lacey's up with the outpost. Shall I have him come back?"

"Leave him there," Lang said curtly. "Somebody said that part of an engineer company latched onto the tail of our column back at the gap this morning. Where are they?"

Lieutenant Haycross shook his head. "I don't know, sir," he said, and went back to polishing the stock of his carbine nervously.

Lang's messenger, a towheaded boy whom Lang knew only as Alabama, came from the inside of the ruined house, where he had been sniffing about like an inquisitive puppy. Steve Lang was fond of Alabama. He alone, of all the battalion, seemed unbothered by the snow and the running and the Chinese who came pounding along behind.

"The majeh askin' about them engineers?" he asked.

Lang nodded. "You seen them, Alabama?"

"Yes, seh. Theah ain't much that I don't see. They're oveh at the far side of this daggone town. You want 'em?"

"Never mind," Lang said tiredly. "I'll go over there. . . . Have the officers and noncoms here when I get back, Haycross."

He picked up the carbine, which he had leaned against the broken wall, and moved off. The afternoon was two thirds gone and it was going to snow again soon, he thought absently. In a way, that might be good. It could slow up the Gook tanks and heavy vehicles a little, maybe. It couldn't hurt the battalion, for the battalion had only the three trucks with the wounded and a few small cars left. No tanks. No weapons carriers. No nothing. Just men.

Alabama swung along at his shoulder, rifle slung, as they made their way among the refugees, who squatted mutely in the shelter of the broken houses. Poor and bewildered people, dressed in soiled white clothes which were too thin for the cold wind which was coming down out of the north. People who had grown used to running; people who were resigned to being shuttled back and forth on the chessboard of war which their country had become. They waited for someone to tell them what to do. For someone to find a way for them to cross the river, so that they could plod on southward with their huge and preposterous burdens hoisted on their shoulders.

Lang looked at them angrily as he went by. He didn't want them. They hindered the movements of the battalion—movements already snail-like in their slowness. But there was nothing that he could do about it, he knew grimly. They were like the Old Man of the Sea, riding his shoulders, and he had to carry them whether he liked it or not.

"Never saw such a raggle-tail lot, seh," Alabama said. "They got an American gal with 'em, majeh. You know that?"

"No," Lang said. "I don't know that. How do you know?"

"Seen her, seh. Pretty as a little red heifeh in a cloveh patch. Got herself a flock of little kids that she's herdin' along. Heck of a thing in my book."

"What's she doing with kids here?" Lang asked. Not that he cared very much.

"She's a Red Cross gal," Alabama said. "Feller in the engineer company told me. Kids are orphans and she was takin' care of 'em when the Gooks busted through. So she brought 'em south."

Lang said shortly, "She's probably used to taking care of herself without any help from us. Where's that engineer outfit?"

"Little fartheh along, seh. By the riveh."

"Officer in command?"

Alabama looked sharply at Lang; grinned a little. "Lootenant, seh. Jest a sprig of a lootenant."

Lang scowled at that. He had hoped that there might be a captain in command of that engineer company, for the job that had to be done was not an easy one. Not something for some young shavetail just out of the Point or Officer Candidate School. He had to have a bridge, and he had to have it in a hurry if the battalion wasn't to be gobbled up by those Chinese divisions rolling ponderously down the valley.

Alabama said suddenly, "Theah's that gal an' her kids now, seh," and Lang glanced in the direction in which the soldier pointed.

There was a house there, bigger than the rest and with a thatched veranda running along its front. A half dozen brown-faced youngsters—the oldest perhaps ten—squatted there in a little semicircle, chewing on crusts of bread which the girl distributed from a musette bag which was slung from her shoulder. She was tall and fair-haired, Lang saw, and there was a swift aliveness in the easy way that she moved. She wore faded coveralls and a lined jacket, and her hair was tied severely back from her face with a narrow ribbon. As he got closer he saw that there was a little dust of freckles across the bridge of her nose. It gave her an oddly little-girl look.

Lang stopped, scowling a little and with his feet spread apart in the snow. The girl gave a crust to the smallest of the kids; said, "Chew it well, Joey. Don't gulp it," and then turned to give Lang a steady and impersonal regard.

"Well, major?" she asked: "What is it? Do you want to inspect our chow line?"

Lang's scowl deepened. This picture was all wrong, he thought angrily. What the devil was a pretty American girl doing up here amid the stinking ruins of a Korean village? Why was she being carried along in this wash of abject refugees? She ought to be at home—Dubuque or Memphis or Jacksonville or wherever it was that she had come from. She ought to be peering into store windows while she finished her Christmas shopping; not running from the Reds here in a land that had been forgotten as soon as it had been made.

"I'm Lang, in command of the battalion," he said curtly. "What are you doing here?"

"The name's Pat Delevan, if we're exchanging introductions," she told him tartly. "And I'm doing the same thing here that you're doing, major. Running to beat blazes."

Lang looked at the squatting children with a faint disapproval. "This isn't any place for kids," he said absently. He saw that Alabama was watching Pat

Delevan with an admiring grin on his face, and that irritated him further. "What's so funny, Alabama?"

Alabama gave him a bright glance, abashed not at all. "Why, nothin', I reckon, seh. Jest thought of a funny story."

Lang shrugged and turned back to the girl. His irritation, he knew, was born of the acknowledgment—which he had already made to himself—of this added responsibility. Now, he was thinking, he had kids to look after and a girl who shouldn't be here.

The smallest of the children was looking at him solemnly, a boy with black eyes intensely alive against the brown of his face. Then the kid suddenly thrust a thin hand up, thumb and first finger making an O—a sign that Lang had long forgotten.

"Lousy refugees," he said solemnly.

Pat Delevan's lips crinkled suddenly and Lang saw that she was even prettier than he had first thought. She said, "Joey! None of that! Eat your bread!" and then swung back to Lang. "A recruit for you, major. Just give him time."

In spite of himself, Lang felt his own lips begin to relax a little. "I'll keep him in mind, Miss Delevan," he said. "Can we help you any? We'll have to stick here until we can throw some sort of a bridge across the river."

"We're doing fine, major," Pat said. "Just fine. . . . And you'd be surprised how fast we can run when you get your bridge built. And the name is Pat, major. The Miss Delevan is reserved for dignified occasions such as Junior Proms and state banquets."

Lang hesitated for a moment longer—he didn't know just how to take this girl with her clear eyes which were unafraid and the soft lines of her mouth which could laugh so easily. He said awkwardly, "I'll see you later—Pat," and jerked his head at Alabama, and together they went on around the corner of the house.

The engineer company—there was little more than two platoons of it left now—was resting in a little hollow by the river where the last of the houses broke the chill wind. Two soldiers, their backs against a wall, spooned beans out of a single can and talked in monosyllables. They looked up with blank faces, bearded and incurious, as Lang came up to them. "Where's your commanding officer?" Lang asked the elder of the two—a man who wore a corporal's chevrons.

The corporal stared back without answering, his eyes passing across the major's leaf on Lang's collar. He slowly scooped up a spoonful of beans, pushed them into his mouth and chewed. Alabama leaned on his rifle, watching, his eyes bright with interest.

"Get on your feet, soldier!" Lang said, and a lash had come into his voice now. "When I ask a question, I want an answer!"

The corporal looked suddenly startled and got slowly to his feet, his face sullen. His companion scrambled up beside him, blinking his eyes as though he had just been awakened from a deep sleep. They were dirty and ragged, and tiredness lay on their shoulders like a blanket, Lang saw. He wished that he could tell them to go on back into the town; tell them to get a hot meal and sleep until they wanted to sleep no longer. Well, he couldn't!

"Lootenant Murtaugh's up by the river—sir," the corporal said, his face settling into heavy lines.

Lang's lips tipped up a little. "A good Irish name," he said. "Well, take it easy. Maybe this thing isn't as bad as you think. We'll get across the river—in case you've been wondering. . . . Come on, Alabama. Let's go."

They went on past the last of the broken houses, empty windows peering out into the dying afternoon like the eyes of old men in a poorhouse watching for the visitor who never came. The river was fifty yards ahead and Lang led on toward it.

"You mean that—about us gettin' across, majeh?" Alabama asked.

"I meant it," Lang told him grimly. "Don't you go back on me, son. Somebody's got to keep on believing."

"Yeah," Alabama answered thoughtfully. "I neveh thought of it exactly that way befoah, but I guess I see what you mean, seh."

"Sure, you see what I mean," Lang told him. "Nothing is ever as bad as it seems—even in war."

"I got my belly full of war right now," Alabama said, grinning. "You wouldn't want to transfer me to the Navy, would you, seh?"

"I couldn't spare you," Lang said. "Where is that engineer lieutenant?"

Back by the corner of the ruined building the two engineer soldiers sat slowly down in the muddy snow again. The one that Lang had spoken to spat and rubbed a hand across the bristles on his chin. His name was Cloister and he was thirty-five—old for war—and he had enlisted in the Army because he couldn't get along with his wife. He wished now that he had tried harder; war had not entered into his calculations.

"West Pointer!" he said finally, and spat again. "They're all the same, kid!

'Stand up! Haul in your gut! Why didn't you salute me, soldier?' They make me sick!"

Rogers, his companion, spooned out the last of the beans and tossed the can away. "Aw, quit yellin'," he said. "Somebody's got to be officers, don't they?"

"Why?" Cloister asked sourly. "Just give me one reason!"

"Nuts! I don't know. To get medals, maybe. You think we're goin' to get out of this mess?"

"How do I know? I wish that I'd never got into it in the first place. I even wish that I was back with my old woman again. Things have got to be bad to make a man wish that."

"There's a gal I used to know in—" Rogers began.

~

Lieutenant Jeff Murtaugh sat at the edge of the river and stared at the dark water which swirled in front of him. Unfriendly water—cold as a lender's heart, he thought. A fifty-yard strip of it flowing between snowy banks. Charred piles showed where a bridge had once been; nothing left now, though, over which you could cross men, let alone vehicles carrying wounded. Just blackened stumps protruding above the water like the stubs on an old man's teeth. Well, they would have to build a bridge here, Lieutenant Murtaugh was thinking.

He took his helmet off and ran a hand through hair which was completely gray. Back through the years during which he had been in the Army, the filed service records read: PRIVATE MURTAUGH . . . CORPORAL MURTAUGH. Finally: FIRST SERGEANT MURTAUGH. Lieutenant Murtaugh now, for they had pinned the gold bar on him two weeks ago when Lieutenant Weeks had died on that ridge at Kung-ri.

Funny, he had thought then. Back through the thirty years of service which stretched behind him, the idea of being an officer had never entered his head. He would have laughed at the thought, for he was a man who believed in letting officers walk on their side of the street while he walked on his. And now he wore the bar and was suddenly acutely aware of the thing which every officer—even the youngest shavetail with fuzz on his chin instead of a beard—had to learn.

Aware that he no longer was plain Jeff Murtaugh, the soldier with no worries except to draw his pay at the pay table once a month. He was Lieutenant Murtaugh, commanding the engineer company—what was left of it. A hundred and two men—if Evans hadn't died back in one of the ambulance trucks—and he was responsible for them. They would live or die according to the way that he did his job. That infantry battalion would live or die, too, according to the manner in which Second Lieutenant Jeff Murtaugh wore his bar. For they had to have a bridge. And it was the job of Second Lieutenant Jeff Murtaugh, engineer, to build that bridge. Such was an engineer's reason for being.

Footsteps scraped over the snow-covered rocks behind him and Murtaugh put his helmet back on and scrambled to his feet.

It was the infantry major and a soldier, he saw as he turned. The major came on up and stopped, and Murtaugh saluted with the ease of long practice and waited.

"You're Lieutenant Murtaugh?" Lang asked, and there was a faint surprise in his voice which he could not entirely hide. A satisfaction, too, for this was no kid—as he had feared—green from school. As he extended his hand his quick eyes took in the indefinable marks of an old soldier which lay on the man in front of him. "I'm Lang, commanding the infantry battalion."

"Yes, sir. I'm Lieutenant Murtaugh," the latter said a little warily. His eyes had not missed the Hudson River school ring which the major wore on his left hand. Then something that he saw in Steve Lang's face reassured him, and he relaxed a little and allowed the stiffness to go out of his mouth. "'Sergeant Murtaugh' would sound a lot more familiar, major."

Lang nodded absently. He was studying the fifty yards of dark water which separated them from the far bank where a snowy V marked where the road crawled away to the south. He noted the charred tops of the piles and scowled. Little help there, he was thinking, and there was so little time left to them.

"We've got to have a bridge across here, Murtaugh," he said abruptly. "I can give you maybe six hours. Can you do it?"

Murtaugh liked that. No long explanations. No crying over the fate which had brought them here, the Gooks at their heels, to find nothing but fifty yards of empty water. Just: "I can give you six hours. Can you do it?" That was good. That was soldier talk.

"Yeah," he said, not bothering with the "sir" now. "Sirs" were not necessary among soldiers, and he had weighed Major Steve Lang in that brief space and found him not wanting—as Major Steve Lang had weighed him and found the same. "I been studying the job. We can do it. We'll saw off those piles and put new stringers on top. Six hours ought to be just about right."

"Can you find enough material in the town?"

"We'll find enough."

"How about tools?"

"We hung onto some." Murtaugh took a worn plug of tobacco from his pocket and worried off a bite; put the plug back while he stared at the river with narrowed eyes. "Enough, I think. It would help if you could lend me some men."

"I'll give you fifty," Lang said. "I can't spare more. We've got to set up a perimeter north of the town if we're going to buy that six hours for you."

"I'll make fifty do."

Murtaugh took a whistle from his pocket, and its shrill blast echoed through the last of the afternoon. As Lang watched, men began to come out of the houses behind where he stood; they formed up in a ragged line. Second Lieutenant Murtaugh went toward them, his head bent a little, and his feet clumping heavily through the snow.

"Cripes, majeh," Alabama said, "You know something? That guy's old enough to be in the Old Soldiers' Home. What is he doin' out heah?"

"Fighting a war," Lang said grimly. "Stay here. If Murtaugh needs help come let me know."

He swung away and went back through the ruined town. As he passed the big house with the veranda he saw that the children were gone, except for the littlest one whom Pat had called Joey. The kid was standing there, his feet spraddled in the snow, and watching as Lang came up. Then he gravely held up his hand, his fingers making that O again.

"Lousy refugees," he said.

There was no sign of Pat Delevan—she was inside with the rest of the kids, Lang guessed. He grinned at Joey, patting him on the head, and then went on, vaguely disappointed that he hadn't seen Pat again. Then he dismissed that thought angrily—this was not the time to be mooning over a girl. Even a pretty girl.

Lieutenant Haycross had the dozen officers and forty-odd noncoms assembled when Lang got back to the temporary CP. They made a tight little group, huddled against the snow, and they watched silently as he leaned his carbine against the side of the ruined house and beat his hands together to warm them. A fresh gust of wind came out of the north, bringing with it a swirl of powdery snow, and Lang could feel his skin tighten as he thought of Murtaugh and his engineers working down there in that icy water.

Well, no use to think of that now. There were other things to be done. He stepped out in front of the tight group and stood for a moment, looking at them and not speaking. Many of them were older than himself, he knew. Many had more service, for he, like Second Lieutenant Murtaugh, had had his insignia pinned on him back there at Kung-ri two weeks ago. *Boy major,* they were thinking. He could see it in their sullen, discouraged faces. *Stand by, boys, for a pep talk from the boy wonder. The old college try, boys. Nuts.* Well, he couldn't blame them much.

"Johnson!" he called sharply and a captain with a dirty bandage around his head beneath his helmet shuffled his feet a little in the snow.

"I'm here," he said, his voice flat and toneless.

"Detach twenty-five men from Baker Company and have them report to Lieutenant Murtaugh up at the river. He's building a bridge. . . . Slayton, you do the same. How many men have you got left in Baker, Johnson?"

"Eighty-nine, maybe," Johnson said. His voice was thick and indifferent. "I don't know for sure."

Lang's face seemed to grow leaner, more pinched, and there was an angry spark which began to glow in his eyes. "Why don't you know how many men you've got, Johnson?" he asked and the whiplash of his voice stiffened the shoulders of the men in front of him. All but Johnson. It didn't touch him. Everything had gone down the drain for Johnson and he didn't care any more.

"What difference does it make?" he asked, that indifference flowing like a drug through his hoarse voice.

"It makes a heck of a lot of difference!" Lang said with his voice tight and harsh. "Haycross!"

"Here, sir."

"You're in command of Baker Company as of now! Get those men up to Murtaugh on the double, as soon as I finish with what I've got to say here. . . . Same for you, Slayton!"

"Yes, sir," Haycross answered, his shoulders stiffening in imitation of those of the slender man in front of him.

"Now give me your attention—all of you!" Lang said, and the metallic bite of his voice cut across the leaden afternoon. "You men have had a rough time for the last few days. We've all had a rough time. Very likely we're going to have a still rougher time before we get out of this and join up with the rest of the division. That doesn't matter. What does matter is that we are going to get out of this and back! Make no mistake about that!"

He paused for a moment, his eyes roving over the men huddled in front of him, and they shuffled their feet and waited. It was as though—so it seemed to them—he was weighing each individual pitilessly; determining his worth and passing on. They avoided his gaze; avoided one another's eyes.

He went on after a moment, "Maybe we could ford the river. If we did, we'd have to leave our wounded behind, and we aren't doing that! Another thing, these refugees are counting on us for help, and you've seen enough of the Chinese to know what will happen if we don't help. So we're going to build a bridge, and either we'll all go on or we'll all stay! Is there anybody who doesn't understand?"

A man at the rear of the little group called out in a muffled voice, "To blazes with the refugees."

Lang paid no attention to that. It would serve nothing to single that man out—if he could find him—and make an example of him now. There wasn't time for that. And, anyway, he understood the bleak despair which lay behind the remark. It was his job to kick that despair out of these men; to lead them back so that someday they would be a fighting battalion again.

"We've got to have six hours," he went on. "We were lucky to break contact last night, and I figure that it will take about four hours for them to catch up to us here. They're moving slow and licking their wounds a little after Kung-ri. The last two hours we'll have to buy here. And the success of the buying is going to depend on you men! Get that! It's going to depend on you because you are the ones that wear the insignia on your shoulders and the stripes on your sleeves!"

He paused again, his eyes roving over those in front of him. Again that cold gust of wind came down out of the north, drifting flying snow ahead of it, and for no reason at all he thought of Joey with his O and his "lousy refugees," and his own lips tightened grimly.

"You've got a bunch of green kids for soldiers," he went on, biting at his words now. "They're good kids—they showed that at Kung-ri—but they're still kids and you've got to carry them. Some of you are green too. That can't be helped. You put your right to greenness behind you when you took the stripes that you wear. Now, you've got to live up to those stripes—that insignia! You're tired. I know that! You're hungry and discouraged and scared. I know that too! I don't feel any differently from the way that you feel!"

Deep silence out there now, and the shuffling had stopped. He could see the steam of their breath blowing away from their lips, and suddenly he felt very lonesome and very old standing there in front of them in the last of the day. They had to carry those men huddled in the razed houses of the broken town; he had to carry them. All the things that he was saying to them applied a hundredfold to himself. But that was the way war was and that was the way things had to be.

Again he thought of Joey with his O.

"You feel sorry for yourselves," he said evenly. "I can see that in your faces. You think that you've been handed a dirty deal. You're saying, 'Why did it have to be me?' Well, forget that! Just start thinking of this: This battalion is going on! It's going to keep on going on until there's not a man left who can lift a foot or pull a trigger! And then it's going to go on after that! Are there any questions?"

There were none, as Lang waited, his hands on his hips and his eyes like gray ice in his dirty face. "All right," he said finally. "Get your companies reorganized. Redistribute the ammunition that you've got left. Then wait for orders here. . . . Lawton!"

A lieutenant with the caduceus of the Medical Corps on his collar stepped forward. "Yes, sir."

"Take your trucks down close to the river. You can set up a temporary hospital in one of the houses; do what emergency work you can. You've got six hours."

"Yes, sir," Lieutenant Lawton said. "You're going to get the trucks across the river, sir?"

"We're going to get the trucks across the river," Lang told him grimly.

The rest of the group was breaking up; drifting away to assemble what was left of their commands. Lieutenant Grosbeck spoke to Haycross as they went. Lieutenant Grosbeck was short and he had been pudgily fat when the outfit had first gone north. Now, the flesh seemed to hang in folds from his cheeks and beneath his chin.

"I've heard better fight talks in high school," he mumbled through cracked lips. "What right's he got to be in command? Captain Johnson was senior before they jumped this boy wonder over his head."

Haycross looked at him thoughtfully—something new had come into Lieutenant Haycross since he had brought back his report from the river an hour ago. There was a tighter line to his lips and his hands no longer nervously caressed the stock of his carbine.

"What would Johnson do that you'd like better?" he asked softly. "Name me one thing."

Grosbeck shook his head and his feet stumbled a little as he shuffled them across the snow hummocks. "Johnson knows that men can't go on forever," he said, a whine creeping into his voice.

"So you'd stay here and let the Gooks gobble you up?"

"I don't know," Grosbeck said. "I don't know."

Haycross struck him sharply across the shoulders and he used the same words which Steve Lang had used earlier. "Get your chin up! We're going out! Can't you get that through your thick head? Steve Lang is going to take us out!"

Grosbeck shook his head stupidly, like a man awakening from a bad dream. "Yeah," he said thickly. "Yeah. I guess that's right, isn't it?"

Back by the ruined house, Captain Johnson was still standing in front of Lang. He hadn't moved when the others had left, and now he was staring vacantly toward the river. Lang went to him; dropped a hand on his shoulder.

"Come on, Bert," he said, keeping his voice low and even. "Snap out of it. You're acting like a baby."

"We're going to have to put the smudge pots out tonight, Sam," Captain Johnson suddenly said in a clear voice. "There's going to be frost. I can smell it."

Lang shook his head soberly and beckoned to Lieutenant Lawton. "Take him with you, Charley," Lang said in a tired voice. "He's back in California in his orange groves. Give him a shot of something—if you've got anything left."

~

Lieutenant Jim Lacey had the outpost a half mile out on the road which led north from the village. He sat a little apart and listened idly to the talk that

flowed around him. Halverson, a towheaded kid from Minnesota, was talking with Corporal Parkhurst, the BAR man. Halverson was twenty, Jim
Lacey knew, and he liked to play the harmonica and nothing ever bothered
him very much.

"You know what I think they ought to do with this place?" Halverson
was asking Corporal Parkhurst.

"No," Parkhurst said shortly. He was a slight man who wore glasses and
he had used to teach the men's Bible class when he was back at home. "Why
should they do anything with it? It's here, isn't it? How are you going to do
anything with it anyway?"

"You got no imagination, deacon," Halverson said. "That's what's the
trouble with you. Now, if you had any imagination you could think up a lot
of things to do with this place."

"Such as what?" Corporal Parkhurst asked still more sourly.

"Such as towin' it out to sea and then borin' holes in it until the thing
sank. I'd like to be in a rowboat watchin' that, deacon."

"You're crazy," Parkhurst said.

Halverson leaned back in the snow, his hands behind his head and his
face alight with satisfaction as he turned the thing over in his mind. "I know
just how I'd go about it. I'd get me a great big saw and saw this peninsula
off right along the Yalu River. Then I'd get me a battleship and a big chain,
and I'd hook on and tow this place right out to sea. Then I'd sink it."

"It's not right to talk about things that way," Parkhurst said angrily. "I
don't want to listen to it! It's blasphemy!"

"What's blasphemy, deacon?"

"Talking like that!"

"Oh," Halverson said. "Like that, huh? Well, I'll play you a tune, deacon. I wouldn't want you to go away mad."

He fished inside his ragged jacket; pulled out a stubby harmonica and
fitted it to his lips and began to play. The reedy notes drifted up in an eerie
melody above the little swale where the two sat—mournful music in the afternoon. Jim Lacey, sitting to one side, shook his head and scowled a little as
he listened. The air that Halverson was playing was vaguely familiar, but it
took a long time for Jim Lacey to remember where he had heard it before.
He got it then—it had been in the little wooden church where he had used

to go to Sunday school back in Idaho. A long time ago, he thought. A long, long time ago. How had the thing gone?

> *One more river to cross*
> *And that's the river of Jordan*

Something like that. Funny song to be playing up here. Then he said sharply, "Break it off, you guys! Here comes the major!"

Lang came on up through the snow; dropped to his heels beside Jim Lacey. "How does it go, Jim?" he asked, his steady gaze going on by to search the valley.

"O.K., sir," Jim Lacey said. "Nothing moves."

Lang nodded absently. "I want you to take your detail a half mile farther up the road, Jim," he said after a moment. "We'll set up a perimeter along here. Stay out in front in observation until I call you in. Got it?"

"Got it," Jim Lacey said. "You figure the Gooks are still after us, major?"

"Don't you, Jim?" Lang asked gently. He liked this lanky lieutenant with the freckled face and the calm eyes.

"Yeah, I guess I do, at that. You think we're going to be able to get across the river?"

"We're going to get across," Lang told him soberly. "We're going to have to make a fight for it first. Send a man back to tell the company commanders to report to me here, will you?"

Lacey nodded. "Halverson!" he said.

Halverson listened to his instructions, then trotted off through the snow.

There were two cigarettes left in his crumpled package; Lang gave one of them to Jim Lacey and put the other into his own mouth. It would probably be a long time before he had another cigarette, he was thinking.

"How's all this rat race going to end, major?" Jim Lacey asked soberly after they had smoked for a moment. "I thought the dope was that we weren't going to have any more wars. What happened?"

Lang sat silently for a moment while he turned that over in his mind. "You'll have to ask a wiser man than I am, Jim," he said finally. "I guess that it isn't a soldier's job to figure out the why of wars. His job is just to fight them."

"I could improve on that scheme," Jim Lacey said tightly.

"Any soldier would like to try," Lang agreed. "Forget it, Jim. A man can go nuts trying to figure such things out. Here come the company commanders; take your detail and move on out."

The company commanders arrived a moment later, Haycross in the lead, and Lang outlined his plan; issued his orders in a crisp, sure voice. The machine guns here; the mortars and the rocket launchers there. Two rifle companies in line, the other in reserve. The heavy-weapons company so, and the CP thus.

As he spoke he felt the spines of the officers in front of him begin to stiffen. This was something that they could understand and get their teeth into. This was something better than the disorganized running back which had frozen their minds and dulled their wills during the past days.

When he had finished, Lang asked curtly, "Any questions?" and was satisfied when he saw that there were none. "Move your companies up and start digging in, then," he said. "We'll buy Murtaugh his six hours here."

~

Lieutenant Murtaugh, wet to the waist, stood on the riverbank by the fire which they had built and watched while men streamed by him with the timbers they had salvaged from the town. Other men, standing in icy water to their hips and on crossbars lashed to the piles, sawed at the tops of the burned stubs. Now and then a blackened chunk dropped, like a sad head under a guillotine, and floated swiftly away on the turbid water. Corporal Cloister came stomping through the shell ice at the river's edge and shivered while he warmed his hands at the fire for a moment.

"That water's colder than a witch's breath," he said heavily. "Two saws! Cripes, we'll be sawin' here for the next ten years with only two saws! How're the stringers comin' along, Jeff?"

Murtaugh glanced along the bank to where a score of men were working, efficiently and without seeming haste, on the scattered timbers which they had dragged from the village. Those timbers weren't big enough, he was thinking; still, they were all that they had, and they would have to do.

"Good enough," he said to Cloister. "The first of 'em will be ready by the time you've got the piles squared enough to—"

He broke off suddenly, swearing with bitter words as a shrill yell came from the river. One of the men standing on the slippery and uncertain perch of the lashed crossbar had lost his balance and disappeared into the eddying water. His head came to the surface after a moment, and then he was swimming heavily.

A thrown rope snaked out toward him, and he caught it and was hauled back to the line of piles. Without argument, he climbed back to the crossbar and took hold of the handle of the saw.

"That Rogers," Cloister said softly. "You can't kill him; he's got nine lives."

"He's an engineer, Mike," Murtaugh said in a heavy voice. "Send a man out to replace him and tell him to come on in here to the fire and warm up a little."

Cloister nodded and went on back down the bank. He yelled to a man who had just dropped a board on the growing pile of planking; the two of them clambered onto the crude raft which they had built earlier, and hauled themselves out to the pile where Rogers was still working doggedly on.

Good men, Murtaugh was thinking. All of them good men. Take that Alabama kid, who had come up with the major, and who was down there swinging a pick with the rest of them as they cleared the abutment. The sound of the tools rang clean and fine in the cold air. Yes, all good men. Too good to die like rats here on the bank of a stinking Korean river!

A slim figure was coming toward him through the snow, and he waited, thinking it might be a messenger from the major. Then he saw that it was Pat Delevan—it was the engineers who had brought her and her flock of little brown kids down from the gap. Murtaugh's craggy face relaxed a little as he spat his cud of tobacco into the fire and turned to meet her. He liked Pat Delevan. She came on to stop at the fire, holding her hands out to its warmth.

"Howdy, Jeff," she said. "Cold for swimming, isn't it?"

"Awful cold," he agreed. "How's Joey?"

"Winning the war," she told him. "I'm looking for Major Lang. I thought that I might find him here."

Murtaugh shook his head. "Ain't seen him since a couple of hours ago. Anything I can do, Miss Delevan?"

"Just Pat," she said. "Nothing, Jeff."

She fell silent for a moment, looking toward the river and her mind busy with the picture that she saw limned there in the last of the day. Against the dropping dusk she could see the stark silhouette of men's shoulders as they swung steadily at the tasks which they had been given. She caught her breath a little, as something of the grandeur of it possessed her. Men down there. Men working to build a bridge so that they and other men might live. Little men who, perhaps, were afraid; little men who were wet and tired and hungry, but who worked on. Little men made in the shape of God—so He must have labored, dogged and tired, when He made His world.

She turned slowly to Murtaugh. "They're wonderful, Jeff," she said softly. "Can't you see it?"

"Yeah," Murtaugh said, and his voice was sober and old. "I can see it—Pat."

Later, she put her hand on his arm and her voice was insistent with a suppressed intensity which Jeff Murtaugh did not wholly understand. "What about Steve Lang, Jeff? Would he fit into that picture down there?"

Suddenly Murtaugh did understand, and he hesitated, looking at the dark river for a long moment. When he turned back to Pat his eyes were honest and untroubled. "He'd fit," he said. "Yes, he'd fit."

Rogers came on toward the fire, his boots squishing water; water seeped out of his sodden trousers. He gave Pat Delevan a bright glance and then squatted in front of the blaze, glancing up over his shoulder at Jeff Murtaugh.

"Do I get me a Purple Heart for fallin' off that pile, sarge?" he wanted to know. "I scratched my leg something awful. You like to look?"

"Naw," Murtaugh said. "You don't get no Purple Heart. You get docked a day's pay."

"Now, that's the Army for you," Rogers said, grinning. "And I thought I was a hero."

Pat's eyes were very bright—a little moist—as she turned away and started back to where she had left the children. Why was it, she wondered, that war—the nastiest business on earth—could bring out the best in even the smallest of men?

～

Steve Lang pushed his helmet back on his head as he entered the building where Lieutenant Lawton had set up his makeshift hospital. A lantern hung on a wire from a beam and its yellow light flowed over the twenty-odd men laid out on the floor. Lawton came to meet him, his sleeves rolled up and his hands stained.

"How are they, Charley?" Lang asked.

Lawton's eyes were bright. "Better than they've got any right to be. If we can get them to a hospital before long—"

Lang nodded and went on down the line, and men's eyes watched him dumbly and men's heads turned to follow as he passed. He spoke a word here, a word there. Not much—just the few words that you said to men who needed the tonic of assurance. At the far end of the building, Captain Johnson sat on a stool, hands clasped between his knees and his eyes on the floor. Lang paused beside him, reaching out a hand to drop it on his shoulder.

"How does it go, Bert?" he asked gently.

Johnson didn't look up, but his lips moved. "Don't bother me, Sam," he mumbled. "I've got to watch the smudge pots."

Lang shook his head wearily—his name wasn't Sam and there were no smudge pots. Well, it was time to get back up front to the perimeter. The heads of the men followed him as before as he went back along the line. Pat Delevan was waiting as he stepped outside the door, and he paused for a moment, watching her face with a faint surprise. Suddenly he had the feeling that he had known her for a long time and he was glad of that.

"They'll be coming pretty soon, won't they, Steve?" she asked gravely. "I wanted to wish you luck."

"Everything will be all right," Lang told her mechanically.

She stepped closer to him; laid a hand on his arm. "Be careful, Steve. Be as careful as you can. The battalion needs you. All of us need you."

He stood looking down at her for a moment, not knowing what to say. Then he murmured, "I'll be careful, Pat," and kissed her on the lips, and wheeled away.

Pat's eyes were bright as she watched him go. Then she lifted her hand and made an O with her finger and thumb. "From Joe and me and all the rest, Steve," she said under her breath.

～

Corporal Parkhurst lay in a shallow hole, his automatic rifle thrust out over the hole's lip. Halverson lay beside him, blowing softly on the harmonica. A gay tune with a hillbilly lilt to it. It seemed out of place here, Corporal Parkhurst thought irritably as he turned in his hole.

"I don't think that you ought to be playing things like that now," he said soberly. "It's not fit."

Halverson took the harmonica from his lips and grinned. "Why not, deacon? Give me one good reason."

"It's just not fit is all."

"Nuts!" Haverson said. "I'm playing me a battle march to heaven, deacon. Like the Indians used to do. You know about Indians, don't you?"

"I don't see what Indians have got to do with it."

"They used to throw a big party before a battle," Halverson said. "Dancing and eats and a big powwow. Well, I ain't got anything to eat and I can't dance. So I play the harmonica. Get it?"

Corporal Parkhurst sucked his lips in disapprovingly and went back to staring up the dim valley. Lieutenant Lacey came presently, dodging through the scanty brush, and slid down into the hole.

"Seen anything?" he asked.

"Nary a thing," Halverson said.

Jim Lacey squirmed on his belly until his field glasses bore up the valley; focused them on the U where the meandering road came down out of the mountains. Then he grunted and the glasses steadied and he looked for a long moment.

Through the dim haze he saw a tiny figure in a padded coat come through the gap. Another followed; a dozen more. They spread out and disappeared into the scrub, and then the gap was empty again. Lacey took the glasses down and spat and spoke over his shoulder to Halverson, "Go back to Baker Company and find that messenger. Message to Major Lang. Gooks in sight. Got it?"

"Yeah," Halverson said. "I got it."

It was ten minutes before the head of the main body appeared. No tanks, Lacey saw, and he let his breath go in a long sigh of relief at that. Just infantry now. A solid column of infantry which flowed down out of the hills behind its sketchy advance guard. They'd come straight on to the river, Lacey thought. He wished that the major would come. He didn't want to open the battle too soon. Or too late, as far as that went.

It was fifteen minutes later and the Gooks were still pouring into the valley in a solid column three miles away when Steve Lang slid into the hole beside Lacey. Without a word, Lacey handed the field glasses across and Lang took them. He handed them back after a little; pushed himself to his knees.

"They haven't suspected that we're here yet, Jim," he said. "They wouldn't be coming on in a heavy column like that, if they did. It'll give us a chance to hurt them bad at first. After that—"

Jim Lacey grinned tightly. "Yeah, after that," he said.

"Bring your men on back," Lang told him in a tight voice. "You've done your job up here, Jim. We'll let their scouts come on if they want to."

It wasn't going to snow, after all, Lang thought as he went back. The sky had cleared a little, and that meant that later on there would be a full moon shining above the overcast. Well, he couldn't do anything about that. He passed through the staggered line of foxholes where Able and Baker companies lay; left terse instructions and then went on to where he had massed the few mortars which were left to him.

The Chinese column was a thick snake on the road, its head only hundreds of yards away, when he blew his whistle and the first of the mortar shells began to crump down into packed men out there in the snow-covered valley.

~

Murtaugh, waist-deep in water, paused for a moment and turned his head as he heard the dull thump of that first mortar shell. Then, trotting close on the heels of the explosion, the yammer of machine-gun fire came crackling back through the cold night. The men on the bridge paused, too, to listen for a brief moment; then bent to their tasks again. That was infantry business. Their business was to build a bridge.

It was taking shape now. Stringers stretching out across the newly squared tops of the piles. Planking coming out, being lashed down with bits of rope, scraps of wire—anything that they could lay their hands on. A makeshift and unlovely thing, but still a bridge. The sound of hammers and axes made a solid punctuation to the steady drum of fire which drifted back from beyond the ruined town.

That firing slacked off, died away and, in his mind's eye, Murtaugh could picture what was happening. He could see the white valley stretching away to the north, and empty now, except for the scattered bundles of padded clothing which lay here and there. The Gooks would have scattered, set back for the moment by the sudden viciousness of the fire which had struck them, but they would come on again presently. They would open with their own mortars, and then their artillery probably, and shells would be dropping in the village. Dropping around the bridge.

Well, no matter about that now. He tested the lashing of a stringer and called to Corporal Cloister, hauling toward him on the raft. "Better put a double lashing here, Mike," he said. "Sounds like the dance has started."

"It does that," Cloister said. "Drop my old woman a line, Jeff, if I don't come out. I guess maybe she wasn't so bad, at that."

Refugees were crowding down close to the growing bridge as Murtaugh splashed out of the river. The ambulance trucks had been brought up close here, their headlights shining out over the working men, and in the glare Murtaugh could see the strained, silent faces of these people who watched.

He called to Rogers, "Keep 'em back. I don't want 'em out there in our way."

Alabama came out of the shadows, his rifle slung over his shoulder again now and his grin pasted onto his face like a mask. He waved a hand. "So long, Jeff," he said. "I got to go fight me a war. It's shuah been nice seein' you, seh."

Murtaugh nodded. "Tell the major to give us another hour, son," he said. "Either we'll have a bridge by then or we ain't going to have a bridge "

"I'll tell him that, seh," Alabama said.

He passed on back into the shadows and, at the house with the big veranda, he paused for a moment. Pat Delevan was there, the children around her with their eyes big in their brown faces. She came swiftly toward Alabama.

"You're going up there now, soldier?" she asked swiftly.

Alabama nodded soberly, his grin gone. For a moment Pat hesitated; then came to stand close to Alabama—close enough so that he could smell the faint perfume of her hair.

"Look after the major, won't you, soldier?" she said.

For a moment Alabama stood looking down at her with his forehead furrowed in a little frown. Then he grinned, and it was the same old careless grin. A grin that said that William Oglethorpe Stanton, of Montgomery, Alabama, was captain of his soul and that nothing the world held could bother him.

"Ma'am," he said, "don't you worry. Me and the majeh are solid. We're indestructible. There ain't anything can hurt us."

Pat said softly, "Thank you, soldier. Good luck," and then Alabama was gone, whistling softly to himself in the semi-darkness.

~

Steve Lang looked at his watch, and it said eight o'clock, and he knew that the bridge would have to be ready soon now. The battalion had thrown back three attacks—vicious assaults with bugles blaring in the eerie half-light which the moon, hung above the light overcast, threw into the valley. They could throw back another attack. Maybe two. Maybe three.

After that the battalion was done. There were more men back in Lieutenant Lawton's ambulance trucks now. There were men who no longer had any interest in a bridge.

Corporal Parkhurst wouldn't complain about the harmonica any more, and Lieutenant Haycross, that new-found light in his eyes, wouldn't go on to keep the command that he had earned. Others. Too many others, Lang thought.

The bugles started again, brassy above the snow, and the mortar shells crumped into the village beyond. The horns took up their eerie calling, and the shadows were full of men in padded coats who came howling in. Then the foxholes blazed with fire again and the machine guns took up their crazy laughter, and presently the snow in front was empty once more, except for new bundles which lay scattered here and there.

Lang crawled along the line and, at its far end, he found Jim Lacey. Lacey gave him a tired grin. "They pretty near got around my flank that time, Steve," he said, and the grin faded from his freckled face. He added, "Next time—" and let the sentence die.

Lang nodded, his face showing nothing, and then Alabama came crawling up to touch him on the shoulder. "Pop Mu'taugh says you can come back now, seh," he said. "They got that theah daggone bridge built. The trucks an' the refugees ought to be all across by now."

Thankfulness ran through Lang like the warmth of old brandy, and he was dimly aware of the almost shocked relief which flowed across Jim Lacey's grimed face. Then he forced his mind back to the things which still had to be done. The overcast was thickening again, dulling the eerie light which lay over the valley, and that would help.

He would pull the companies back one by one, he thought. He and Jim Lacey and Baker Company would be the last to go, holding a screen out here until the rest were across the river. Then they'd pull back. They might not make it. He said that to Jim Lacey, and the latter nodded while Alabama crouched there with his face suddenly old in the last of the light.

"Whatever you say, Steve," Jim Lacey said. . . .

The night was full of shuffling noises now which grew gradually fainter and then died away altogether as the rest of the battalion pulled back. He'd give them fifteen minutes, Steve thought. It should be enough. Alabama came crawling back up to the foxhole.

"Theah across, seh," he said. "Bridge is ready to blow as soon as we get back. Pop Mu'taugh says—"

He didn't finish, because the bugles had suddenly set up a howling crescendo and the world seemed suddenly to be full of shadowy figures which sprouted out of the snow around them. He had been afraid that this might happen, Lang thought as his carbine took up its spiteful bark again and the foxholes spouted fire. Too few foxholes now.

~

Jeff Murtaugh stood with what was left of his engineer company at the near end of the bridge, while he stared worriedly back into the darkness and waited for Baker Company and Steve Lang to come. The last of the others had passed ten minutes before and time was running out for all of them, he knew.

Behind him, Corporal Cloister shuffled his feet in the muddy snow and spat. "Why don't they come?" he asked angrily. "That West Point major lookin' for more medals?"

"Why, sure," Rogers said, his teeth clicking in the cold. "Majors are always lookin' for medals. Didn't you know?"

A figure materialized out of the shadows beside Murtaugh, and a voice asked quietly, "Jeff, why don't they come?"

Murtaugh turned slowly; saw that it was Pat Delevan, Joey clinging to her hand. "What the devil are you doing here?" he asked, making his voice rough to hide his concern. "I seen you go across a half an hour ago!"

"What the devil are you doing here, Jeff?" she countered.

"The engineers always go last, blast it!" he told her, his voice still more rough. "Now, get the—"

He didn't finish, for the distant howl of the bugles drifted down on them out of the night and the air was hideous with the sound of gunfire again. Mortar shells crumped down into the village at their backs; began dropping closer. The center of the bridge suddenly disappeared in a flash of blinding flame.

"Oh," Pat whispered in a voice which was shocked and disbelieving. "Oh, God. You couldn't."

"Cloister!" Jeff Murtaugh yelled, his voice rising harsh and unafraid above the racketing hell of the gunfire. "Start replanking her!" But Corporal Cloister was already going forward at a run, his men pounding after him.

Other men were trotting back toward the village—burning now—returning with planks on their shoulders. . . .

The last of the planks were going in as Baker Company came out of the village, the light of the burning houses smoky and red against their faces. They carried their wounded with them, and Jim Lacey came at their head and Steve Lang followed them in. The rest of the battalion, across the river, had taken up the fire now, and the racket from beyond the town died away again. The boots of Baker Company echoed hollowly on the bridge and Lang swung out beside Jeff Murtaugh as the last of them passed.

Murtaugh blew his whistle and the engineers—frozen clothes crackling stiffly as they marched—moved on after Baker Company. Pat Delevan, standing unnoticed with little Joey, watched them pass, a knot in her throat. Men. Just men. But good men.

"You built it, Jeff," Steve Lang said. "Good job." There was no emotion in his voice. No elation. No praise. No nothing. Jeff Murtaugh liked it that way. Soldier talk.

"You bought us six hours, Steve," he said.

Then Steve noticed Pat and little Joey for the first time, and he frowned thoughtfully, not saying anything. After a minute, he slung his carbine over his shoulder, took their hands in his own and the four of them went across the bridge that the engineers had built here. The red light of the burning town lighted their way.

~

The bridge blew with a shattering, crashing roar which laid a red smear of flame across the sky, and presently there was nothing left there but a few shattered stringers and the dark water flowing coldly beneath and the snow which was starting to fall again.

The column was on the road once more, slogging tiredly through the night, but there was a difference now. The hopelessness had gone and men marched now with a certain sure swing to their tired shoulders. They would get back to the division, they knew. Nothing could ever stop them now. They were indestructible.

Pat Delevan marched beside Steve Lang, and he made no protest, for he was glad to have her there. Little Joey marched between them, his short legs trotting. They had squeezed the other children into the trucks, but Joey had refused to leave.

"We must keep him with us, Steve," Pat Delevan said softly. "When all of this is over."

"Yes," Steve said. "We'll keep him with us."

Little Joey lifted his face, understanding somehow. Then he thrust his hand up, his fingers making the familiar O. "Lousy refugees," he said.

In Baker Company, Halverson took his harmonica from his pocket and began to blow on it softly. The reedy music had a soft and caressing quality as the snowflakes drifted down to stick on Halverson's face. A sound like Taps in the night.

One more river to cross
One more river . . .

Halverson played it only once; then put the harmonica back into his pocket and went clumping on. Alabama, beside him, looked curiously through the curtain of snow.

"Concert ain't oveh, is it?" he asked. "Go ahead. Blow some moah, seh."

"Nope," Halverson said in a stolid voice. "That was just for a guy I knew once. I'm goin' to miss him, I guess."

Rolando Hinojosa

~ Hoengsong
(from *The Useless Servants*)

February 18–19. Capt Bracken joined the 219th on 2/18; he'll be the CO for our battery again; this is his first command since the war started. He's the O who calls me Tex, for God's sake.

~

Were promised some days in a rest area after last January's long, hard fight, but this was cut short.

About six days ago, some US Army and Marine Corps units were caught in an ambush on a twisting road between the towns of Saemal/Hoengsong; we were assigned to a death count detail to recover the dead there. We'd been promised some days in a rest area, but this was cut short, and we learned why when we got to the Hoengsong road.

The battle must have been a horror; as we drove up, we could see nothing but devastation: burned trucks and tanks; jeeps and weapons carriers also burned and on their sides or blown upside down.

And the dead. No idea how many, but for a short route, the death count will rank as one of the highest in the war. Some of the men with us broke down right away, and I've no idea why I didn't break down with them. That I didn't doesn't mean I'm brave, God knows.

The cold is unbelievable; colder than last Nov-Dec in northern Korea; brutal. But noted that glass melted and embedded in some GIs in trucks.

Before we started out as a group to help with the recovery of the bodies, a runner brought news about the gauntlet at Kujangdong last Nov. This was the first hard news regarding Charlie Villalón; we were told he was killed in Kunu-ri along with three other guys during the crossing back and forth of the River Chongchong. My guess is he prob died saving someone who didn't deserve it.

I have no idea how long I'll be able to sit and write about what goes on here; words fail when I write the word "horror," and the word itself means little unless one speaks of bodies that are torn, burned and unrecognizable . . . but even that becomes tiresome and repetitive, which is what war is: repetitive. How many ways can a person die, anyway?

Some continue going to Mass now and again, and I do too, but I refuse to go to confession.

Receiving absolution for killing doesn't make sense to me, no more than being wounded, surviving and then seeing someone die, next to me or across the way . . .

Add Charlie Villalón's death to this, plus my state of mind at the start of the death count detail on the Hoengsong road, and that completes the picture of early February.

On the first day of the death count, I got off the two-and-a-half-ton truck at the assembly point and threw up. Tried a cigarette and got the dry heaves immediately afterward. I then wandered off, canteen in hand and rinsing my mouth. Done in, I climbed in the back of a covered weapons carrier, had a good cry, and that brought some peace.

Feb 19. The Hoengsong fight/ambush took place about a week ago while we were fighting at Chipyong-ni. Today we joined the Marines and went back to the Hoengsong Road for our dead. No wounded here; no one survives in an open field at ten degrees F.

We found the dead well-preserved due to the cold. This made ID easier too. Graves Registration Os and enlisted came with us. I counted eleven dead Os, all ranks, with the highest being two Majors, and all the Os within 50 yards of each other. Leading small groups, I'd say.

The bodies were frozen, and this too made it easier for us to stack them. We then lined up the dead on the road while the trucks waited their turn to load them up. We were asked to identify guys, told them we were artillery and found seventeen from our battalion. Graves Reg EM recorded the names as we handed them the dog tags.

Joey identified seven from a 37th Field battery, and I came across three others I knew: Dutch Evitts, Robert Boatwright and Richard Delaney. Their outfit had been through the Naktong bridge explosion and Kunu-ri with us, and then to die in this ugly, desolate, frozen house of the dead.

At the end of the second day, we told Graves Reg guys we'd ride in the truck with the dead from the arty unit, and was told this was not necessary, but we insisted. Joey nodded, and he also refused to ride in the cab. "We'll go with the guys in the back," is what we said.

I'll never get used to any of this.

Once again at the assembly point, we learned that more men had been killed at Hoengsong than at first reported.

We returned twice after the initial trip and found two more artillerymen: Pete de León and Wilburn Rice.

Since the cold continues, the bodies will remain frozen. We found many GIs under trucks; some had been run over by trucks and tanks; others wounded by enemy rifle or arty fire. Some GIs were also found inside trucks. Charred hulks of burned vehicles stood all over the place; the bodies inside were in bad shape. Medics say the wounded must've died in their sleep.

A disaster. No civilian photographers from what I've seen. This prob due to Army censorship; someone has a lot to answer for here.

Four guys in our detail broke down. They'd been through the Kunu-ri ambush, but they couldn't take this detail and cracked. Got to feel sorry for guys who crack. Os and Old Guys say this: "No reason to chew them out. You pick them up, feed them, give them some rest, and they'll be back to fight. Army doesn't give up on people."

We from Kunu-ri recognize that crossing the Chongchong was worse than this, but as the Old Guys say: the dead stay dead, and they've all got relatives back home.

True enough.

Lt Vitetoe was in charge of our unit's work detail. Hoengsong being called Massacre Valley; that sounds like civilian talk, but it was baptized by the Marines. USMC lost many, many men here.

Still no civilian reporters here on our final trip to Hoengsong; the photogs consist of EM and Os.

Worked on open fields first, then up and down roads. Found dog tags, shoes and boots, socks and rings, etc. Petey Sturmer, the runner from Donora, Pa., worked with us and handled the bags carrying the personal effects.

Said he had seen hundreds of photographs of Gettysburg Battle and no diff from bodies here.

Talked about Penna a while. Says Donora is mostly Polish and German. The Gettysburg Battlesite, though, is near the state capital. I've no idea where any of this is.

Petey asked if Joey and I were cowboys in Texas. Told him no; my brother farms and Joey's dad is a printer and a newspaperman. Petey says his father works in a foundry of some sort.

Passed the time of day talking and I think we all knew we jabbered on to forget what we were doing.

~

Petey: "As I said, this is no different. As a runner you get to see more war. While this shit is bad, it's bad because these are our own guys. CCFs died too, you know."

So we kept up the work and the chatter. Stopped for a cigarette, and I waited to throw up again, but got through okay.

Petey says runner's job has changed: using jeeps more now. Easier since Gen Ridgway doesn't go all over the map. (We take land, fight, hold and move on, but not at breakneck speed.)

Then Joey said, "Possession for all time."

Petey looked at me when Joey quoted Thucydides again and said: "Catholic school, right? Jesuit?"

"Marist," and we both laughed.

Put out the cigarettes and back to work. In one hour we picked up 80 M-1s and over one-hundred helmets. We then filled more barracks bags with abandoned webbing, ammo clips, etc. Petey said that temptation remains the biggest risk for runners; he also said that dead NK and CCF are usually booby trapped. Asked me if I joined in, said no. Told me I was crazy, and Skinner working with Stang on some helmets and helmet liners, said, "He's not crazy, just dumb."

And we went on like this until time to quit.

~

As soon as we assembled again, we were broken off into small groups; Lt Fleming talked first and then Hat, and both said the same thing: we'll live with this for a long time. Don't fight it, admit what you've seen and done here, and you'll be done with it in less time.

That, too, is easier said.

In all, we spent three days here. I was glad to get off the detail and back to my binoculars.

After late chow we were rewarded with some beer.

Old Guys took over. Two battles shaping up, according to the Os. Maybe we'll go back to Seoul. Who knows?

Kitchen trucks arrived and the briefing was over. Ordnance guys came in and replaced two blocks, and we checked them out. Frazier scrounged a couple of mess kits for Ordnance guys, and they ate with us.

Mail. Three letters from Aaron, two from Aunt Mati and six from some letter-writing group in Tennessee, of all places. Never been there. They're form letters: "Thinking of all our troops," etc.

Heard of Hollywood actors on USO tours again. In this cold? I would like for them to get a load of the frozen dead at Hoengsong. It's all propaganda, and the shows are so bad not even Skinner would go to them.

Old Guys say they used to corral troops in Europe to watch the shows. I told them I used to see smiling faces on the Paramount News and all.

"Ha!" from Hat. And then, "I don't see you putting in for a trip to go see 'em."

Floodlights went up, and we went to work. Gearing up, taking in more ammo, which arrived after late chow. Rechecked new blocks again (perfect). I got me a new pair of gloves and a pair of mittens to go with them. Cleaned my two scarves by dipping them in hot water barrels, and hung them to dry across our gun. Scarves were getting rank. Froze in a matter of minutes, the steam rising at fifteen degrees F.

Work over, wrote to Aaron, Israel and Aunt Mati. Since it's close to early March, the ground will be turned by now and the cotton seed planted. The last of the oranges were already picked, is what Joey said.

And then, out of nowhere, Joey said, "Orange juice has the same color and consistency as rattler venom."

Stunner looked at us as if we were mad and said: "Is that true? Really, guys?"

I said it was, but that the smell tied with Korean rice paddies for first place. Sturmer laughed and said that was the runner's motto: "Avoid rice paddies at all costs."

During this, Skinner, of all people, brought me ten books. Haven't read a line in a month. One was another copy of the biography of the actor John Barrymore, plus a biography of a New York lawyer named Fallon. The rest is a mixed bag: Amer Lit from the 20s and 30s. Still, books are books and meant to be read.

Before sacking out, Dumas came up and said, "We'll spend one more day here. The Bn CO says you guys deserve to take a day off after the last three."

We asked if we were going to Wonju, but Dumas said he thought we'd go northwest, to Seoul. To take it back, he said.

Joey brought his arctic bag and a couple of blankets and said he was going to spend the night in our battery area.

Talk got to rumors as always. Part of unit is going to Seoul, but we, this arty Bn will go to Wonju, etc.

We talked a bit about Cloverleaf and Obong-ni and the two stubborn knobs and hills. This is the same site of NK atrocities: burying an O alive and tying up GIs, then shooting and bayonetting them; some were buried alive and suffocated.

Wherever we are to go, we're to meet units we're supporting when we get there. Dug out my next to last USMC cap and read the Marine's name: S. Boers, but pronounced Boris. Some Marine forces are out here again, and maybe I'll run into him, if he's alive. Boers's outfit transferred to Northeast Korea and no idea how fighting went there in Nov and Dec when we got whacked at Kunu-ri.

Cooks came by and said there was plenty of hot chow left over, and out we went. Luxury's lap: two hot meals in one day.

Got sleepy soon after and told to be ready to move out tomorrow at 0530 with early chow from 0430 to 0500.

(I'm scared to talk with the guys about Hoengsong; I'm trying to forget the dead, but it isn't working out. Please, God, don't let me go crazy.)

Stanford Whitmore

~ Lost Soldier

On the morning of the first day Corporal Wolfe had lain near the base of a scrub pine with his mouth in leafmold and snow as artillery fire shredded the trees where his platoon had been. That afternoon he had crawled some eighty feet into a shallow ravine. He had discovered a cut on the back of his left hand.

On the second day he moved out of the ravine and crossed three smooth hills. He heard only scattered small-arms fire in the distance. At night he ate a handful of snow and a fruit bar, checked his Garand, and slept in the lee of a drift.

Now, the third afternoon, the war seemed to have stopped. Since a half-hour past daybreak he had moved in the general direction of south, plotting his course by the infrequent, cold sun and taking care to avoid contrasting himself against the many troughs of snow. He estimated that he had traveled nearly five miles. At any time he might meet an American patrol. Once he heard the chilling whistle of aircraft far away and high, but could neither locate nor identify them. Crouched, running across a clearing with heavy, clubbing strides, crouched again, watching from behind shelter, eyes slitted at sounds, he heard only his openmouthed breathing.

As he rose and went on and moved up the side of the ridge, his confidence increased with each step. The war was almost behind him.

From the crest of the ridge, then, he saw the road. Two hundred yards to his right only a short length of the dry, rutted strip was visible as it flanked the draw between the ridge he stood on and the opposite hill. The road was thin and deserted and unchanged, and he knew it wound southeast to the American lines. He was no longer lost.

At his first short left-footed step down into the shadowed draw, he saw the lone Chinese soldier.

Without panic, mechanically, as he had been taught, faintly surprised at his calmness, Corporal Wolfe pivoted and flung himself full length on the frozen ground and rolled down behind the crest. He waited. He counted to fifty, slowly, listening between each number, his eyes focused on nothing so that he might hear better. Then he cradled the M-1 in his bent arms and crawled along the rise towards the road. He reached a heaved-up shelter of earth and rock. And listened again. After a minute he released the safety and looked over into the draw.

The Chinese was sitting about a hundred yards to the right and below, with his back to Corporal Wolfe. He was alone. It was evident that he had seen and heard nothing. In the brown quilted coating he looked like a rag doll stuck in the snow. No communications equipment was in sight. Every so often the miniature right arm bent and the hand went up to the face. A weapon lay nearby on a pile of something like straw. The doll sat quietly behind the mound of raw earth that commanded the twenty yards of unprotected road.

Only the road looked real. There was something deeply cold and dead about the silence weighing over the entire tapering length of the draw. The depression itself had a diseased quality in its outcroppings of stumps and pockmarks of rough stones, even to each shadow that lay on the snow like a bruise. Except for the brittle, tiny movement of the far-off arm, there was nothing else—nothing real but the wind now, cold and dry, blowing into Wolfe's eyes as he searched.

After a while he pushed down behind cover of a rise and rolled onto his back. The air seemed to have become colder. Lying there absently rubbing his thin, rough jaw, he watched the thick scud of storm clouds fleeing northeast and spreading their shadows over the rippled water standing in the fields. He longed for a canteen cup of coffee.

He decided that the best thing to do was to kill the Chinese. There was the road but the Chinese commanded it. There was the closed end of the draw but to circle it would involve at least a mile of walking along the steep slope. And there was always the chance that more Chinese might be sitting hidden in snow-caves. The only thing to do was to get this single Chinese. The sound of the shot had to be chanced. It had to be good. One shot—one firm slow steady squeeze of the trigger, and the war would be finally behind in the wood and the paddies and the patches of snow.

Like a lizard he moved across the stubbled ground towards the road, his head angled up and to the height of the protective crest ten inches above his vision. When he had carefully estimated the distance he stopped, rechecked his rifle, and looked over the rise.

The Chinese was not more than forty yards away and presented his quilted back as a target.

Wolfe could give and he could take away. There was no one in the world—the feeling was new. He thought about himself. There was not much thinking to the killing before. It was different noises and everybody clumsy, running into things, and when it was over he had been neither proud nor feeling guilty. What had impressed him most was the way in which the faces smeared and melted and were then nothing in the smoke. It was not the same as this.

The Chinese turned his head and Wolfe, after flinching, saw that he was young. Again the arm and hand moved, the short fingers touched and scratched the chin. The hand withdrew and the young Chinese inspected his bent forefinger. There was a peculiar saneness in the action. Alone and sitting like a small boy behind the hump in the snow, he picked at his chin and stared into the gradual gray haze of late afternoon and paid no attention to the submachinegun which lay nearby with its stock of thin metal like the framework of a crutch.

Wolfe looked at the road and then down at the Chinese. One shot was all he could afford against the machinegun. He brought the tip of the front sight up and held it steady just below the right ear of the Chinese. The corporal breathed once, his nostrils flaring, realigned the sight, and saw the head jerk suddenly as the Chinese stiffened and sat upright.

Wolfe slid below the ridge and waited. Voices, faint and fluttering in the wind, came from the road. He listened and shut his eyes. He wanted to throw up and he wanted to cry. He had waited too long. Any moment he would hear the shouts of greeting and then he would have to lie with his eyes in the leaves and pray they would not discover him. He was dead. He had almost made it, and he was dead.

The voices did not seem to grow louder. There was no sound from the Chinese in the draw. Wolfe waited, very slowly wet his lips with his tongue, and edged his vision over a cluster of spiny leaves.

The greasegun still lay within arm's-length of the mound behind which the Chinese sat drawn into such tight watchfulness that he appeared ready to spring six feet into the air at any second. But he did not move. He looked at the road, and Corporal Wolfe looked at the road, and on the road were three American soldiers, none of whom acted as though he was within twenty miles of danger.

They came slowly along the road until they reached the open stretch. They kicked at frozen mud-ribs and walked wide-legged. None of them wore helmets. One had on a brown knit cap; the others wore fur-flapped caps tied together at the top. The three grouped on the road as the one in the knit cap lighted a cigarette into the wind.

Wolfe snapped his front sight back to the Chinese and waited for a movement in the direction of the machinegun. The Chinese raised his hand to his chin and continued watching the road.

Wolfe could not account for it. The range was point-blank and the scouting-party was in a three-yard circle, their carbines slung over their right shoulders, thumbing the slings like suspenders. There wasn't a chance of getting away if the machinegun opened up, and still the Chinese did nothing. And still the three stood together, now and then stamping their boots, taking turns at the cigarette—scouting nothing, Wolfe thought, thinking about nothing except the tobacco taste and dogging it until they could report back that no contact had been made.

For an instant Wolfe saw them cut down by the machinegun while he watched. They went down on all fours on the cold hard ground and then their stomachs and just when the Chinese was congratulating himself Wolfe put a bullet in his ear. He shook the image out of his head, feeling a mixed sense of guilt and anger. Why didn't the Chinese go for them with the machinegun?

So, it occurred to him, he's afraid of giving himself away. Three Americans mean more are coming, and he doesn't want to draw the artillery. He'll sit there and wait like a statue, and when they go back to report no contact, he'll come back over this ridge and head north. With his muzzle unwavering, Wolfe lay quietly and considered.

One of the scouts began to beat his arms against his sides to keep off the cold. The one in the knit cap put his hands on his hips and quite deliberately studied the draw. Nothing happened. The third soldier stood beside the second and they both looked around. The first soldier stopped clapping his arms and packed a snowball. He threw it at a bony tree and missed. All three of them made snowballs and threw at the tree. One puffed white, there was a thin shout, but Wolfe could not tell whose aim had scored. The first soldier moved his head and neck, and together the three scouts turned and walked back along the road, carelessly closing the open space as though there was nothing, not a sign of danger, almost behind the shelter of the base of the hill, and then they were gone.

Wolfe watched the Chinese. The arm bent across the chest and inside the quilted coat; the hand extracted a cigarette. The Chinese held a match to the white stick and smoked. It was getting dark and cold.

There was no telling how far the scouts had to go before reaching their troops—but it was probably less than a mile. Still, judging from the silence, from no sounds of trucks or jeeps or tanks, and feeling the cold pressing onto the fields, Wolfe was sure that the Americans would not advance until morning. The Chinese knew it too, he thought. At some time during the night the rag doll would get up and come back over the ridge. Meanwhile the face stared from behind the mound and the mouth tasted the rich smoke and sucked it in warm and thick, and the cold came down.

The cold came through Wolfe's jacket and boots and made his feet feel like stumps. The cut on his hand started to hurt, and began to throb the more he thought about it. He rubbed his ankles and felt nothing through the heavy leather. He could be eating hot food and in warm clothes in an hour or less. By going just one hundred yards west, behind the cover of the ridge, he would reach the road. But then he would have to cross the open stretch in front of the Chinese. He squinted into the dusk at the machinegun lying within reach of the hand that held the cigarette. Why hadn't it been used on the scouting-party?

It was getting more difficult to see. In a few minutes he would he able to run across the short open space and out of sight almost before the Chinese saw him. The cold brought his teeth together uncontrollably. His hand pulsed at the end of his sleeve. A moving target would he impossible to hit. Still, there was the machinegun. There was the cold and the Chinese and the machinegun.

He fixed the front sight on the neck of the Chinese. He took a breath and held the black point steady. Dimly the small head rested on top of the cold barrel. A pinpoint orange glow lit the flat features.

"Yo!" Wolfe called, and the face turned, full face above the barrel, the cigarette-ash pale green for an instant, and then was the explosion as he fired. The head disappeared.

The Chinese lay on his back in the snow with his right leg bent under the left. His arms were outflung, palms up and half-gripped. He did not move. He lay in the snow as if he had been hurled from a cliff.

Wolfe came down into the draw and went over to the quilted coat and dull gleam of upper teeth. He saw that the cigarette had fallen on end and was still burning. He covered it with a scrape of his boot. Then he slung his M-1 on his shoulder and picked up the submachinegun. It was cold to the touch and surprisingly light. He handled it clumsily and even looked into the bore. There was a magazine clipped behind the trigger. He did not look into the magazine.

Snow sprayed from his legs as he carried the weapon by its thin canvas strap. When he was almost at the road he stopped and stood for a long time without looking back. Then he lifted the gun and detached the magazine.

It was full.

He weighed it in his hand and clicked it back in place. Holding the weapon by its muzzle, he turned to face the draw, coiled, and threw it as far as he could. Through the dusk he saw it lurch against the sky, and fall, and tear a dark gash in the crusted snow. Then he hitched his rifle on his shoulder and walked.

John Deck

~ Sailors at Their Mourning: A Memory

One night in November, 1952, a Navy patrol aircraft crashed into a freezing sea a few miles offshore from the North Korean port of Wonsan. It was an old seaplane, a PBM, loaded down with electronics equipment, depth charges, and fuel for a full night of flying. It flew in over the task force that blasted North Korea from international waters, cruising at two thousand feet; one engine quit and the ship began to fall away to the powerless side.

There was probably time to jettison some fuel and arms, but there was not enough time to lighten the load so that a single straining engine could maintain air speed. According to men who had seen or experienced single-engine flight, the weak side would be low, and the ship would go into a descending spiral. When it hit, they said, the pontoon would catch the crest of a swell, pulling the wing tip under, and the aircraft would probably flop over on its back, break up, and catch fire.

Witnesses aboard a destroyer in the task force confirmed the fire. They steamed up to it, skirted it looking for survivors; they searched through the night. They found nothing. By morning a storm blew up from the south, dispersing the oil slick. There were thirteen officers and men aboard.

The lost plane was one of twelve belonging to an antisubmarine squadron that patrolled the east coast of Korea, the Tsushima Strait, and the Yellow Sea from a base in Japan. The squadron had arrived from the States only a month earlier, and the sudden and complete disappearance of one ship and thirteen men was an awesome thing for some of us. I was a second radioman, radar operator, and titular gunner on one of the planes. Like many of the younger sailors, I had enlisted in the Navy so that I would not be drafted into the infantry, and I had spent a good portion of my enlistment in training schools. When I was assigned to a flying outfit and managed to learn the Morse code, I was given a chance to fly. It meant extra money and an easy life. Air crewmen stood fewer watches and did less work. I was not at all prepared for death.

There were older men in the squadron who warned us that our planes were dangerous, untrustworthy always, absolutely defenseless against attack. (We didn't worry about attack.) The squadron lost planes regularly. It spent eight months in the States, training pilots and new men, and six months overseas. Never in its history did a full cycle of fourteen months pass without a crash, and never did all the crew escape death.

But the men who admonished us were career sailors, veterans of World War II who had developed those peculiar enthusiasms and loyalties that permitted them to make a life of the service. A few were sincere, hardworking, intelligent. Most of them were wretched men, good at their work, but their work was stupid.

The Navy, clumsy and official, tried to awaken in us a sense of purpose and an awareness of the threats. At briefing sessions before each flight the intelligence officer reported what enemy planes had been sighted. It was generally known then that the Chinese used the Korean War as an extension of cadet training.

On a huge briefing-room map of the area, circles were drawn over sections of seas. Grease-penciled into each section was the current water temperature and a translation of that into minutes that a man would survive if afloat there.

Once, I remember, we were told that, should we go down off Vladivostok, we would have something like seventeen minutes. The planes flew up that way for a weather check after leaving the task force, so it was not out of the question. But we didn't worry. We weren't going to cream in, but if we did, we would get into a life raft.

Some clear nights a jagged, self-sustaining lightning flash visible off the starboard wing marked the fire line of the ground war. Our boys were out there, American soldiers, dying in the snow for free men everywhere. They could have enlisted rather than wait out the draft. We had enlisted. It was possible to be prudent while assuming one's share of the national risk.

Only once in that orientation period were we confronted with the unquestionable proof that we were engaged in a deadly business. We had a lecture on survival in North Korea, delivered by a Lieutenant Commander Birdwell, who had volunteered to go behind the lines and do his best to open up escape routes for downed fliers. In the event that any of us went in near the mainland and decided to try our luck on foot, we were advised to stay close to the coast, avoid settlements, bribe farmers, and eat either cats or dogs—I cannot remember which animal was recommended.

The lecture should have been convincing, but Birdwell made it all seem like more propaganda. He had been burned terribly. His face was plated with skin grafts, none of them matching, and his hair was linty and grew in little bolls scattered over a tortured scalp. He had a tiny nose with unmatched nostrils, and his eyes peered out of rough, irregular sockets, like holes torn in a paper bag.

He was so disfigured, and so obviously delighted by some of his shocking counsel, that it was like that famous, unheeded VD film, where the man with advanced paresis, sitting in the wheelchair, kept trying to count to ten.

"If I looked like that," Kramer said, "I wouldn't eat dogs or cats."

We didn't listen; then the first plane crashed and the first men died. Three were officers, remote from us. Three or four were veterans. But the remainder were fine young men, like us.

~

The day before the plane was lost, my crew had flown out over the Tsushima Strait, a short gravy hop during which we photographed shipping. When we came home, we were pulled up on the seaplane ramp for minor repairs. We had liberty that night. As the storm front moved through, and two-boat was flying toward its doom, I went into the small town outside the gate, drank beer, and danced with bar hostesses.

The girls were perfect. They were humorous and gentle. And they needed us. I had never been around a collection of pretty, young, intelligent girls who needed me—not as a civilian and certainly not as a sailor. It was a blessing, a whiff off a dream, and another eloquent argument against worry.

I came back to the barracks late, probably staggering, but damned happy, I'm sure. And there were all the men in the dorm, wide awake, dressed for flight. They sprawled about on the big picnic table, the single piece of unnecessary furniture in the room. They wore bulky winter flight suits and fleece-lined boots. They were silent; they all looked up when I walked in, grinning.

"'Bout time you got back," Pat Fanning, my plane captain, said. "Two-boat's missing."

Pat was another battered man. Once, not too long before I met him, the husband of the woman he loved had got him drunk one night and had almost killed him, laying him out first with a bottle and then kicking and stomping him. He came out of that with his face a fine mesh of scars. He had been handsome—he showed us photographs when he was on a friendly drunk—and now he was blurred and broken.

When he was full of contempt, which was his usual state, he could say "Two-boat's missing" and somehow imply that it would not be had I stayed on base and had the husband, a first-class storekeeper, not beaten him.

"Missing? Where? What happened? Who flies in two?" I was worried about friends first.

"Some poor bastards *we'll* never see again," someone said.

"Nobody said they creamed," Harper said.

"Listen, they don't put the whole outfit on standby if it's just radio failure. You'll see."

"Get your gear on," Pat commanded.

"I will. But who's in two?"

"Nobody we know," Kramer said, too loud.

"What do you mean you don't know them? They're your shipmates. You pukes don't give a damn about this outfit, do you?"

"I mean no one we know well."

Kramer, Harper, and I had gone to electronics school in Memphis. Scattered through the squadron were other classmates from whom we selected our close friends. All of us had at least started college, and Kramer had finished it. We talked a lot, and loudly, about our futures in the civilian world. We read books and criticized movies, and Kramer even went so far as to write poetry. We disturbed the atmosphere of the dorm. We were snobbish in a ridiculous way, but in the Navy it helped to feel superior to your superiors.

Kramer ticked off the names of the missing men while I pulled off and folded my uniform. I knew only one man well. He was a thin, nervous bespectacled mech, who had a clear tenor singing voice. At squadron parties he and I and two men of the ground crew formed a quartet and sang barbershop music and college songs. I had gone off for beer a few times in the States with the metalsmith of the crew. The first radioman was a squadron legend. He was a devoted alcoholic with a tricky stomach. He could tell if his gut was up to boozing each morning when he brushed his teeth. On a bad day, toothpaste made him sick. In the head we could hear him retching and spitting. If he passed his toothpaste test, he would announce it.

"Made it, by God! Anybody want to go into town tonight?"

I dressed and stretched out on my bunk. The steam heat had been left on, the suits were hot and heavy, and Pat told us to keep them on, allowed us to leave the zipper open, but that was it.

"If they call us, they'll want us at the hangar right now."

"If those guys crashed, by now they're frozen."

"The poor bastards."

"Aw, it's a radio. It's gotta be. It's just *gotta* be."

"It don't *gotta* be nothin'."

I was sleepy. I lay in the bunk, trying to stay awake, trying to remind myself that some men were missing, a ship might be down.

"'Member that time down in the Pescadores, Pat? When some dumb fuckin' radioman forgot to pull the control locks? Jesus, that dumb sonofabitch."

"The last locks he ever forgot to pull."

They talked of crashes; they always spoke of death.

I fell asleep.

$\sim$

We had three days of rain and wind in Japan, and the storm prohibited our searching for survivors. The bay that served as our airport was too choppy. PBM's were stubby-winged, heavy old ships with none of the grace of the more famous PBY. Swells of four feet or more were considered too hazardous for taking off and landing. We were grounded by weather, kept on standby, and restricted to the base. We could not leave the dormitory without informing our plane captains of our destination. The three captains, all of them first-class mechs, ruled off sheets of stationery and made check-out lists the first morning.

"You people know what this list is. This here list is a list for you people to check out on. Any sailor moves his ass out that door for anything that takes longer than it takes to crap had better get his name down on this list. You people know we're on standby and that some poor fuckin' shipmates may be out there freezin' their asses. . . ."

I remember those three days as dark and wet, with the wind grinding on the barracks and shaking the glass in the windows. I didn't enjoy the storm, but it was appropriate, the only contribution to our feeling that did not follow regulations or have a stamp of government control on it.

Everything was suspended. We slept in our clothes. When the door to the dorm opened, we expected a man to enter with news—good or bad—which would guide actions and feelings.

I tried to recall the face of each man on the crew, even the officers, because I required sorrow from myself.

On the third day, the master-at-arms, a chief petty officer, came around to say that all hope for the aircraft was lost. The search we had never engaged in was being called off; the men were considered dead. He also told us that it would be a good idea to write home, quickly, for news of the missing airplane had reached the press; no names were given, but our squadron had been publicized.

"You know how them papers are at home," he said. "They want to scare people, to sell papers. If you don't want to cause your folks some real pain, write. I knew a guy who creamed in a helicopter, and he was saved, see, but the papers printed as how his outfit lost a ship, see, so his old lady, she was pregnant, she dropped the kid. You men ought to write, specially if anybody in your immediate family is sick, got a bad heart or something.

"The whole lash-up's got two days off," the chief added. "There'll be some kind of memorial service in the hangar on Saturday, at oh nine hundred. All hands *will* be there, *in* dress blues."

We climbed out of the flight suits, went off to the showers, took out the stationery for letters home. In the dorm it was silent and solemn. The men were dead. No question now.

It was then that the sailors began to mourn.

~

We had all been forewarned. Pat and others swore they would get drunk as hell if those guys weren't found. During the three days there had been ripping, spontaneous curses from all of us, born less of sorrow than of the sudden sense of our futility. One man, Frank Franconi, said, "Guys dying really drive me nuts. I just fall apart." Others confirmed this.

"Boy, if those guys *are* dead, old Frank will really be hurt. He hates it when guys die."

Frankie was a short, fat man, extremely strong, with an almost hairless, pale body, the color of white cheese, which he displayed in states of nakedness or near-nakedness whenever weather or room temperature permitted. The steam was left on during our days of anguish, and he wandered about in his skivvies or bare. He had a single-cratered moon for a belly, and he patted and soothed it when clad in shorts. Naked he divided his affection between gut and genitals.

He was the squadron banker. He loaned at two-for-one rates, plagued those who didn't pay up every payday. A welsher was under seige. I saw Frankie urinate on a man's bunk one night, dousing blankets, pillow, and all, because the man had returned only the principal on a ten-dollar loan and was boasting that Frankie would have some trouble getting to him for the interest.

Frankie had a sexual cast which disturbed others, even his friends. He was an exhibitionist, and when he went after women in town, he went in to get his "knob polished." He brought back details of the fellatio, which he shared with the dorm. He was too kind and solicitous toward those tender sailors who often got into flight crews because the complement of gunners was not complete. They were usually unskilled and anxious to please. Frankie was first ordnanceman in his crew, and a good one. He schooled novices, advised them, befriended them. Sometimes he drank with one, and it was not unusual for Frankie, in a moment of drunken camaraderie, to suddenly clutch the sailor and kiss him on the cheek.

It was a mistake. Horror and abashment would come flooding into the boy's face. But Frankie was equal to anything. If any man in the squadron accused him of deviation, Frankie would fight and probably beat the man. That was refutation enough. If the sailor was just mad, but sensible enough to know Frankie could crush him, then Frankie would begin with one of those senseless boot-camp tirades.

"You little fuckin' greenhorn pukes. You people come around to a fightin' outfit, a real lash-up, so goddamn dumb you don't know your ass from last Friday. And they stick you in a Peter Baker Mike. You're a goddamn danger to your shipmates. You can't do nothin' and you don't know nothin'. You guys could kill us all. Do you know what it means to do a job that could kill your buddies if you screw it up? Do you?"

It would continue. The right bluster, intimidation, and rank-pulling. The kid's outrage would give way to a sense of worthlessness, of being a burden. I have seen them mumble apologies when Frankie finished. He was an expert.

That was the trouble. Frankie was good at his profession. He took excellent care of guns and turrets. He was able to fill in for others. In his spare time he had picked up the code, he could operate radar, he was checked out on the flight panel so that he could do the mech's job. His greatest achievement was his ability to fly the planes. Few enlisted men knew how to land and take off.

"In the *old* Navy, they figured that once in a while the pilots might get shot up. So they taught us how to fly. In them days wars were real."

My memory is cruel to Frankie, and I won't vouch for its accuracy or freedom from prejudice. Of the twenty-seven men in the dorm, probably a half-dozen were equally despicable and competent; we who criticized them were totally dependent on their skills. To challenge their authority would have required us to become sailors, full-time and devoted Navy men.

I suppose one of the reasons why the wake for the dead remains so vivid, seventeen years later, is that the Navy men failed completely to convince us that they were human.

It began the following morning when four or five men came back from mess hall and brought out their bottles. Good whisky could be purchased tax free at the NCO club. Men bought it and hid it in their lockers, used it for home entertainment and in preparation for a night ashore. When the drinking began, Frankie was still in bed. He moaned about the "poor little bastards." He called for a flunky to fetch his whisky.

He was a finicky sailor; his gear was always neat and his locker sacrosanct.

"Don't touch nothin' else. It's rolled up in my seabag, down by my shoes. I can tell if you mess anything else around. And roll the bag up and put it back where you found it."

The sailor obeyed.

Frankie rose on an elbow, uncapped and drank from the bottle, capped it, got back into his bunk and took the bottle in under the covers.

"Did you lock that locker?"

"Yes."

"Did he, Pat?"

Pat was among those seated at the table. "Yeah, it's locked."

Frankie stayed in bed until noon, drinking occasionally, calling crewmates to him. Kramer went over and listened to Frankie's scheme for single-engine practice.

"We're gonna shape up," Kramer said, imitating him. "We're gonna get so's we can empty that fuckin' tub of every piece of gear in two minutes. We won't let you boys cream in. Nobody in crew nine's gonna freeze his nuts in the Sea of Japan."

At the table others were passing bottles to their friends and taking drinks in exchange. As they began to feel their alcohol, they began to pay impromptu tributes to the dead men.

"When a bitchin' guy like Jim McCracken gets killed flyin', you know damn well the world ain't worth tin shit. That McCracken was one of the *best*. A real radioman. Jesus Christ. What a fuckin' good guy, goddamn. Wasn't he, Pat? Hub? Bill, you knew him. Wasn't he? Oh, shit. What a good guy."

From Frankie's bunk came frequent groans and the rasp of the bottle being opened. Frankie was up after the noon meal. He walked around the dorm, stark naked, bottle in hand. He said nothing at first. He paced about, his huge feet slapping the wood, sighing. He had a wide face and big black eyes and they were sad; they belonged in a *Pietà*. They turned away from people, looked longingly out the window, studied the floor, pierced the ceiling. He began tossing his head.

"The poor guys. Jesus, I can't stand it when guys get killed. The poor guys."

Out of respect for Frankie's legendary torment, the men at the table began to rise and stand in the path of his perambulations, pat him lightly on the shoulder, utter calming words.

"Ain't your fault, kid."

"Can't do nothin' about it."

Pat Fanning didn't rise and, since I liked him, I was pleased with that. But twice he called me over in descending stages of his drunkenness to reassure me that Frankie really meant what he said, what he was doing.

"I've seen him this way before. He just can't stand it. He really can't."

Frankie was crying before long. The bottle was not half empty, and he often paused in his pacing to force a drink on some bystander. He strolled, and suddenly tears popped out on his cheeks.

"Oh the *poor* sonsofbitches! Some of them nothin' but babies. And some, like Jimmie, *real* sailors, good men. What a *rotten* thing! It rips me up!"

Those were real tears, and they soon were streaming down his face, slicking the thick cheeks. He stopped walking and began a general tremble. His shoulders shook, his belly wobbled in opposition, his huge white butt swayed.

"Now he's really started."

I noticed then that the dorm had filled up: people from other crews were coming in, taking seats on the bunks of friends. A squadron tradition was being celebrated and the word had gone around.

Frankie began to scream curses at the aircraft, the squadron, the war, the Navy, the country. There was no smooth transition. The change was sudden and complete. His eyes narrowed to fierceness.

"They give 'em planes that ain't worth a damn, that spin out and stall and can't even land in four-foot swells. They load 'em up with gas that ain't nothin' but explosive, so the whole goddamn ship is one big bomb, and then send 'em out over freezin' water. They just *killed* those guys, just murdered 'em, that's all. They don't give a flyin' fuck. Because there's always more of us. Right? We ain't nothin'. Cheap help. We ain't shit. They can kill us off. They don't lose nothin'.

"They send us out in ass-freezin' weather in obsolete airplanes that ain't any good for anything. And the crews are loaded down with dead-beat punks who don't even know what a ship smells like. In the old days we were seamen first, airmen afterwards. We could tie and knot and throw a line. We were *sailors.*"

No applause for that, not even from his peers.

He went through the sailor's plight. The bar owners that sucked up the monthly wage and wouldn't give you a free drink if you came at them with a belaying pin. ("You can sit there, smilin' at 'em, night after night, and they don't even know your last fuckin' name.") The used-car dealers who sold them junk machines. ("I bought one and the heap threw three rods in one hour after the warranty wore off.") The idea of trying to pick up women. ("The only ones you can *look* at without gettin' a gutful of whisky won't talk to you.

Unless the bitches are married to a shipmate in the alternate squadron.") The treatment by civilians generally. He quoted a boot-camp adage: If a civilian, staggering drunk, fell in a gutter and covered himself with geysers of vomit, the civvies would say: "The poor man is sick." And if a sailor, chest covered with ribbons, twisted an ankle and stumbled while trying to save a child from rape by gangsters, the civvies would say: "Arrest that drunk."

Frankie was wet to the collarbone when he came around to his mother, and all the mothers whose sons were perishing in rotten ships with rotten pilots and crews made up of amateurs.

"Right *now* they're gettin' a knock on the door. Right now they're readin' those telegrams. Think of that. Good-fuckin-bye, son. Dead out here, froze or ruined."

He began to grope the air with his hands, a fat mime, holding the telegram. He tore it open, read it, and howled. Howled again and again, with a shrillness I'd never heard from animal or man before. I haven't heard it since.

It was the only time in his whole performance that I believed he was hurt. And he didn't give that time to sink in. In the midst of all his blubbering, he raised his eyes and crossed himself.

"May the Holy Father protect Mama from ever becoming a gold-star mother like the old ladies of all them poor bastards who died out there the other day."

His bottle was never emptied; there was always the suspicion that he was not drunk. But his stagger rapidly became dangerous. He would appear to lose balance on one side of the room; and in order to catch it, he would have to trot, knocking aside people and banging into lockers. He fell once against the edge of the table, cut his forehead so that blood gushed down into his eyebrow and along his nose and cheek. It smeared with his sweat, splattering throughout the barracks each time he jerked his head. He seemed not to notice the blood.

He asked for the names of the dead, many of whom he couldn't place. "What did Joe Moody look like?"

"He was the little guy with glasses. He could sing."

"Oh, yeah, little Joe with the glasses. What a fine kid. Little guy, yeah. I know. Jesus, why should a little turd like that die? I mean, who'd he ever hurt?" He would shake his head and distribute the gore. "Who was the third mech?"

"That was Joe *Moody,* for God's sake."

"Oh, sure, sure. Little Joe Moody. I thought he was a metalsmith striker. Little Joe. Who the hell did *he* ever hurt?"

In the evening we went off to eat again. Frankie was once again in tears when we returned.

There were others asleep at the table or sprawled in their bunks. Pat Fanning and another mech were talking about Alaska. Once in a while Pat, alone among the career sailors, considered getting out when his hitch was up, going to Alaska to homestead. He spoke this way in spite of ten years' service and his ruined good looks.

"Sure," Frankie said. "Go to Alaska. But what about Jimmie McCracken? Ain't no Alaska for Jimmie McCracken."

Pat nodded, went over to Frankie, who was blubbering, and patted his shoulder.

"Poor Jimmie, huh? Poor Jimmie. Ain't that right?"

"Oh, yeah," Frankie wailed. "The poor shit."

It went on most of the night. Those who fell asleep revived later. There were sodden prayers uttered at impromptu funeral services, several thick tongues struggling through the intricacies of the Lord's Prayer. Someone sang a portion of the Navy hymn over and over.

A sober sailor screamed out for silence sometime after midnight, and all the mourners gathered at his bunk and threatened to turn him out.

"Get down, you prick, and we'll kill you! We'll kill all you punks who don't care when your buddies get killed! Wish to Christ that plane had been loaded with you cruds and we still had Jimmie McCracken with us."

"'Member how old Jimmie used to run his toothpaste test every mornin'?"

"Yeah. We'll never have another guy like Jimmie."

"Poor old Jimmie."

~

At nine the next morning the squadron met at the hangar, all sailors dressed in blues and wearing peacoats and winter hats. We lined up by crews. At the gap in the rank were thirteen small, hastily-prepared floral wreaths, unsteady on their bamboo tripods. Pinned to each was a hand-lettered card with the name, birth date, birthplace, rate or rank of the deceased. The storm had broken but the wind howled in through the hangar door, and two personnel men had to stand among the wreaths and keep them upright during the chaplain's talk.

He was a thick-necked, blond man, built like Frankie, with a curt, uncomfortable manner. He prayed once. Then he told us that these dead were good men and heroes. That they died for a cause which had the support of God. That no man was free until all were free and those who perished in the struggle for freedom never really died.

The captain said the same thing.

There were almost two hundred men in that rusted tin barn on that cold morning. Their heads were bowed. Many of them had colds and were sniffing and snorting. But some were crying openly. Frankie Franconi was. And Pat Fanning.

The next night the captain's plane flew up the coast of Korea with all the wreaths piled in the after station. They were directed toward the general area of the watery grave of our shipmates by the command ship of the task force. The hatches were opened, and the wreaths were quickly dumped into the sea. No words were said. Enough had been said.

"There's a war to be fought," said the captain.

Mark Power

～ Graves

On almost the incendiary eve
When at your lips and keys,
Locking, unlocking, the murdered strangers weave . . .
—Dylan Thomas

After getting off the train at Chilsongmal, Captain Graves decided to walk to his old outfit. It was cold: a thermometer at the railhead had read fifteen degrees below zero; he thought perhaps it was colder than that, in the country away from sheltering buildings. Maybe twenty below, twenty-five; a little colder and even a man's urine would freeze before it hit the ground. He struck his thigh from time to time, as he walked, with a walnut swagger stick . . . in Germany the officers wore ceremonial daggers, and the Japanese their samurai swords . . . which could sever a man's head effortlessly: two hands on the hilt, thumb and little finger interlocked, the way one would hold a golf club. Imbedded in the head of his stick was a fifty-caliber cartridge case . . . he had been wounded by the same caliber pouring with mechanized ease from a plane's wing tips to pierce his flesh with the easy velocity of a samurai's sword, dirty yellow bastards to use a ritual of steel in the twentieth century: lead was the honorable man's weapon . . . no, U-235, the flesh rotting invisibly, shine of bone. Thank God he would be too old for that war . . . give me lead, an honorable death strewn like nuggets through the Lieutenant's body, where was he now? In Arlington, flag-draped, bugles, rifle shots, wreaths, tears.

After a while Captain Graves stopped for he saw Wendell squatting in the snow like a Korean. It's me, your Captain, he said but Wendell was too far away to hear. He was waiting indifferently, his arms resting on his thighs, his eyes on the motionless Captain. Guess who, he said to Jackson but Jackson was asleep beside his radio in the dugout. Sergeant Hopkins heard: he turned his pocked face to the side and spat. I thought they locked him up. Pfc. Luvars lay on a camouflage net, silent but listening. I ain't about to get off my ass, said Hopkins, not for him, not for MacArthur, not for Truman. Jackson stirred and emitted a bark like a dog in agony. Wake up, prick, said Luvars stirring him with a boot, guess who's coming to pay us a visit: Captain Graves. It's him all right, said Wendell from the road; Jackson opened his eyes and threads of dry saliva fluttered from his lips.

Fifteen degrees below zero, said the thermometer at the railhead, the Captain read it with some difficulty as it was several feet above his head, nailed to the corrugated iron of a fuel hut. A gray sky seemed to join the snow-patched earth without sound. Effaced in the thin mist were two rectangles: the fuel shed and a ruined boxcar scrawled over with the sentiments of soldiers, Chinese, American, South and North Korean. He wondered how long they had been there, the old woman and little girl who were staring at him with solemn eyes. He stamped his feet, impatient for the train to Chilsongmal. He wondered how they would feel when they saw him. They had been waiting for three months for their commander to return. My men, your Captain, a man like yourselves. The little girl was motionless as if on the end of an invisible string. How many of yours have I trampled into the snow, one by one lined them up, ready, aim. Machine-gunned, more humane that way. Bodies fall left and right, a curious dance, jerk, twitch, convulsive carrion. How many have you killed, Captain. Who wants to know. The Lieutenant. Well, *he* knows. I can't say more, you'll have to take my word. My duty is to lead, I can't be concerned with tallying death. The child's face blunted by cold crossed his vision. The old woman was wearing trousers made of U.S. Army blankets. Thief, the word lodged in his mind tenaciously; he looked away. Fifteen degrees below, perhaps twenty, it was difficult to tell because the thermometer was several feet above his head. Nothing smells in cold weather remember that. Yes, Captain. Be grateful. There was a stick by the child's foot; it shone like a fresh bone. He looked away to see the skeleton of a machine gun, a derelict from the skirmish when the railhead had changed hands twice in one afternoon, years ago, at least two, long before he bumped into the Lieutenant hanging onto a tree with both hands: excuse me, sir, he had said foolishly in the dark.

The girl bent and touched the stick and the ground suddenly trembled. Ah, the train, thought the Captain with relief. His wrist watch said two thirty, the damn thing was almost an hour late. He peered down the tracks. The ground was no longer shaking. A fine fury slowly drew him tight as the girl crossed in front of him, the stick in her hand. Whore, you whore. The Lieutenant found the tree, flames, flares, umbrellas of bare light, blood or tears were on his face, he embraced the tree with both hands, the Captain thought he was a Korean, Gooks, head-down, unspeakable, they killed my Lieutenant, how I hate them, his mind singsonged, they killed my Lieutenant.

—Come now, said the doctor, you know better than that.

—Excuse me, sir, he said fatuously. No answer as the Lieutenant released the tree and settled into the snow. Fifteen degrees below zero, he thought, too cold for snow . . . nevertheless it was covering the Lieutenant's face.

Overhead, the sky moved from left to right; behind him were the railroad shacks, to his right the boxcar pierced by shellfire. There was a stick by the boxcar, yellow and stripped clean as a bone. The girl leaned over to pick it up and the ground trembled. The train, thought the Captain, it's coming at last.

He shook Wendell out of his sleeping bag. You're driving me to Seoul. The morning was cold and secretive, a pale gray light stained the horizon. Wendell's profile was rapt, absorbed as he drove Graves along. It seemed as if the jeep were on a treadmill revolving in front of a painted backdrop.

—How come you're in such a hurry, Sergeant, I mean Captain?

—I have my orders.

—They puttin' you away?

—It's for a rest, you know that. It's not a mental hospital. Come on, step on it.

—That's not what I heard, Captain.

—I'll be back, I'm your commanding officer, don't forget. I'll be back.

—We'll be waiting for you, sir.

—I'll be back.

They passed several Koreans their heads sourly lowered. How I hate . . . he thought absently, to Wendell: watch the speed limit.

—Yes, Captain.

The road shuttled between the wheels of the jeep and a broad plateau covered with pines spread out before them.

—I've had three hours of sleep, the Captain inexplicably confided, I'm a little depressed—no, just gloomy—you know what I mean.

No answer. The train to Chilsongmal was late. In Germany, war or no war, the trains were on time. He tried to form the village in his mind: burnt spars like teeth protruding from the snow, dawn staining the sky like acid. A dog on its back four legs sticking straight up. Dog; dead dog. Drop it, he cried, drop that stick; the child's eyes darted to his face.

The doctor hammered him with questions pausing now and then to take an indolent drag from his cigar. Finally Graves answered:

—I waited until noon.

—You said before it was night.

—Night?

—Yes, said the doctor, rising and plucking his trousers from his thighs, you said it was dark, remember?

—Snow. There was blood on the Lieutenant's face and snow drifted through the trees like hundreds of little white birds of course you're right, it was dark, I remember now.

The train leaned around a curve, squeaking, and the Lieutenant rose in the Captain's mind, faceless, a creature of his imagination, a puppet incongruously clothed in U.S. Army standard issue. . . . Adams, he whispered, the name rusty on his lips after so many months, Adams.

Villages unwound in the train window, their edges marred by a common scorch mark; he blurred his eyes so they registered as an anonymous gray line. Behind the villages, hills, inside the hills guts rotting, bodies turned inside out, flame-torn. Rain-soaked. No, that's snow, men. Wendell, Jackson, Luvars, Hopkins. They're only five of us, Captain, think five men can lick five million Chinks? Orders. Duty. Your orders are to fight, not to think. One by one they looked away. Men, my men.

—You mean you can't remember his name? The doctor gave him a deliberate look of slow incredulity.

—No.

—Does Adams mean anything to you? First Lieutenant Richard C. Adams, RA 13625289?

—No.

A hill, a cone in the dark and soon snow began to fall as he paused breathlessly in the middle of the village surrounded by bones and a dog on its back protruding from the snow as if it had been recently vomited from the whitening earth.

The train clacked through a valley erupting cinders; in the far distance, he could see the remains of a camouflage net, absurdly brown against the snow. Next to it a spavined rusting 155 howitzer. At the foot of the hill a farmer gazing placidly into a rice field, his hands clasped behind his back. In the hill, his men. Turning over and over in the black earth, their bones picked clean by time. No headstones for them: frail stalks of rice, here and there sheets of ice holding for a moment, the sun's glare.

—I've noticed various things about them.

—Such as . . .

—Filth, poverty . . . dirt . . .

—And . . .

—Mud. Standing in the mud . . . smiling.

—Smiling.

—Yes, mocking . . .

—Ah . . .

—They were mocking me.

—You.

—You see, the first Korean I ever saw was dead.

—Was dead.

—Yes.

The Captain's eyes came to rest on the doctor's pale fingers methodically shredding a cold cigar butt. Maybe they just didn't like you, he said, maybe they just don't like foreigners destroying their houses and farms, killing their children, wives, husbands . . . or maybe they just don't like you personally. I bet that's it. You know most of my patients always assume everyone's going to like them. The thing is most of them dislike themselves, so naturally no one else likes them. I like them though, he added, allowing a complacent sigh to gently pass his lips, in fact I love them.

The train whistle howled and echoed off the hills in faint parody of itself as smoke rolled in front of the Captain's eyes. He probed an old cavity with his tongue and thought of his men. Now that the fighting had moved north they were no longer soldiers but whoremongers, black marketeers, pimps, gamblers, drunkards. something inside had collapsed . . . in all save him: Captain Graves. He had no use for whores: lascivious limbs bowed by a diet of rice and *kimchi,* faces as round as the moon, teeth like worn pearls smeared with American lipstick. He saved his manhood for the battlefield. Where he had fired a pistol once, twice. The stored seed. Hanging onto a tree with both hands. The snow buries all. My men. Search out, kill the enemy. Your mission. Not whoremongering. Yes, my Captain. Black-market *hwan.* Tory's whisky. The dice: five-and-two: seven. Dollars tucked into the cavity between the breasts. My men. Don't sell your seed. Yes, Captain. You are soldiers not machines of pleasure. Remember that. The Lieutenant remembered it: he died a soldier's death. Shots rang between the trees and then the snow fell blotting footprints, erasing sound, whitening blood, burying bodies: the merciful shroud.

—The flames, said the doctor abruptly, a faint smile illuminating his teeth, what about them. The flames.

When Wendell was driving him to Seoul, he saw a boy in a rice field making a sound *ai ai* a doubly intoned note of bereavement.

—He was scaring crows.

—Crows?

—Of course it was too cold for crows.

The doctor's eyes widened with anger and he probed the Captain in the ribs with a derisive middle finger.

—The hell with crows. What about the flames.

—What about them.

—What about them, the doctor repeated suavely.

—Flames. I could hear a gasoline engine and then three sharp cries, O, O, O . . .

The doctor rubbed the heel of his palms into his eyes and gave Graves a regretful look. You bastard, he finally said, you miserable bastard. You were afraid to die. That's what it boils down to, doesn't it? That you were chicken? Just a Goddamn coward?

The thought crossed Graves's mind that the doctor was an agent. C.I.D. or something similar. Of course he knew his drugs (the Captain's throat burned from an injection given him moments before) but then any agent hired to investigate the minds of Army officers would know about such things. He coughed into his hand trying to think of what to do. Because I didn't die, I'm a coward. What about you. You're not dead. Finally he told the doctor that it wasn't dying that frightened him, he wanted to die, he wanted the airplane to kill him, when he turned over (or was turned over by the fifty-caliber bullets) and saw his blood on the snow he had felt a vast relief, he thought he was dying. There was no pain, only peace. The lieutenant was smiling too as snow drifted into his open mouth. I've been wounded three times, he said, three times. Count my purple hearts. Twice in Germany, once here. Each time I wanted to die. It's not my fault I'm here.

—It's the Lieutenant's fault, said the doctor. He winked.

Charred bits of wood on the road, and in the village putrefaction, the stench of wet ashes and the stony soil hidden by snow that covered their bones, the violent calcium of recent death.

—You know what they say, said the doctor casually, they say you wanted the Lieutenant's job.

—What do you mean, they?

—Your *enemies*, Captain. You know who I'm talking about . . . don't you?

—It was a coincidence that I got his job. You know that I was highest in command. A master sergeant. I had seniority over Wendell, besides I was given a field commission. If I had been killed Wendell would have become commander of the battery. It's all in the report, didn't you read it?

—Oh, yes. The doctor's smile deepened. A most inspiring document of war. You're right, of course. Silly of me to forget.

The train entered a tunnel with a shattering roar and the Captain's face leapt out from the window glass like a mirage before his fixed smile vanished as the countryside streamed by, a string of huts, the mud flats of a village . . . the train seemed to be slowing down, children's faces—laughing soundlessly—drifted in front of the window; the train stopped, although perhaps only the children had stopped: they stared at him, motionless.

I haven't anything to give you, he muttered, do I look like a Goddamn candy salesman? Mud-daubed fences; an old woman clutching a dirty shawl about her neck. The Captain suffered her malevolent gaze until she dwindled away then he lifted his eyes to see the cloudless sky, empty of snow, picking up speed.

—I hate them, said the Captain.

—Those poor innocents? What do you have against them?

—I just don't like them. Is there a law saying I have to like them?

—Well, there're a number of laws saying one has to treat them well; I suppose that's the same thing . . .

It was warm and the only light was the random stabbing of fireflies in front of the screened and barred porch where several madmen quietly gibbered to one another.

—I hate them.

—O.K. Next time we'll arrange a different meeting place.

—I'm glad I don't have your job, said the Captain conversationally.

The doctor barked with laughter. Don't feel sorry for *me,* friend. My job is easy, all I have to do is move reality (which is relative and unreal, you understand. "It was the Germans who discovered the mechanical clock, the dread symbol of the flow of time . . ." Spengler said that you know), all I have to do is move reality into a different time-stratum—in your case anyway. Erase the cumulative force of that day and a night or whatever it was—look at it this way—I believe the Army prefers this interpretation: you are a fighting machine with a stripped gear. I am the retoother of that gear. It's that simple. I'm a mere mechanic. His laugh stabbed through a haze of cigar smoke.

There rose a stench of antiseptic as the train eased into the Chilsongmal railhead with deep and lengthening sighs. The Captain found himself humming several bars of "Colonel Bogey's March." In the States, a long time ago, he had gone a hundred and fifty miles to hear Sousa . . . when he was in OCS the first time . . . if it hadn't been for that . . . queer Major . . . he might have . . . *Colonel* Graves, one-star-two . . . when men were men not whoremongers . . . cymbals crashed, the bass drummer's hands crossed, they all stepped fiercely through the streets, men of war . . . past the Germans who stood silent clutching remnants of black wool about their shoulders.

—His dog tags were under his shoulder. I lifted his arm and eased his face away from the snow and pulled his tags free and fitted them into his mouth the way they taught us so that his front teeth would catch the little notch when I tapped his jaw with the butt of my .45

—Captain . . .

—I could hear myself breathing over and over like a machine and somewhere a gasoline engine running and a man who cried out three times like a woman: O, O, O . . .

—Captain . . .

Like a plucked guitar, the brittle afternoon snapped into light and the Captain was suddenly aware his hands were trembling. He inspected their pale lengths critically and decided it was the cold. Fifteen degrees below zero, or perhaps twenty, it was difficult to tell because of the instrument's height, silly of them to nail it that high. He found himself looking in a mirror that hung in the door of the boxcar. Somebody living in there. Ah, the old woman. Her clawlike hand gathering morsels of wood. They'd live anywhere, these Koreans. Beer-can houses in Seoul. Pack rats. A pallid sun was burning in the center of the mirror. After a while he noticed rice fields stretching away in the glass. Then the old woman's legs and the stick lying on the snow like a yellow bone. The child. Girl-whore. Drop that fucking stick. He turned away, peered down the tracks. She looked steadily at the stick. Her face had a greenish cast. Windy flames, he mused helplessly, the fire unwatched, flames blowing across the striated earth. The stick like a newly bleached bone in her hand.

—I saw him. Through the flames.

—Of course you did.

—I noticed his eyes didn't blink.

—Then you buried him.

—Then I buried him.

Koreans, their heads bound in white rags. Hands folded in a womanish way across their genitals. Dog: dead dog. The Captain hurried on. The wind, a voice in the distance, touched the back of his neck. He tucked the swagger stick under his arm and paused to adjust his scarf, blood-red embossed with the crest of his regiment. Clouds scudded overhead; his boots pressed into the snow releasing a cloud of sluggish dust. A small girl holding a tray of apples. Surrounded by an immensity of snow. He heard her voice long before he could distinguish her features. The pinched flesh of her arms, ah, you whore. He stared incredulously at her closed eyelids, the red scarf bobbed violently, the polished swagger stick struck his thigh. A man squatting in a doorway raised his head at the sound of the Captain's voice: a suppressed whisper, men, my men. Two linked bars of silver were pinned to his collar, one on each side. Men. He spat the word into the snow.

On the side of the hill given one of those homely picturesque names he had since forgotten, his men were bathed in a violent phosphorous glow that revealed them clinging to the snowbound slopes like upturned grubs. Then the machine guns began their impersonal thudding and his men, his trained animals, rolled slowly out of sight.

—They decorated me, he told the doctor.

He stood on the parade field, a scarlet ribbon pinned over his heart. The crash of martial music. For extraordinary valor. Shadows stretched across the field. A field commission to the rank of Captain, someone read in a deafening singsong. The band swung solemnly, glitteringly through its maneuvers.

The doctor again raised his weary, slightly strident voice.

—All right. Let's pin this down. When did you last see Lieutenant Adams?

The Captain sitting under a hard blue light, did not answer immediately, instead he touched his bony forehead with the tips of his fingers. A gray gown fell from his knees to the floor in one straight line.

—I suppose . . .

—Come now, said the doctor, picking his teeth with his thumbnail, I'm not interested in what you suppose. When did you last see him?

The Captain closed his eyes. I've never told you about Julia, have I?

—Your wife?

—I've never seen her entirely naked, not once . . .

The doctor found this information enormously funny. My, you do have your troubles, he finally managed to say. He lighted a cigar, shaking his head. Well, maybe it was for the good. This remark provoked another burst of laughter; the Captain did not alter the tentative smile his face had assumed.

—You sonofabitch. Quit stalling, said the doctor.

He dragged the Lieutenant up the hill, then sat down to rest. My glasses, Adams whispered; he took them off and put them in the Lieutenant's breast pocket. Close your eyes, sir, he said, you'll feel better if you do. But the Lieutenant kept them open.

Ice torn by rice stubble. The Captain's boots sounded like the strokes of a defective drum. A cross of wood stood in the center of the rice field, its arms draped with frozen rags; clouds drifted, sullen rifts in a sky without weight.

—We have no flag to lower. Folded about Graves's neck was a meticulously pressed red scarf embossed with the regimental shield. His voice emerged, thin, strained, almost feminine. Dusk gradually enclosed his men: Jackson, Hopkins, Luvars, Wendell. The Captain stood at a stiff attention, his fingers pressed into the seams of his trousers, and his men stirred in the twilight that effectively masked all detail. The imaginary flag descended the imaginary flagpole and the imaginary bugle rang bravely against the sides of the hill. Several prostitutes sat watching the ceremony: they warmed themselves at little fires which burned like black flowers against the snow. The Captain opened his mouth, licked his lips, spoke: We'll be getting our orders soon. I am going to Seoul for a rest. Someone snickered and he slowly colored but continued without moving his eyes. They'll send us replacements for the men we lost and then we can return and help our comrades. Friends, he hastily amended in a high voice that sank into the snow, without an echo, as cleanly as a knife blade.

The blue light shone along the doctor's face from his hairline to the edges of his swollen lips. I'll tell you about my God-damned job, he said irritably, carcasses all day, trying to find the shadow of a heart behind ribs, wears a man out listening for heartbeats that aren't there. In the head, you understand, he added, winking.

Old leaves protruded from the snow. The Captain's boots trod by furtively and a bird cast a shadow of portentous wings, as overhead the sky moved, assembling masses of clouds.

Soldiers passed him carrying rifles across their shoulders like sticks; a few nodded, one even said, good evening, sir, as if he were in basic training. Graves pressed his boots together, opened his mouth, no words came, his ponderous lids drooped, he inclined his head, an overweight ellipse, gravely towards the snow; weeds shook in the wind. Ah: my men. Alpha six-two, this is Dog seven-one, Lieutenant Adams dead, Sergeant Fowler dead, Greever dead, Jones, Berg, Williams, my men, I will return, I am your commander. Good-by, good-by. I'll be back, I'm your Captain. Your Lieutenant. Dead. Fuck him. I'm in command now. Sergeant Graves, fuck Sergeant Graves, Captain now. Field commission, bravery on the field of duty, fuck bravery, fuck the field of. To the rank of Captain for extraordinary fuck valor. The Lieutenant in the fucking snow fucking asleep dead dead fucking dead: shot, once, twice to bleed. Am I my brother's keeper? Fuck him. My men, yes, my men. I am your fucking Captain. Good-by. Good-by.

—Miss Warren? Miss Warren? Where is that bitch?

The Captain sat erect with his gown falling stiff as a board to his ankles.

—Oh, there you are. Two coffees, one black, one with cream and sugar. Where the hell were you anyway? Screwing around with the patients again?

—I am forty-one years old, said Graves.

—Interesting.

—I can't carry you any farther, sir, I said. He just lay there looking at me breathing between his teeth.

—Poor bastard didn't breathe much longer, did he?

—I am forty-one years old, the Captain said, his eyes roving above the gray of his gown. It was very quiet as I ran through the trees striking one then the other—he turned, he was smiling. Excuse me, sir, I said. Two streams of blood were running down his cheeks from his eyes, he was holding onto a tree. There you are Graves, he said, did they get you?

—And you said, no, they won't get me until an hour or two after you're dead, Lieutenant.

—I began to drag him up the hill.

—You heard them coming, so you said to the Lieutenant, look I've got to go, I'll be back for you later, but he just lay there looking at you.

—A gasoline engine was running somewhere and I heard three cries like O . . .

—I'll take the black, Miss Warren.

—She never did like moving around, she was always sorry she married a career soldier, she wanted a home in the suburbs, near Chicago, with some maples and a big lawn.

The doctor patted him on the head. Look, let's forget the home front and concentrate on the business at hand.

—I had to do it. Excuse me, sir, I said, you see I had bumped into him in the dark. He let go of the tree and fell into the snow. He was so heavy, I had to do it. He wouldn't let me go. Excuse me, sir, I said . . .

Strangely enough, Graves could still feel the unpleasant sensation of the doctor ruffling his hair before he pulled away and stiffly informed him he was not a child. The doctor smiled in an enigmatic way and handed him his handkerchief: the cold linen against his face. It was fifteen degrees below zero yet all about him the snow glittered strangely as if it were about to metamorphose into water.

He noticed Wendell was standing. Probably recognizes me. He flexed his hands waiting for Wendell to speak.

—So it's you.

—Yes, Sergeant, I've come to say good-by.

—We figured you might, said Wendell.

Donald R. Depew

～ Indigenous Girls

Army life in a headquarters has its advantages, and mine were Miss Pok and Miss Kim. I thought of them at first as "the little girls," and later as "my girls." They weren't quite five feet tall. Both girls said they were eighteen; the Army does not hire indigenous laborers under that age.

They spoke a few words of English and I knew only a little market Korean, but with that, some pidgin-Japanese, and a great deal of pantomime on my part we understood each other.

The first day Miss Kim came in she looked too frightened to speak. A Korean interpreter from the labor office led her into the room. He bowed. "Sar-jent," he said with a wide grin, "I present to you Typist Kim. This intelligent girl goes to school altogether four weeks for the typewriter. All graduates of school, number one. You try." He gave a light, gracious laugh for me, then hissed at the girl and turned her by the shoulders so that she faced an empty typewriter.

She stood staring at the floor, where the snow was melting from her canvas shoes. The Army typist and the two file clerks were enjoying the diversion.

"Four weeks?" I asked, thinking the interpreter had mistaken his word. "She couldn't learn typing in four weeks."

"Yess, yess," he smiled with delight, "she learn all letters on typewriter very good. Number one school," he assured me sincerely.

The Captain walked out of the inner office with his overcoat on. "That's right, Sergeant. When these Korean girls decide they want a job with the Army, they go to school for a few weeks, learn the keyboard, and think they're ready to work. You'll have to make typists out of the ones we get, if they stay on the job long enough. Try her on a copying job, and if she can do that we'll keep her." He bent toward the motionless girl. "What's your name?" he asked as to a child. "You name hava-yes?"

"Kim," I said, while the interpreter smiled, "Yess, yess, Typist Kim."

"Give her a try," the Captain said, leaving. "If she can copy, keep her."

The girl still faced the typewriter, showing black braids and the high corner of a red cheek. Her wet shoes were in a little puddle of melted snow.

"Take off your jacket, Kim," I said. "Will you type something for me?" There was no response. I picked up a letter from my desk. "Kim, you can copy this?" The interpreter said something to her with many harsh gutturals.

She flashed a glance up from brown eyes, and in an almost inaudible high voice she corrected me: "*Miss* Kim." Then, terrified, she snatched the letter and ran light-footed to the typewriter. I never knew, after that, just how much English she understood.

Miss Pok came in that afternoon with the same interpreter and his same recommendation. The eyes of the two girls locked in gratitude, each for the presence of the other, and instantly they were friends and allies in the face of the United States Army. Miss Pok was more frightened and more candid than Miss Kim. She glanced at the typist and the clerks, and then fastened her unblinking gaze on me. "I go to school," she said slowly. "I now . . . number ten type . . . but soon . . . I learn." She held her breath and stood awkwardly, conscious of being watched.

Miss Pok tried copying a letter, and in less than a minute she stopped and sat tensely with her hands in her lap, crying noiselessly. I sent my three men out for a coffee break and left her alone. Soon she came to my desk with her copy of the letter and said softly, "All now. I am sorree."

~

It took a week, with all of us trying, to get the girls over their fright, and another week to get them to laugh. Even the Captain helped now and then; he had three girls at home. When the office wasn't busy we made clumsy attempts to learn Korean words, with the help of a dictionary. We taught them words in German and Spanish; we discovered that a *Dummkopf* in German is a *pahbo* in Korean. One of the clerks taught them tick tack toe, and they beat him easily. We made something close to pets of them; we told them that they were number one girls, and they shyly assured us that they were number ten girls. There were times, at last, when I had to say, "Too much *tok-san* yakkity yak," and then a thick, abashed silence drowned the office until one of us opened a bag of popcorn or peeled an orange and passed the sections around.

The girls became personalities to us. Miss Pok was the leader. She was quicker to grasp a new problem, more eager to learn English and Western ways; Miss Kim was the more meticulous worker, and the more charming in her pretty reticence. Miss Pok asked many questions about Americans, and had a quick understanding of our explanations in Army slang, tortured Korean, and ridiculous sketches. Miss Kim startled us occasionally with a quick, brilliant imitation of the mannerisms of some American, then ran from the room in a modest panic at what she had done. But both girls took their jobs with grave earnestness. They would spend a day recopying one page, letter by letter, rather than give it to me with an error. When they finished each job we exchanged multilingual thank-you's, not-at-all's, apologies, disclaimers of merit, and polite self-recriminations.

Once, on Miss Kim's second unsuccessful attempt at a letter, I tried to relieve her disappointment by saying, "Very good letter. Number one job, but one mees-take," and I showed it to her.

"Oh," she whispered.

"Close, but no cigar."

"Cee-gar?" she questioned sadly.

"Ah, you don't know cigar. Miss Pok, you understand cee-gar?"

"*Anway me-on-homneedah*, I am sorree," she said. "Dictionary?"

"No dictionary." They remembered words better when we worked them out. "You understand cigarette?" Both girls said, "Ah," and smiled. They had probably handled cartons of them; cigarettes as currency were second only to military scrip. "Okay. Cigar *tok-san* cigarette, very big cigarette, all brown."

"Ahhh," came a dual relieved sigh of comprehension.

I drew a picture and showed it to them. "Yess, I understand," Miss Kim fluted, and sketched in a glowing tip and a column of smoke.

"Okay. You number one. Now, you understand no cigar? Cigar *upsaw*?"

"I understand very good," said Miss Pok, while Miss Kim said, "Yess," with a look that wondered how anyone could fail to understand "no cigar."

"Okay. Now, in America we have carnival. You don't know carnival. Is big place with many tents. You know tent?" I made a shape with my hands, and they understood; they had seen hundreds of them. "Many people go to big place; in tents they play games."

"Carnival," they whispered to each other, trilling the "r", ecstatic that the strange Americans should have such a common thing as a carnival.

"Good, *chowah*. Now: One game, you pay ten cents, you get three balls." I cupped my hands together. "Throw three balls," with the motion, "at hole in wall. Man put head in hole. Okay?"

They were aghast. "Head hurt!"

"Head not so hurt," I reassured them. "Very long distance, not so heavy ball. Also, man take head away."

They giggled with relief. They were all on the side of the man with his head in the hole.

"Okay. Now if you hit head, then you get cigar. You understand?" They did. "You no hit head, no cigar."

They give soft screams of delight. "No cee-gar!"

"But," I shook my finger slowly, "if you almost hit head—if you hit very close to head, you understand? —" They did. "Then they say 'Close, but no cigar.'"

They got it; they shot gleeful bursts of Korean chatter at each other and giggled in delight. But Miss Kim sobered with tragic suddenness. She picked up the letter.

"I close, but no cee-gar. I am sorree. I number ten girl. I *pahbo*."

"Ah, no! You no understand yet. You listen; if you get cee-gar, you number one girl. Okay?"

"Yess," she whispered woefully.

"You close but no cee-gar, then you number *two* girl. You not close, no cee-gar, you number three. But maybe you throw ball in back, maybe you hit somebody else, you hit old lady stand behind, then you number ten girl."

It was a new concept, but they had stayed right with me. "Hit old lady, then I number one hundred girl," Miss Pok decided soberly, and then the giggles rippled out. But Miss Kim's laughter was controlled, and she backed away with the letter. "I now *tosh-chigun*," she said quietly. "No more mees-take."

After that, when they had done something particularly well, I held out a pack of cigarettes to them and said, "You number one. Cee-gar!" and they ran from the room in unbearable laughter, which was their highest expression of joy.

$\sim$

A gift of an apple or an orange, accompanied by the formula "Presento you," and "Ohh, denk you!" made a daily bright spot. We all knew that the Army paid its indigenous laborers just enough for food to continue working, and we made our small illegal gifts from the mess hall as regularly as we could. The Captain had explained to me once, "These Koreans can get along forever on a diet that would kill an American in a month." With his pride in the delicacy of Americans, he did not approve of friendship with indigenous laborers. But he liked our girls, and he chose never to become aware of our gifts to them. Miss Pok, hesitantly, offered him a section of her first orange, but "Oh, no thanks," he said quickly, "I get them in the mess hall. Army plenty oranges hava-yes. I eat Army orange, you eat Korean orange."

Once in the spring I received a package of food from home. It had been mailed six weeks earlier, and contained such winter treats as powdered coffee, bouillon cubes, tea bags, and cocoa powder.

Toward the end of the day I made two small heaps of these rarities on my desk and called the girls. "Presento you," I said, pushing one pile toward Miss Pok, "and presento you," moving the other to Miss Kim.

Each girl gasped, stepped back, and put a hand over her mouth. A sibilant burst of Korean broke from both at the same time, then as one they were sorrowfully silent.

"You no like?" I asked. "*Sirri-aw?*

"Is too much," said Miss Pok, while Miss Kim breathed a troubled moan. "Why you do?"

"I cannot use. Is for cold times. Must have hot water, but I hava-no hot water. Water *towah upsaw.* You must take to family."

In the end I convinced them, and they put the food into the little square kerchief-wrapped bundles that they carried on the street. "*Ote-keh?*" asked Miss Pok, "What shall I do?"

"My mother denk you," Miss Kim said. "My father denk you. My brother denk you. My sister denk you. You number one."

"Everybody welcome," I assured them. "I number ten."

$\sim$

The next morning I came in after the girls had arrived and asked Miss Pok what she had in her kerchief. It looked like a square box, and was sitting on the floor in the corner. Miss Pok raised her eyebrows and smiled in pleasure. "That for later," she said. Miss Kim clapped her hands in that awkward, maidenly manner, pushing them together with her elbows extended horizontally. The girls jabbered swiftly to each other and giggled. We had a surprise coming.

It was a busy morning. The pressure didn't let up until nearly eleven, when the Captain left the office to talk with the Adjutant. Miss Kim appeared beside my desk, all broken out in a smile. She clapped her hands and said, "Sargee, pleas-a you," which meant I had to go to her table to see something.

Miss Pok had three boxes of big red strawberries lined up in front of her typewriter, and she stood there with a smile just rising on her face, waiting for my surprise.

One of the clerks, beside a filing cabinet, watched with no expression.

Miss Kim opened her kerchief and pulled out a folded paper, which she opened beside the boxes. She had brought the sugar. The two breathless producers waited for their effect.

The clerk and I stared at each other for a second, trying to delay what was going to happen. We put on big grins and used the ritual phrase, "Oh boy, strawberries!"

The girls, reassured, chorused, "Oh bo-ee," which was one of their favorite words, and waited for us to try them.

The pause stretched out, and I had to begin, "Miss Pok and Miss Kim: These number one strawberries. You very number one girls. But now you listen . . ."

The Captain and the Adjutant stood in the door with clear faces, as though they might want to join in the fun. They became serious when they saw the three boxes. "Are those indigenous strawberries?" the Captain asked, and no one answered, because in the silence he knew that they were.

Miss Pok piped up determinedly, pointing to the inner office, "One box in there, two box here. Everybody eat." She knew she was carrying the whole burden of enthusiasm.

The Sergeant Major and my typist chose that moment to walk in, and they joined the group standing around the berries. "Are they native grown?" the Sergeant Major asked, and the Captain said that they were. The newcomers shook their heads.

"Why everybody not eat?" Miss Pok asked. She sat down on a chair in the corner. Miss Kim stood beside her.

"They sure do look good," said the Sergeant Major, "but I wouldn't touch them. You know what higher headquarters says."

So I picked out a strawberry and held it in the sunlight and said loudly, "They look wonderful. I haven't had a strawberry since I left San Francisco."

The Adjutant's tone was low and quick. "Eighth Army has a medical circular out about that, you know. Indigenous restaurants and indigenous food."

"That's right," the Captain agreed uneasily.

"'Really?" I said.

"You know how they grow things over here."

I said, "I don't see much to choose between bovine fertilizer and human. You're eating the plants, not the soil."

The Adjutant became cold at my tone. "The cows in the States are injected, and they're healthy. Cows back home are cleaner than these people."

Miss Pok was sitting in the corner looking at the floor, and her big warm cloud was lying around her feet like frost. I held up the strawberry and said, "Very good, Miss Pok, very good," and when she glanced up I ate it.

The Captain made a good try. "I'm going to take mine back to the mess hall and have them sliced up and eat them with sugar and cream. You understand slice?" He made a slicing motion with his hand. Miss Pok and Miss Kim looked at him briefly. The Adjutant walked out stiffly, and the Sergeant Major followed him. The Captain went into his office.

The clerk and I stood there eating strawberries, dipping them in the sugar and enjoying them as visibly as possible, but Miss Pok wouldn't look up.

Miss Kim joined in after a while and ate with us, piling sugar high on her berries. The clerk said that he was full. The shy Miss Kim urged Miss Pok to have some; but the eager Miss Pok, having spent her pay for three boxes of strawberries to make a picnic, wouldn't eat them. Miss Kim, a little reluctantly, profited by the chance to shine alone.

Miss Pok stood up and tried to put the third box of strawberries in my pocket, saying, "Only you eat."

"Captain's strawberries," I told her. "He eat at mess hall."

"Captain no want. Only you eat," and she walked out of the room.

That afternoon Miss Pok didn't come to work. "She say head hurt," Miss Kim explained in her high, frightened voice. "She go to house, sleep."

Robert O. Bowen

∼ A Matter of Price

After they were through cutting the whole course of pathology samples out of him, and they had got most of the steel out, and the scars were coming all right, they used to bring other doctors, sometimes civilians, into the ward to see Carson's case. Only with him it was not simply a case. It was the man. The new ones always paused at the foot of the iron VA bed and studied him with a drawn, unprofessional pinch at the outer corners of their eyes while Major Kimmel spoke the prefatory, unheard, "This is Doctor So-and-so, Carson, come to look in on your case." The little major had been very patient with him in those days, treating him with deft routine efficiency, not stiff but not particularly bending either.

There had been a time when the major's guests had swung quickly from Carson's look to the clip-boarded charts and safe prognostic gibberish, and he had marked the cowed eyes of each in the examination, and after, propped and motionless, watched their consciously professional backs as they left the ward, chatting as in an unpeopled and painless hall. At each of those early visits he had drawn a pleasure from thrusting toward their second's subjective eyes his protest at their violation of his ruin. He despised in them the same curiosity that fetched clerks and housewives to theatres where they cheaply thrilled at other deaths and agonies in photoed news and called their thrill an interest in the world.

He had not learned this hate in the hospital; rather he had survived there on its strength. He had earned it slowly and at great cost through months

of frostbite and combat stench and frozen rations, through ammunition shortages and being those several times cut off completely when confusion had
become more total than even he had thought a war could breed. In those
months he had learned to enjoy killing. He had killed for two years in the
ETO, but it had taken Korea before he enjoyed it. In Europe that element
of action had been a numb thing, firing on a target, always *the target*. In his
mind he had never recognized it *man,* and with the others in his squad, gab-
bing, he phrased it *one*. "I got that one." When the war had been over for
almost a year, it occurred to him that he had never seen the face or looked
closely at the body of a man he had killed. In Europe this idea had not sur-
faced in him, and when he did think of it later, it seemed an odd quirk of
his mind, an evasion to no purpose he could understand.

In Korea the last several men he killed he had watched fall and cease,
and once, taking a loner in a little draw, had let him close to within ten yards
of his bush so he could get the full kick of smashing the guts out of him.
He had not understood this but had wished it, knowing it his reward for
enduring the frostbite and the grenade-stiffened elbow and the bitter of his
own past-harvest life. It was the look of this that he had turned on the major's
neurosurgeon colleagues as they stood defenseless in their curiosity by his
bed in the long ward with the nineteen other patients that he had never spoken ten consecutive words to.

He was alone within himself, almost beyond physicality, so lone that he
did not resent even the nurse's prodding his depleted butt with needles or
the one noticeable ward boy's mumbling about the ward with the adolescent surliness that comes out on some noncombat medics. Since the first
weeks, after they had flown him back and got him in a decent hospital, the
pain had held him like a tentacled thing, from his head downward through
his neck and across the shoulder and swathed along his side and back, tapering out into the right thigh; and in the beginning he had felt, with constant
shock at its continuance, the pulse of the pain. Major Kimmel had told him
that the pulse was his own, his blood throbbing the damaged nerve at the
back of his head, but he had denied this for long, believing the pain to be
alien, invading, not of himself. The doctors who had come on the guided
tour then had been as part of the pain, a tangible part that he could look
his defiance on though he could not harm them, being still in the big cast.

His hate was real enough. He did not simply daydream of attacking them.

With a weapon in his hands or with strength enough, he would have killed any of them. Back in the ETO, a long way back, he had seen a black-white difference between soldiering and murder. There he had been even less likely to murder than he would have in college before the war. Until he had got his field commission in Germany, he had been a BAR man, a good one; and in the scramble of rummaging Germans out of town after town, door-by-door and room-by-room, he could have killed officers or anybody else and never been caught up on it. But no.

His sergeant then had been a Bronx Irishman, the political type, loud and beefy and backslapping and shrewdly yellow. Going through towns they had always worked in pairs; and, because Carson had been what they called "dependable," the yellow sergeant had partnered with him, sidling up and saying: "What about you and me, Car?" and tailing him up the road, though it had been an order, not a question. When they had gone through one house, there was always the next. They would break for the front and flatten out, one on each side of the door. Then you had to move fast because the man going in has motion to make him faster, and a German in a room somewhere is a second slow because he's sitting. But if you loaf at the door, the German can get nerved up. The second at the door, between the time you hit the wall outside and the first guy on the team goes in, is very precious. It's your handicap over the German.

The yellow sergeant with the blue eyes and black hair let Carson take the first house. The next was the sergeant's. That was the system. But at the second house, stiff against the wall, the sergeant didn't move. Carson jerked his head toward the door, but the sergeant wouldn't take it. That first time Carson saw in the man's face the yellowness. Not fear only, the simple paleness around the mouth and the dry swallowing. Not only that, but the cornered habitual lack of control over the fear and the recognition of Carson's contempt, but no shame at that, only a touch of a don't-give-a-damn privilege to be yellow behind his stripes. When too much time had passed for them to have cleared the building, a three-story French hotel, the sergeant had got control enough to use his politician's voice again and said casually, "Go ahead, Car," ironically even. There was no argument; it was an order. Carson went. He went again and many times, always at the sergeant's ironic Irish smile, always wishing he could gun him down in some hall or alley.

They were together on the sergeant's buddy-buddy orders through a whole campaign; and through all that Carson thought of killing him, not pondering it really or plotting, but in each high-ported rush into a house wishing it. When he steadied afterward, he always remembered that he was alive because he was dependable and he was dependable because he never let down. To kill the sergeant would be letting down a long way. Once he'd done it, he might take to officers. By then, with the general sloppiness of his technique, he'd be sure to get casual about keeping his butt down, or maybe he'd just quit digging in when they stopped in the dark and the 88's would get him. Carson kept his discipline, and finally, one cold afternoon by a watering trough in a village, the sergeant took two machine-gun slugs in his right thigh. Lying on the litter, he was so blatantly glad to be out of it alive that he giggled and repeated over and over like a kid at Christmas, "Class B, Class B."

Carson had gone on, not so much pleased at having the sergeant unhooked from him but satisfied at his own handling of their relation, his control of himself, proof of his competence. There were bits of style that went into soldiering, the tight circle the muzzle of his BAR always swung in so he could snap a shot off at any point from a start already made in that slight weaving, other touches that a man had to teach himself. But it had been the yellow sergeant that put the polish on Carson's military education in the ETO. Before the sergeant he had been a good armed fighter; after, he was a soldier.

In his high VA bed now with the pain that companied him, he could remember the campaign with that sergeant nostalgically. He recalled sitting against a stable wall one afternoon, waiting for ammo to come up so they could push over a little river and on across the hedge-rowed fields. It had turned warm after a spell of rain, and he sat sunning and smoking for an hour until they moved out. A moment only, of springtime pleasure, but he remembered many like it in that war. It had been a good war, that one, a sensible war with clean issues that you could believe in. It didn't poison a man's insides to want to knock out the Germans and break up the gas chambers. The world had needed it. At the end of that war he had felt proud, not noisy but satisfied, and he had written to his mother simply, "I have fought the good fight, and I have kept the faith."

From his bed, where he looked across the ward through the window and out over the brown hills to the mountains twenty miles away at the state line, he remembered his campaigns, those first sane ones in Europe when he had been young, then the Korean affair. He thought that most of the other guys in the ward were Korea cases, but he did not talk to them. That had not been his kind of a war. Only his own doctor, Major Kimmel, struck him as an ETO soldier, and though he did not allow himself consciously to like the doctor, he did not resent him. He had learned not to be fond of people. That was a point of style. Still, there were other points: you trusted a dependable man.

At sick call the major managed always to see him alone before he left the ward. Nothing buddy-buddy, only a word sometimes, no sympathy, no encouragement about the pain, only the calm questions and the steady cut of his gray eyes, and the nods to Carson's terse answers about the pain, and those not encouraging either. Dependable was what the major could be called. Carson had never been ugly with the major. Even before he realized that to irritate this doctor would let him in for twists of agony when they changed his dressings, even back then he had not stared at him sullenly. He was a pretty good doctor at that. Dried up and thin, wiry, hard. It had been Major Kimmel who told him straight about his case, with no Gray Lady crap. In his own field the major was a very competent soldier. Often now as Carson waited the days past until they released him, he went over that interview with the little major.

He had been two days out of the big cast, technically ambulatory, and was sitting on the bed, dangling his legs to get some strength into them. The surly ward boy, the one who disliked combat men because he was jealous of them and so figured they despised him, the blonde, acned one, came down to his bunk and said: "Get in the chair, Carson. You gotta see Major Kimmel."

"*Captain Carson,*" he said, and the punk echoed it as if he could have got up and wrung it out of him. He groped into the wheelchair, and they moved off, and the pain sawtoothed and peaked each time the medic accelerated the chair or swung it hard on a turn in the terrazzoed, institutional corridors, and through the pain Carson thought of a time when his strength would fill back, and he did not complain. In the dressing room, waiting for the major, he watched the ivoried door in front of him and flexed his hands and counted the pain down silently with that mental trick the major had taught him, focussing on his tally to lull the shoulder and side and today the arm. Across the room at the glazed instrument cabinet the surly medic asked him something that he let slide unrecognized beyond his count. The medic repeated it in his adolescent superiority, but Carson held on, ". . . twenty-three, twenty-four, twenty-five . . ."

The medic came over to the wheelchair to yell whatever he had asked, and he got out, "When I . . ." Then the major pushed open the door, checking him. Carson lost count.

"You can go," the major said over Carson's head to the medic.

From the other side, the medic, "Shall I wait outside, sir?"

"Go back to your ward."

Carson flexed his hands and watched the open door. He never looked up at talk that wasn't his, and he spoke only to answer questions. The door closed behind the medic, and alone with the major he stopped flexing his hands.

"Turn around, Carson."

He labored the chair around, very weak still, and faced the major on the white stool by the washbowl. He was in suntans as always, his tie tucked in like a soldier's and his face lined as if weathered though he never seemed to leave the actual hospital building to sniff air, let alone get marked by it.

"Carson, you've never asked me anything about your case. You listen when I talk to you, but never ask a question. Do you realize that?"

The remarkable thing about the major was that his expression never changed. Looking at him, Carson wondered whether it had been this that checked him from staring him down as he had the others. They'd been soft for a second, vulnerable in their gawking, and he'd gotten to them. None of that stupidity had ever come out on the major, and he didn't slide off behind any GI bedside manner. He was himself, alert, alive, uncallused, but tough. Yes, Carson thought, it's maybe the toughness. He looks at a thing head-on so he can see it. The others skulk around being clever, or they gush, but they never see anything the way it really stands.

"Why haven't you asked, Carson?" curious, non-professional.

"What d'you tell a guy like me?" looking up at the major. "When I first came here, you explained how close I was to it. 'A good sneeze,' you said; one good sneeze would shake my head apart and I'd be done."

"You don't like doctors?"

He worried the question a moment. "It's not the profession, Major. I'm tired. I hurt. I was worn out before I got this." He jerked his hand awkwardly toward the shoulder and head. "You know how tired I am."

The major nodded.

"I want rest, peace. You know how I relax. You write the orders. They knock me out in there three hours a night. It helps, but it's not rest. It's just a blackout. I don't exist in it."

On the stool a few feet away the major leaned with his forearms on his knees and looked steadily into Carson's face. "Carson," his voice was very low, as it was with those little questions he asked each sick call and didn't write any notes on. "I told you when we first patched you up how badly you were hit. That was so you'd be careful and not kill yourself falling out of bed or getting hysterical about your pain."

He reached some Chesterfields out of his shirt pocket but seemed to change his mind and offered them to Carson instead of taking one himself. When Carson got lit up, he went on, "The only difference between you now and when you came in here is that a bump won't damage you much now. Otherwise you're almost as bad off."

Carson looked a question but didn't speak.

"It's not a particularly rare case as these things go. Unusual that they got you to a hospital intact, but not a rarity. I've told you enough about it in the ward, the nerve damage and the other. Would you like me to go over the records with you?"

Carson puffed the cigarette. "I wouldn't understand the technical stuff anyway, Major."

"Well, it's unusual in a case of this type to get the patient healed at all. You're the first I've had that lived more than nine days." He stopped.

"It's better than two months." Carson raised his eyebrows for corroboration on what he was thinking, but the major gave him nothing back to that.

"I don't know whether the two months are lucky or not. The condition is degenerative. It's advancing now. The pain aggravates it. It keeps you exhausted. The drugs push it along that much faster. As I told you, it's rare that you're alive this long, but the condition isn't rare. Any neuro-surgeon would confirm my diagnosis. I'll get others for you. The ones who've come in to see you have more or less accepted my diagnosis without any real examination."

"Yeah." Carson reached out with the cigarette butt, and the major said: "Throw it in the sink."

"The thing is, Carson, you don't have very much time. I don't know how much yet. Several years, possibly only a year." He slid the cigarettes out again and this time lit one for himself as well as Carson.

They smoked, and in the wheelchair Carson's face did not change. He sat patiently, unshocked at the death he had foreknown. Beneath his listening he felt himself a part of death already, like any combat soldier who knows grief but not the lamentation of a workaday world where men die seldom, die then in age or ill, rarely in strength as soldiers always do, leaving comrades but neither kin nor home, having lost them already miles, months, and lifetimes back. Like that he knew death, had not time enough and life since the Korean hills to unlearn, perhaps undesire it. In the major's low, clipped tone he heard it not as a sentence but as an old soldier takes a briefing on a patrol, not that each patrol is death but that the total is, and each is a part; and in times of steady combat, when all go early to it, death seems past and not future, already accumulated and waiting issue like one's pay. Carson had rated it so long that he simply marked it down as an incidental in the plotted advance of the condition building it. A problem of logistics, one expendable immortal soul to be replaced by issue.

The major went on in that personal but not familiar tone, explaining the tests he wanted to run, the series of pathology samples spanned over the months so he could gauge the rate of degeneration and estimate the time. He glossed over a possible recovery as too rare to hope on. His last point was simple. The lobotomy. It was optional.

"Actually," he said, "none of us know what pain is like to someone else. I have a reasonable idea of what you feel, but that's a guess. If the condition goes beyond your endurance, we can do the lobotomy. It won't stop the pain, but it will cut off the part of your mind that the pain troubles. You'll feel easier because your worry will be cut off. It's a matter of how much you want to pay to control the pain."

Carson flexed his hands very slowly on his lap. "You said it was a kind of mental castration."

"That's the simplest way to describe it."

"What about the other? Cutting lower down so I can't feel?"

"We can do that. You'll have an arm and a leg that you won't feel at all. If you lay your hand on a stove, it can burn to the bone and you won't know it unless you smell it. The pain in your head, that can't be cut out."

There in the tile-sterile dressing room, in the wheelchair with his hospital gown tucked around his sick-bony frame, Carson had a flickered memory of that last Chinese he had killed: the quilted field-coat and brown face with the eyes shut and the mouth hardly open as he slid sideways at the burst from the BAR. There had been something very clean about that, complete. Less a job than a pleasure, that one, but a very efficient piece of workmanship anyway.

"Think about it," the major said. "If you get troubled, I'll talk to you." He got up and slid the white stool back in the corner by the sink and stood there a minute, saying what he'd held back. "About the lobotomy. It'll help in one way, but I can assure you that it'll make you careless about a lot of things. No philosophy, no moralizing. You won't care much what people think any longer." He caught Carson's eyes. "If I were you, nothing would make me request the lobotomy."

He had wheeled Carson back to the ward silently, not helping him into the bed, just giving him a tight-lipped nod and turning on his heel.

That had all been months ago, and the tests were run and the "guess-work," as the major called it, tallied up. Carson had about four years. He had the pain, of course; there were four years of that. He could get it out of his mind if he wanted, cut the wires to the frontal lobes and have . . . what? Not rest, more like as tired and not able to care. Not peace of mind, have in a way none of the good of mind. Be like an old, blind, and asthmatic dog, too gone to live, too animal to know it. Through the long nights until his shot at three each morning he learned to weigh it all, looking at each dawn to come as the lingering dawn that had fetched to him behind an overturned jeep the shell that maimed him, recalling the slow clenching of hate in those months before, and the encumbering weariness that leached through him, striated beyond physicality; and often in the long pain-pulsing hours, among the sleeping patients to whom he never spoke or even turned aside, he felt that he recalled in the falling face of that last Chinese a great and lasting peace.

The Korean thing had not been a war that he could take pride in or find order in. The shortage of experienced infantry officers out there and his old field commission had guaranteed him his captaincy, but there had been little pleasure in the bars. There seemed nothing behind him as there had been in Europe, and no real object in front. They killed gooks and they helped gooks. He had not liked World War II for itself, but it had been needful to wipe out the Nazis, and after it, back in the States, when he saw how the fast bucks had been handled, he had not soured on his belief in an ideal in that war. In Korea he had no such constancy. The Commies he could feel as a proper enemy, but the field was never clearly sided. He located nothing that he could stretch into decency in Rhee's mob. From what he saw of that he got the same impression the yellow sergeant in Europe gave. Rotten to the bone and beyond giving a damn for the contempt of a whole world. The Commies up north were bad, but they weren't Nazi-bad so far as he could judge, and he felt no deep faith in the rightness of his fighting them. Rhee's people questioned prisoners with gun butts too, and left them often in a Commie peace, dead. Carson felt lost among it all, killing and dying purposelessly, evilly.

The various contingents that he touched confused him. On one ridge his company had shared holes with some Turks, and once a slender Turk corporal had shown him with mimetic explanation a trophy. A tobacco pouch crudely worked from the flayed hide of a North Korean. Carson had been too long at war to be repelled physically; but after, as he looked out over the frozen valley to the Commie lines beyond, he thought on that drying skin, seeing in it, beyond the simple proof of killing, a more subtle Turkish pleasure in cutting off the flesh and barrening the land. He remembered now the confusion of that winter after Yalu, among the polyglot packs that roamed the iron earth and as often killed South as North Koreans and were not above ambushing a quartermaster truck in their scavenging. In those months the wrinkled brown leather that the Turk had secreted within his blouse came to be a symbol of the fight to Carson: the end of ordered future. A real war forced order, was fought for that purpose; this marred it in anything it touched.

He had known in Korea, among survivors of those early days, many who were skilled killers, black, white, and brown, men with the hardness to squat on raw earth and eat frozen rations without turning their lean backs on those they had killed in the same hollow; men who endured pain and privation and despair, whose flesh would knit without rest or warmth or a full belly;

men from whom all the honor and the pride and purpose that a war is fought for were shorn; godless men whose real hate was turned, not forward against the brown peasants that they shot or stabbed or trapped with mortars, but back toward the white Christmas-card churches and the thoughtless home-people that leched and marketed and bitched at taxes and offered neither ammo nor ideal to an unrelieved and weary mob on the Korean peninsula, to the armed victims caught in a shifting rush of pure attrition from which all must suffer, none gain. Hard men in a hard land, and he among them.

In his VA bed, months from it, but never to unhitch himself from the pain it taught him, Carson lay silently from day to day, brooding out over the hills his window framed, and wondering always whether the spawn of that winter's chaos would multiply itself, or whether, like the Turk's tobacco pouch, it would one time come to be a curio to men, harmless of reprisal, abstracted from the past and dried of living warmth and pain, resting, almost forgot, in an enduring calm. A time when men might cease to kill, when men might think and war be a matter for scholars only. A dream which a wise and tired man could meditate without the need of hoping.

As his last days in the hospital checked off and his weight bulked out his uniform, Carson lost the look he had once turned on those doctors who drifted in to study Major Kimmel's case and paused that human moment to see the face of the man. Now, in the mirror as he shaved, it was an old face, gray-templed, with fixed lines creased deep around the eyes and across the forehead, heavy-featured but almost gentle with fatigue. Now, too, these final days, the major's friends did not turn from the eyes. They were not embarrassed, touched, puzzled. They were like city-bred hunters scanning a slope on which an antlered buck stands clear, and stands unseen.

On the morning of Carson's discharge, the major walked with him down the long drive to the cab at the gate, slowly but like two well men, for it was not the flesh but the nerves that withered within Carson. They walked pleasantly through the May sunshine and the breeze from the wooded valley below on the left. The hills were green now, and far back toward the mountains moist air dimmed the ridges, softening them. Carson and the major smoked a cigarette together in silence at the gate, and across the road the cabby slouched impatiently against a fender.

The major tossed his cigarette out on the cropped grass, watched it smolder out from dew, and swung back to speak. "Carson, I appreciate your decision against the lobotomy."

"Yeah." He measured the hills slowly. They had been his view for most of a year, and he had watched them come alive this spring. "I can handle the pain all right now." He put out his hand and, as the major took it, said: "That cutting wouldn't be the right thing for me."

"Yes." The major's gray eyes were hard and steady as always. "Pain isn't the worst thing in the world." Then abruptly, "Good luck to you, Carson."

They left it at that, and Carson crossed the road.

James Drought

~ From *The Secret*

The unfortunate thing that I discovered next, in the years of the Fifties, working like a slob for the finance company, not much different from the slobs I was trying to pump some money out of—was that the fat-cats are not content to exploit us, bleed us, work us for the rest of our lives at their benefit, but they want us to win them some glory, too. This is why every once in a while they start a war for us to fight in. Like everybody else, I suppose, I read about the North Koreans invading the South Koreans, and just like everybody else—including the South Koreans it turned out later—I just didn't give a shit. Somebody was always invading somebody in our God-forsaken world and I couldn't keep up an interest in who was taking over who. And I can tell you this: I sure as hell didn't think this invasion was a threat to me, my family, my country, or even the whole goddamn world. But Harry Truman did. He decided that Americans—under the age of twenty-five of course, which left out him and the Congress and the businessmen and doctors and teachers and scientists and ministers—that we were going to defend South Korea. "We'll teach those bloody Communists!" Harry said, waving goodbye to the troop-ships; and Congress agreed and began appropriating all kinds of money to pay to the businessmen for weapons and war materials—plus a profit, of course. It's a funny thing, but a lot of the experts say we were surely headed for a Depression if it hadn't been for the Korean War; and the shot in the arm that this war gave to production, to business, and even to religion—since right away everybody returned to church to pray for their brave sons overseas—was something that the fat-cats had to have or they might have gone under and suddenly become poor folks like the rest of us—a situation they are quite ready to try anything to avoid. So suddenly we were at war, although the term applied was a little more subtle—"a police action," Harry called it; but still it was the same old thing, the flag-waving in the newspapers and on the movie-screens, the speeded up draft, the processing centers, the crazy uniforms, the guns, the firing ranges, the squad-training, the troopship—and then war, death, murder for all under twenty-five, while Congress resounded with virulent speeches, much chest-thumping, and the artists began to "soul search," and the businessmen pocketed the profits, as did the elderly war workers, the housewives, the physically unfit, the "professional patriots," and the grey-haired ministers who gleefully led their flocks again in something worth praying about. Again the fine and free Americans were being inflated with death. Oh, there was much band-playing and march-tingling and "we'll-kill-them" shouting, and everyone including General MacArthur predicted the war would be over in a few weeks. The military journals explained "Korea will be a useful testing ground for our young field commanders," and everyone expected to gain something except, that is, those under twenty-five. And even for these younger souls, slipping into their uniforms provided them at a tidy profit, there were voices like old Ernie Hemingway's which told them that war gave them a one in a million chance, a way to test their manhood, their courage and all that was in them. You can tell how great you are, the young were informed, by how willing you are to give up your life, to charge the blazing guns for your buddies and for your country; and when it is over you will never be afraid again, because you will have discovered yourself. Nobody mentioned what those would discover who lay ripped open after the battle, bleeding, dying, dead from monstrous wounds.

I took my Basic Training at Fort Campbell, Kentucky in 1951, along with other suckers of my kind and age. We learned a simple skill, how to make war and how to murder and how to hate and how to obey orders no matter what—a fine and splendid Basic Training for the future mature citizens of this our great democracy, no? Well, this is what we were taught; and I hope no one ever tries to lie to me again for when I see the beatific expression beginning, the hands held high, the head thrown back and the voice starts to say "we are the finest, the most splendid . . .," then I remember Fort Campbell and what I was taught and I must laugh at the speaker who thinks we are all so fine and splendid. Please do not think I am telling you something you never knew, or something you are against, or something you abhor; please accept that I, we, the young, did what you told us and nothing else. First we were given guns, fine and shiny and new M-1 rifles that clicked easily and worked, and we were taught how to walk with them, drill with them, take care of them, shoot them straight at silhouettes of men, and then clean them so they would be ready to shoot again. "Sometimes you may have to kill with your hands," said the realistic sergeant, and he taught us how to do that, too—at your direction; and we learned it all as well as we could. Some of us made poor killers, some of us fair ones, and some of us good ones, and a very few made excellent killers, but we were all trained to be killers, the quick and slow of us, and nothing else. There was no pretense of freedom in the army. "You must obey the orders of your superior instantly with no thought, because the lives of your entire unit, including your own life, will almost always depend on it," they taught us, and who among us knew whether or not they were right? No one of us could say for sure, so we listened and learned and accepted, because if we didn't we were dead. They were going to throw us into a war—everybody knew that for sure— and we knew we had to learn quickly how to survive the situation they were going to place us in. When someone tells you they are about to throw you into the water, you listen hard when they tell you how to swim, whether you want to learn how to swim or not; when someone tells you they are going to lower you into a pit of snakes with a gun, you listen hard as they tell you how to work the gun—or your days are numbered, because you can be damn sure they are not going to change their minds about where you are headed.

Basic training is a simple school, devised to tear down any moral instruction or inclination an individual might bring to it: It must teach him to kill, while unteaching him "thou shalt not kill," and convincing him he will not be punished by the electric chair or God or anyone; it must teach him to obey unthinkingly, while unteaching him that he knows right from wrong in his own mind, and convincing him that his group is much more efficient if he gives total obedience to an appointed dictator who has been through West Point or Officers Training School; it must teach him to be willing to die, while unteaching him how free and fine it is to live, and convincing him that it is better to be a good soldier than to be a good human being—why?—because the time, his country, his "loved ones" require it of him, as well as his "God," who has given His word that it is the young man's flag which is right, and not the flag of the other young men he is sworn to kill. If he fails to comply he is thrown into jail, executed, or dishonorably discharged in disgrace; if he refuses to perform the role of killer, he is branded a coward and punished; if he disobeys, he is punished—so he learns and he accepts and he obeys and he complies and he performs as a professional killer, and that is it.

He is taught to fire a rifle, pistol, machinegun, artillery piece, bomb cities, sink ships and all the rest; he is taught to keep good ranks, to march, to make his bed and to keep himself, his clothes and his weapons clean and ready; he is taught to think only when he is told to, speak only when spoken to, go where the others are going, and all the rest of that, too. And on Sundays he is sent to church where he listens to a chaplain made an officer, and he prays when he's ordered to pray and kneels when he's ordered to kneel. When he can be trusted not to surprise his superiors he is placed on a ship and sent to the war.

We had a guy in my training barracks named Elmer—and where was he from?—Davenport City, Iowa, I think. He was always rumpled and saying the wrong thing, and on weekend passes when we'd all get dressed up in civies Elmer would put on tennis shoes. I can remember talking to him: "For Christ's sake, Elmer, get hold of yourself, and wear normal shoes and look alive!"—but he never could make it. He was only five-foot-four and somehow he looked like the world's worst soldier. He was always afraid. One day he disappeared rather than pull KP, not because he was lazy but because he was *afraid* to pull KP and walk into the messhall. He knew he would do the wrong thing so he ran away. When they found him hiding under the barracks with mud up to his ears, they decided to punish him, and they made him walk around with his rifle on his shoulder guarding some empty boxes for twenty-four hours. When he was almost finished I saw him, like a ghost walking, and he couldn't even talk. I don't know what was keeping him up, unless he thought he deserved it, no matter how lousy he felt. He just moved through the night, clumping along, not even knowing where he was, around and around the empty boxes. When they let him go he clumped into the barracks and fell on his bed, still holding the rifle, so the sergeant who was a nice guy let Elmer stay behind and get some sleep while the rest of us went out to the machinegun range where we were scheduled.

When we came back that afternoon for lunch, Elmer was hanging by his belt from the barrack's rafter near his bed, and he had been dead for a couple of hours. I guess he thought he deserved to die, after the way he screwed up, and nobody had bothered to remind him that like everyone else even he had a right to live. I had the honor to cut him down, and the next weekend I got the truck-detail to take the pine box into the railroad station at town. It was shipped home to Davenport City, Iowa, and I bet the folks there weren't in the least surprised. Elmer was the kind who was probably a screw-up since the day he was born.

There was another guy named Van Strappen, and he must have been at least five years older than the rest of us, because I remember he had all his teeth out in the first few weeks when they offered it for free, and then he got the free glasses, too. He was tall and skinny, and he said he had twins at home with his wife. Although he tried hard to laugh and make jokes and sing songs and get high on three-point-two beer, and although he was a model of a soldier, sometimes he'd tell us how they had screwed him. In the late Forties he had served eight months in the army, stationed in Italy, and then they forced him home. At the time he had told them that he wanted to finish his hitch because he didn't want to be called later when he had started his family and everything, but they informed him that he had to get out, and go home, and that there was nothing to worry about—the war was over. He had gone home in 1946 and married his Bohunk sweetheart in Berwyn, Illinois, and then gone into the bulldozing business with his brother. Twenty thousand bucks they had laid out between them to get two bulldozers, and they were in hock up to their ears, although they were making a lot of money digging holes. Then, as Van Strappen told it, his brother had gotten hurt by somehow taking a bulldozer blade in the back when some idiot started it up by mistake, and Van Strappen had had to work fourteen to sixteen hours a day, keeping both 'dozers busy, supporting both his family and his brother's—and then along came the army and told the skinny guy he had to go back in and serve a full hitch of two years. He got documents showing the debt he owed on the 'dozers, and he had his twins which were proof enough he was needed, but in that great goddamn fairness of mind and idiocy the army was determined to take him. So here he was at Fort Campbell, getting new teeth and new glasses, and telling everyone how he was getting his money's worth; and then when he'd get drunk he'd tell how he had to sell those 'dozers for a fourth of what they were worth, and how he was still in debt up to his ears for them although he didn't even have them anymore, and how he had to send extra money home for his brother's family, when his own was not eating too well on the allotment dough as it was.

(Everybody got screwed in the army. There were ball players sitting out the two best years of the only ten they could make money playing ball. There were husbands, fathers, farmers, storeowners, all of whom had to sell out everything in order to come into the goddamn nation's service. There were skilled workers carrying rifles; there were lawyers carrying machineguns; there were engineers pulling KP; there were inventors and artists, the crafty and the gracious—and all were just sitting on their asses, killing time until they could kill or be killed for the greater glory of South Korea. There were scholars carrying cans; mathematicians peeling potatoes. There were historians cleaning the johns; accountants carrying flags. There was only one rule that I ever heard of: those who wore glasses became clerks and those who didn't became infantry or artillery. It didn't make any difference about skill or intelligence or education or desire or what. Just whether or not you wore glasses.)

Meanwhile we were getting cookie boxes from home, and letters from Mom saying, "Everyone asks about you, son," and notes from Dad saying, "Just do what they tell you to do son, and you'll never be in any trouble." The *homefront* was solidly behind us we were told; it was the *nation* that had put us where we were—so we accepted this, and for the bastard mess we were in we blamed (that's right and why not?) the whole damn *nation*. When they told us that it was the *nation* itself that spoke through the voices of our officers (and that this was why our officers deserved our unthinking obedience), we looked at our officers and saw right through to their pompous and shaky stupidity, and we knew right away that our *nation* was pompous, shaky and stupid. And when the young girls in the towns near our camps were buttoned up by frightened fathers and mothers and were told never, never to date a soldier because a soldier couldn't be trusted—well, we knew the *nation* was a little afraid of us, too. And when we counted our money each month, we knew the *nation* was exploiting us, there was no doubt about that; and when we bought a car or insurance or beer or a sportshirt or what-have-you in town at high prices, we knew the *nation* was also out to con us out of everything we had, from our blood to our time to our money. Grad-ually, we came to have little respect for our *nation,* and I hope this piece of information won't shock you. Don't choke up and say, "My word," or any horseshit like that. You know, as well as we do, in your guts that you were out to use us and nothing more—so if you are shocked then it is your own guilt that shocks you and not anything I am saying. We were never as stu-pid as you thought we were, and I think you always knew it. You must have known that someday you would have to answer for how you turned us to your own profit, while you were waving the flag and we were marching a long way off to war.

The Korean War was a blinding nightmare of muck, blood, strange and slant-eyed faces both in front of us trying to kill us and behind us begging from us, offering us women and wine for money. The Chinese charged with trumpets blaring, as if they were fighting in the Fifteenth Century, and although they went down, wave after wave, they kept right on coming and no money or bright metal could stop them. They overran us, surrounded us, killed us, captured us—and all after we had won the war and forced the Koreans way up to the Yalu. The only thing we could remember about our brief victory that Christmas was the running, running, running, leaving behind the legless, armless, headless, bleeding bodies, leaving behind the dead and the captured. And then we turned at the 38th Parallel and fought war to a standstill, digging in with all the fine and expensive modern weapons that government money could buy at home from the homefront.

All day and all night in the same goddamn hole, going nowhere, dying a little bit, killing a little bit, standing there on either side of a valley like two great trees brushing each other in a static urgent fight for life, always a little bit, day by day, with no daring, no great movements, no spectacu-lar attacks, just small patrols, the taking of a hill then the losing of it, the blowing up of one square patch and then watching it get rebuilt, always on the alert for an attack that never really came, probing, nothing but prob-ing, losing a little here and winning a little there. It was war fought on a con-tinuous basis, as if no victory were possible as well as no defeat; it was more a boxing match from across the valley—but then suddenly someone would die and you realized this game could kill you. There was no pretense here.

War was being fought for the sake of war, not for the victory of one nation over another, not for right against wrong, not for rescue, not to free a people, just the red-line tracers jabbing across a worthless space, poking out lives as easily as removing checkers from a checker-board, losing lives in return. It was all supposed to be so important, but it was absurd. There were strange rules which had nothing to do with "liberating a captive people" like *you can bomb this but you can't bomb that* and *you can win this but you can't win that* and *you can go here but you can't go there.* They even called us "The Army of the United Nations," because it pleased them, when the truth was we were an American army, fighting with a handful of Allies. They called it a "Police Action," too, rather than "War," also because it pleased them. It was a game of Monopoly fought for real estate but with weapons as well as money, an athletic contest where the losers were taken out under the stadium and shot, a play where the actors fired real guns while the audience applauded one side or the other, it was a game of odds that you played with your own life as a stake almost as if you held your gun at your own head and fired at random. You couldn't win, you could only survive. You couldn't be defeated, you could only die. You couldn't quit playing, you could only be captured. You were in a helluva mess that meant nothing and you couldn't get out, you had to play; it was like a nightmare with someone waiting to chop your legs off if you didn't run the 100-yard-dash fast enough, only you never woke up, it never ended, you were there, day after day, and you knew that the longer you played the higher the odds became that you would make a mistake and die.

There was even a "time-out" or a kind of "half-time" respite—they called it "R&R," and you were "rotated" to Japan for some rest leave where you could relax, see the sights, drink, screw the Jap women, take a bath; and believe me, it was odd to be in a ditch in Korea one day and then be walking the streets of old Tokyo the next. It wasn't war, it was an "exercise" in strategy, a contest played for time, a kind of hot psychological battle, a political contest that needed gunfire to prove its importance, a training grounds for the more military-minded, a testing terrain for new weapons and fresh men, a splendid Maneuver Area in which to practice under ideal conditions that were only too real, a human safari for both sides, a weird, sadistic reverence of the deepest reflex of mankind—killing for the sheer excitement of killing, and for the breathtaking anxiety about being killed yourself. A new general came every few months to lead us in the sport, so the Pentagon could test his mettle, and we were his pawns, we had nothing to lose but ourselves. It was all so clear and cold, after they told us we couldn't bomb the enemy's supply depots north of the Yalu River. "We are not at war with the Chinese," said our government in Washington, "and we don't wish to be." The Arena was limited to Korea, because that way it could never become dangerous to "the folks at home," and nobody knew this better than those of us who were there, young, risking death every day, the goddamn gladiators of the free sparkling moneymaking Western World.

When we were asked to believe that we were fighting for such wondrous things as "the freedom of mankind" it sounded more than just a little absurd. Like all gladiators, we were simply fighting so that each of us (the poor saps who had been thrown into the Arena) would survive in order to get the hell out of the Arena and return home where everyone else was. We weren't even allowed the dignity of being mercenaries, because we were paid very little for our trouble. The absolute end, the only thing we could gain, the best we could ever hope to get was simply *Out!* We weren't allowed to conquer, we were denied victory, we couldn't expect fame or loot, we weren't even decently paid. We had been placed deliberately in an intolerable situation for no reason that we could understand, and the very best we could hope for was someday to get *Out!* It was like telling a boxer that he had to step into a ring and fight fifteen lousy rounds to a predetermined draw, during which time he and his opponent would try to kill each other, and when he asked "Yes, but what for; what do I get" you tell him that if he does well and survives then he won't have to do it anymore. When the fifteenth round is over, you ask him to fight five more, and when these are finished you say "Don't worry, it will all be over soon, just a couple more rounds." Well, as you can imagine, before long your boxer ceases counting the rounds, and he stands in the ring dull and uninspired, hammering away at his opponent, who thank God is just as dull and uninspired as he is, and if some slob yells from the sidelines "Give him a good one in the gut for the freedom of mankind,"—well, my friend, you have the very picture, the allegorical image, the representation of all that was the Korean Conflict. I hope that it grinds in your guts as much as it grinds in mine.

But I have to tell you the story of Frank Nolan, because his is a typical case; if you can't understand what I'm talking about at least you will have to accept Frank Nolan as I do, because he is a friend of mine and a fellow citizen of yours. He was young and was drafted and was made a soldier, and he fought in Korea. Let me tell you about him.

Like the rest of us in Basic at Campbell, Frank Nolan came from the Midwest, as a matter of fact, Chicago on the Southside. He was born of poor folks. I think his father was a taxicab driver. His mother had a plain, straight face that looked blank and undisturbed. There was a sister who had gotten into trouble a couple of times and then married a salesman, before moving to the West Coast. Frank had come from this drab, dreary life, all freckles and bone and brown hair, with a slightly tilted face and a small round nose, and a way of being awed by the Army, the officers, the Post and by all of us whom he considered his new friends. "I'm the luckiest sonofabitch," he would tell me. "If it hadn't been for the army I would've never met you guys or had the chance to do any of these things." He was convinced that, like the rest of the kids on his block, he would have gone to work for the big Ford plant on the Southside of Chicago, and without the draft Tokyo would always have been just a name to him, while here he was walking the streets of this bright, wild city, a conquering hero to be bathed by women, followed by boys, and going out with us, laughing and drinking and carousing, as if he were as good as anyone.

He was trained as an infantry rifleman, like the rest of us, and he worked hard at it and was a good shot, took care of his weapons with great skill, shined his shoes and kept his uniforms neat and sparkling, as well as his bunk wherever he was and his footlocker, too. When we got to Korea and were all busted up to be sent as replacements to different regiments, Frank almost cried at leaving, and I remember the lug standing there in the Repo Depot with his big duffel bag slung over his shoulder, pumping my hand and telling me he would write. The next time I saw him was in a hospital in Pusan just before he was shipped back to the States, and there wasn't a tear or a smile or even any emotion left in him because his right leg was gone.

Bit by bit it came from him what had happened. He had worked hard, done all the right and brave things, and he had ended up a squad leader on the line, taking his goddamn patrols out every fourth day and somehow making it back with his notes that never seemed to mean anything to anyone. Then one day the word went down the line that four Congressmen were "coming to observe conditions," and immediately the men had been set to work building a fine and safe concrete bunker facing a nondescript hill that the Gooks had been allowed to occupy since they did hardly any shooting from it, just sat there looking. But the politicians had come to observe the fighting conditions and so some good fighting had to be whipped up for the politicians to see. An attack was planned weeks in advance for a regiment of ours to take the hill, and even programs containing the schedule of events were printed so the big-wigs would know exactly what was going on and when and where and why and how. The only trouble was that, naturally, the Gooks up on the hill got hold of copies of these programs, too, and everyone knew it, but if the attack plans were changed then the programs would be useless, not only to the Reds, but to the politicians, too, so it was decided to go ahead.

The day came and there was a big inspection, while the Congressmen walked down the line and shook hands with everyone, especially firm and heartwarming with those GIs from the areas of their constituency, and then the politicians were handed helmets, led to the bunker and the show began in front of them. Frank was in that show.

For hours the hill was blasted with artillery, mortars and skip bombs, napalm and all the rest. Then in the beginning dark, up went the infantry to secure the position. They got slaughtered. The Gooks had zeroed in on all the routes and raked through the ranks at long range until there was nothing to do but fall back down the hill defeated. Frank lost his whole squad, and he figured he was the luckiest slob on God's earth just to make it back down the target range of the slope of that hill with puffs of death kicking up all around his heels and mortars blowing caves in the ground ahead and behind. It was like running through lightning, he said, and when he got back to his emplacement he sat down and cried and it was an hour before he could even bring himself to take a drink of water. It was a bad show all around, and especially bad for the politicians to see. So it was decided that the next morning in broad daylight the whole lousy scheme would be tried again, and this time there had better not be any running back until the hill was secured!

By the time the regiment could be pasted together for another assault, the whole hill was sunlight coming right over the top into the eyes of the upward advancing GIs. Frank said that little more than a platoon of men made it to the top, and then only because the Gooks withdrew down the other side.

Frank wasn't one of the inspired handful who made the rock's pinnacle. He lay instead in a ravine with his hand covering the bloody right mess where his leg had been. It was as if the whole hill was groaning, speckled with the bleeding figures of the rest of the regiment, while down in the bunker the Brass shook hands with the four Congressmen who now had something swell to report when they got back to Washington. Although the battle had taken only about two hours' running time, some sixteen hours were spent by the Medics dragging the bodies off the hill, Frank included, although he didn't remember leaving since he had passed out soon after the cheers went up.

He came out of it in the hospital. Soon the general himself walked in with his staff and pinned the bronze star and the purple heart on Frank. Two days later word hit the field hospital that the hill had been given back to the Gooks as "untenable," and it was all over, positions had slipped back to exactly the same place they were before the Congressmen had come. Frank, along with the many, many others who would never be whole again, was shipped to the big hospital at Pusan, from where he was to be sent back to Hawaii and then Seattle.

"I told the cocksuckers they could cram all the goddamn medals up their ass," Frank told me. "You know what they did? They smiled at me. They said they understood."

"Understood what?" I asked him.

"I don't know. The dirty cocksuckers just patted me on the shoulder and said they understood."

Poems

William Childress

Soldier's Leave

Beside the river where he walks
boulders like green and moldy loaves
resist the downward pull of water
and hold their own in ordered grooves.

It is October, and the leaves,
once so flexible and green,
grate on each other in the wind
like a surgeon's knife on bone.

Soon ice will form among the trees
in lean cinereous splinters,
but he will be gone before it does
on a cold campaign of winter's.

Korea Bound, 1952

Braced against the rise and fall of the ocean,
holding the rail, we listen to the shrill
complaining of the waves against the hull,
and see the Golden Gate rise with our motion.
Some hours previous, bearing duffels
as heavy as our thoughts, we wound inward
like slaves in some gigantic pyramid,
selected by our Pharaoh for burial
against our wills. Now we watch Alcatraz
sink into the water, and visualize
the pale, amorphous masks of prisoners,
whose lack of freedom guarantees their lives.

Letter Home

Mother, they line the roads
like broken stalks,
children with bellies swollen,
and O, the flowers
of their faces, petals all torn,
and the flags
of their threadbare garments.
Mother, we give
them everything in our packs
and still they moan
so sadly. More with eyes
like stone.
These kids will never sing
again.
O, mother, wish me home!
With just one field of Kansas grain,
what I can do for them.

The Soldiers

In Korea, decomposing shit
chokes the perfume of the stray flower
still seen occasionally on hills,
and the paddies, heavily seeded
with napalm mines, can grow red flowers
at a touch, with a blossom that kills.

From the dark immobilization
of earth bunkers, our probing patrol
infiltrates forests. Distant searchlights
paint ridges with something like moonlight,
and a grey rain chills us. Winter's cold
is not far away. It too will come.

Our ghosts meet other ghosts in the trees:
They appear pallid and luminous
in the eyepiece of a sniperscope,
a tool too complex for the Chinese.
But their simple burpguns never stop,
and their simple power murders us.

In December we start pulling out,
having done little but christen hills
with proper names: Million Dollar,
Triangle, Heartbreak; names that matter
to no one but us. We taste defeat
and like it. Victory is what kills.

No soldier can ignore tomorrow,
though finally it does not matter
as much as it should. We have today,
and by the grace of Generals a stay
of execution. Our lives narrow
around living's uncertain center.

It is not likely a solution
to human problems will come of this,
but soldiers can't be soldiers and be
human. The cold rain descends softly
on scorched graves, where, beyond human praise,
men lie in stiffened resolution.

Shellshock

I am MacFatridge as he was then,
torn by the mine he was defusing;
at the aid-tent door his arm fell off,
and a Medic stooped to retrieve it
and stood as though lugging a melon
that had burst in the sun.

There are those of us who are not tough
despite all they told us. If I cry
now, no one seems to care, but before,
I would have been punished with a laugh.
I wish that underneath the green sky
of this room, images of terror
would come again: that the emerald door
I can't pass would let me out to sleep.

Combat Iambic

Once in a distant war which was no war,
mired in the unclean paddies, bleeding clean
my buddies died while tracer bullets tore
through earth and armored vests like acetylene.
Our General, in rearmost echelon,
with fancy unfired pistol near his thigh,
barked militant commands and acted out
his manly role untouched by fire. O, sir,
I pray Beelzebub, Lord of the Flies,
to rear his maggot children in your eyes,
where curled like living lashes they can give
the atmosphere that suits a General's mind.

Trying to Remember People I Never Really Knew

There was that guy
on that hill in Korea.
Exploding gasoline made him
a thousand candles bright.
We guided the Samaritan copter
in by flashlight
to a rookery of rocks,
a huge, fluttering nightbird
aiming at darting fireflies,
and one great firefly
rolling in charred black screams.

There was the R.O.K. soldier
lying in the paddy,
his lifted arms curved
as he stiffly embraced death,
a tiny dark tunnel over his heart.
Such a small door
for something as large as life
to escape through.

Later, between pages and chapters
of wars not yet written up
in Field Manuals or Orders of the Day,
there came shrieking down
from a blue Kentucky sky
a young paratrooper whom technology failed.
(I must correct two common errors:
they are never called *shroud lines,*
and paratroopers do not cry *Geronimo.*)

I wish I could say
that all three men fathered sons,
that some part of them still lived.
But maybe I don't, for the children's ages
would now be such as to make them
ready for training as hunters of men,
to stalk dark forests
where leaden rains fall with a precision
that can quench a hunter's fire.

Burning the Years

Solemn as a priest, he gives
himself to fire. His shining face
wrinkles and turns brown,
a Kodak soldier
writhing in paper pain.

Goodbye to the slim youth
in paratrooper garb,
with boots like mirrors
and ribbons straight as his spine.
He knew all there was to know
about honor and duty.
But duty changes with each job,
and honor turns ashes soon enough.

Deeper in the cave of years
he's joined by man of War
who's still a boy.
Fists full of detonators and TNT,
he smiles murderously
for the folks back home.
At night he scrawls
on sweetheart letters
inscrutable Oriental signs.

Smoke rises like morning fog:
shadowy pictures, enlarged by time,
dance and preen. Girls of months or moments
feel again the fires
that once swept them and him.
But now the act is over. The fires
go out. All that's left
are the ashes in his mind.

The Long March

North from Pusan,
trailing nooses of dust,
we dumbly followed
leaders whose careers
hung on victory.

The road might
have been the Appian Way
except for the
starved children lining it.
We gave what we could

to hold back the grave,
but in Pusan the dead-truck
snuffled through frozen dawns
retrieving bones in thin sacks,
kids who would never beg again.

When we bivouacked
near Pyongtaek, a soldier
fished a bent brown stick
from a puddle. It was
the arm of someone's child.

Not far away, the General
camps with his press corps.
Any victory will be his.
For us, there is only
the long march to Viet Nam.

Rolando Hinojosa

The Eighth Army at the Chongchon

Creating history (their very words)
by protecting the world from Communism. I suppose
One needs a pep talk now and then, but what
Gen. Walton H. (Johnny) Walker said
Was something else.

Those were darker days, of course,
And the blinding march South
Cannot be believed
Unless you were there. But the point is
That the Chinese
Were stoppable, so Gen. Walker believed.

And he was right; later on he was killed
At one of the fronts, standing up
On a jeep. We understood.

This wasn't Ketch Ridge or Rumbough Hill
Or the Frisco-Rock Island RR junction at Sill,
But then, it wasn't the Alamo either.

And those who survived
Remember what he said:
          "We should not assume that (the)
          Chinese Communists are committed in force.
          After all, a lot of Mexicans live in Texas."

And that from Eighth Army Commanding
Himself. It was touching.
And yet, the 219th
Creating history by protecting the world from Communism,
Brought up the rear, protected the guns, continued the mission,
And many of us there
Were again reminded who we were
Thousands of miles from home.

The January–May 1951 Slaughter

I'm sick. They didn't stop coming,
And we wouldn't stop firing.

At the beginning, in January,
It looked like the Chongchon action for us again,
But we stopped them.
Brutally.

I passed on the beer ration again.
Drink? I don't even want to eat . . .
Our counter-offensive started on January 21;
      Happy Birthday, Rafe.

In February, it was just as bad. If possible: it was worse.
No one talks about the cold anymore, nor about the dead,
Theirs or ours, but mostly theirs.
Also, we never seem to run out of shells.

March, and Seoul's been retaken. We took our time.
I don't want to look at the Chinese dead.
There are hundreds of them out there. They died in the city,
They died in the fields and in the hillsides.
They died everywhere.

At one point,
It was artillery against artillery in the city.
It's early April.
I am not going to talk about this again, and so I will say it
This once:
    We fired twelve thousand rounds of 105 mm. in twenty-four hours
In support of the Second Div.
    I don't see how people can understand what
I am saying when I say
    12,000 rounds of 105's in 24 hours.

It means this:

Seventeen of us were wounded. Minor wounds they were,
And all wounds bleed, but we kept firing.
There was no pain . . . the blood caked and we kept up the fire.
We're animals,
But then, so are they.

At the aid station, Sonny Ruiz said it best:

"They came at the infantry down there like pigs in a chute,
    And we just cut their necks off from up here."

The officers are now ordering us to eat,
But we notice that their appetite hasn't improved either.

May, and I'm overdue for an R&R; I'm one of the medicals;
Personally, I think it's mental.

Night Burial Details

It's been raining most of the day,
And our dead and their foolish grins
Are still out in the field down there.

The wind is blowing this way, but the stench won't drift over
Until the heat is upon us
And them.
And who's to pick up our noble dead?
Ah, the regimental dregs,
The deserters, the cut-and-runners, the awolers, too,
Malingerers all of that screwed up regiment.

And so the night passes and with it comes the warm day.
The two and a halves motor in
Laden with canvas bags of the finest, heavy duty, waterproof material
Found anywhere in this man's army.
The hasps are also first-class, rustproof affairs
With shiny, yellow plastic tags that are toe bound.
In short, the best canvas bags that sealed bid contracts can buy.
The M.P.'s with side arms and with nothing to do,
Mill around and ponder: just what the hell did *we* do to deserve *this?*
Well, it's join the Army and learn a trade, I say.
Just then a chopper hovers over,
But it's waved away:
You're in the wrong territory, chop.

The laws of physics are then observed: Heat rises and with it the diesel fumes,
And the smell of the friendly dead.
It matters not to them, of course,
But the Army's made arrangements some forty miles away
For a pit that's half as much again the size of a football field;
Neat as a pin it is and lime-caked, too.
Someone really knows his business there.
The job's unfinished here, and now it's starting to rain again.
(It's the season, and you have to expect it.)

As always, rumors are that some of the dregs are officers,
But this is wishful thinking;
Although officers must surely have their private little hells somewhere.
This is just a work detail that needs to be done,
And done not your way, not mine, nor anyone else's, save one:
The Army Way: tag and count, tie the bag, the wallets go in that pile there,

And for Chrissakes watch what you're doing!
Out of the wallets dribble the pictures and the condoms, and the money;
From the wrists and hands, the watches and the rings,
And out of the pockets, here and there,
A rosary, a GI missal, and a French postcard or two,
Printed in Asia and on the back of which usually reads:
In case of accident, notify the President of the United States,
1600 Pennsylvania Avenue. (He's the Commander-in-Chief, don't you know.
At home, it's usually a telegram from the Secretary of Defense who sends
His regards,
And regrets he cannot attend.)

The trucks are now stuffed with close friends,
Tighter now than ever, rid of worldly cares,
Each encased, snug and warm, in his private GI womb;
From here they look like so many mail sacks.

Double clutching, the two and a halves manage to get out of the mud;
The drivers are very good at their jobs.
One more turn around, and the trucks will form a circle
And head for home in time for the night burial.
The regimental dregs stand guard over the bags,
And the M.P.'s stand guard over them;
They've all earned their pay today.
The last truck is finally out;
Its fragile cargo shifts and is shaken up a bit,
But except for shattered nerves,
There are no visible casualties.
And then Hatalski says,

    "Give it a rest, Rafe;
    You've been at the binocs all day."

But I wave him off
And now the trucks are rounding the bend,
Lights on, thirty yards apart, all in step, and very proper.

    "Take a break, Rafe, and say, Hooker,
    See if you can raise the old man."
    "No use, Hat, the trucks've churned up the wire by now.
    "Try 'im anyway, we need that right forward ob. bad."

Hook goes through the motions,
And I find I need a drink; I check the canteen;
It needs filling and what must be for the very first time,

I take full notice of the Lister bag,
And judge it would do nicely;
Just right, in fact:

It too is heavy-duty and waterproof
And of the finest canvas available.
    "No use, Hat; can't get a rise out of HQ."
    "Keep trying, Hook."

And Hook shakes his head,
    "Hatalski's becoming Regular Army,
    And he wants us busy."

But that can't be the reason.

Since some of our dead are still down there the trucks'll be back tomorrow.
The M.P.'s, fewer this time, will also be back.
Hook'll be at the phone; I'll be at the binocs,
Hatalski will fill shell requisition forms,
And he'll continue to look for our mystery man,
The right forward observer.

Hook says five will get me ten
That the dregs will skip early chow now that they know.
Hatalski spits and says,
    "Okay, go down and check the guard."
Hook sets the receiver down and falls in with me
While I go see to the rookies.
The rookies are still shaken, but they'll survive this
Although tomorrow they and the dregs and the dead
Will all skip early chow.

Jacob Mosqueda Wrestles with the Angels

Mosqueda doesn't believe it for one minute,
    but it's true;
And although he swears he'll never forget it,
    he will
As we all do, as we all should
    and do.

The scraps of flesh on Mosqueda's sleeve
Belonged to Hatalski or Frazier,
    one of the two;
And when they splashed there, Mosqueda screamed and fainted
And soiled his fatigues. And yet,
Unhurt and all,
He was carried off as if a casualty, and maybe he was . . .
But he'll forget it, in time;
In time we all do, and should.

On the other hand,
If Mosqueda had lost an arm or a leg or an eye, a nose or an ear,
He'd not forget it nor would others let him, but
One man's meat is not another's souvenir,
And so, Mosqueda will forget;
If not, he'll become a bore, and a bother, or a public nuisance.
But Mosqueda will forget;
His skin wasn't even pinked, let alone charred or burned
Or blasted into someone else's clothing
When the rocket burst. And,
When the rocket burst, Mosqueda was between the gun
And Joey Vielma, a casual visitor who came calling,
But this proves little except, perhaps, a law of probabilities.
The burst took off Hatalski's face
And Frazier's life as well; Joey Vielma caught it in the chest and face,
But Mosqueda was unhurt . . .

    He screamed anyway,
And the other gun crews froze for an instant.
Some came running in time
To retch and gag and vomit over the dead
As the fainting Mosqueda screamed and cried and sobbed
    And yet

He was unhurt
When the rocket burst.

As for me, my hand was nicked a bit, my eyes and face peppered,
When the sun glasses broke in half;
Later, in a stagger, I came upon the binocs
Some fifteen yards away.
But, as I've said, Mosqueda was unhurt, and,
Given time,
    he'll forget.

A Matter of Supplies

It comes down to this: we're pieces of equipment
To be counted and signed for.
On occasion some of us break down,
And those parts which can't be salvaged
Are replaced with other GI parts, that's all.

And so, in the 219th Field at least,
On another burial day,
The *newer* newer officers stay away, being busy on more important
    matters
Than seeing to the junking of replaceable parts;
And tomorrow or the day or the week following that,
A two and a half or a weapons carrier
Bringing the shell supply will dump other replaceable parts
On our doorstep:
       "Sign right here for the shells and equipment.
       Anything to take back?
       No? See you in a couple of days, then; oh
       And by the way,
       Here's a past issue of *Time*: It says,
       Among other things,
       That we're winning the war . . . Isn't that nice?"

       "Yes, isn't it . . ."

And one signs for the shells, and
The men are received and made welcome,
For tomorrow's another day, and one must earn one's bread;
       And what's that that the Chaplain just said?
Was it something about violent hands upon themselves?

No matter; he's reading it from a book,
And I suppose anyone of *us,*
Could have done *that,*
Except
For the fact
That we don't belong to the same union;
Our guild furnishes the bodies;
And his, the prayers. Division of labor it's called.
But why the long face, Man of the Cloth?
Truthfully now, aside from us,
Who cares?

Native Son Home from Asia

Pepe Vielma, himself the picture of indifference,
Has just arrived on the nine o'clock train.
There are those who say that his body is preserved on ice;
Most likely it isn't.
It is also possible that the dead man in the box is someone else.
It's S.R.O. at the Klail City cemetery where the dead
Are stacked three-deep.
The three acres of bones are disposed and ready;
The land, accustomed as it is, awaits the pickax.
Inside of two months, perhaps three,
Six, at most,
The government will send a piece of marble from Vermont:
Co. D., 160th Regt., 40th Div.
With any luck at all, they won't misspell the name.

James Magner, Jr.

The Man Without a Face

Gutted, tangled—sprawled like a broken crab,
Glorious in enstillment, in encrusted crucified
      entanglement.
Near-dust now, but sometime alive in night-fires
      of high-men's thoughts.
He, dead and alone in his body,
Seaweed shredded upon assaulted wire;
      without a face.
Far from the reach of our hands,
Entombed in the heart of our mind,
Victorious in forward sprawl;
One of those who fought.

Zero Minus One Minute

The dawn has come
to sleepless night
again
and it is time for us to answer
from the gray, crystal holes
that seem to womb
just northern night and nothingness;
but we are there;
our eyes electric,
our bodies splinters
in bundled rags;
we are there
and we shall creak
our frozen bones
upon that crystal mount
that looms in silence
and amaze the world.

There is no sound
and the world doubts
that we exist
—that we will creak
like brittle crabs
upon that skull,
consummate mount,
into the very hollow of its eyes
that will flash us death
or simply stare us life
and frozen day
again.

Repository

"Be one on whom nothing is lost"

A reader asked
The Sportsline
what college quarterback
named Adam
died
in The Korean War.
No record.
Even from the army and alma mater.

I remember an evening,
lit by lantern of a tent
in Jimungi of Kyushu,
before we sailed from Sasebo,
a second in silence
thirty-two years ago
in hills above Beppu
(strange, that I retain the face
of a man I never knew;
perhaps, in the secret of things,
a gift of him to you.)

I remember
a tall dark quick body,
alert dark-eyed gaze
(How can I see, now, so clearly!)
above his golden bars
caught in lantern
and the shadows
of what was to be
his austere and steely way
to memory.

Impossible to mind, impossible to heart
that one so quick,
who stepped so quick
in pocket
and rifled passes forty yards
for alma mater and the infantry
could die
and be forgotten

(even by his academy)
by all except me
who see
his face still,
dark eyes, dark hair—dark God
who disappeared
with him.
(How does heart, do eyes remember?)

Vanesca!
(Do I spell his name correctly?)
Vanesca!
(I say it again, so someone will remember.)
Vanesca!
(What is this repository that keeps the names,
the souls of men!)

Reg Saner

Re-Runs

All that flying iron was bound to hit something.
His odd nights re-visit a stare, let a torn head
trade looks with him, though the incoming whine
was only a power saw. If what's buried won't cry
and won't go away, if in some field on the world's
other side all crossfire tracers burn down
to old movies whose re-runs he's sick of,
who's to blame then for what's missing?
Odd nights, a clay pit or two may waken him
still, alone inside a nameless grief holding
nothing: their faces, grass shrapnel—which some field
on the world's other side bothers with. Like seed,
the shapes that won't go away without tears.
They just lie where they fell, and keep going.

They Said

They said, "Listen class attention before sorting
your blocks put the red ones in the tray
and yellow in the bowl." So most got all but one
or two of them right and drank from paper cups
of pre-sweetened juice voting later to stuff
them nicely down the trash-clown on the way home.

They said, "Now color Holy Manger brown
the Virgin Mary blue the Christ child pink
and St. Joseph anything you like." So this one boy
colored him polka-dot but was allowed to try again
on a fresh sheet getting a green paper star on his
second St. Joseph he colored him pink a suitable choice.

They said, "Democracy is at the crossroads everyone
will be given a gun and a map in cases like this
there is no need to vote." Our group scored quite
well getting each of its villages right except
one but was allowed to try again on a fresh village
we colored it black and then wore our brass
stars of unit citation almost all the way home.

Flag Memoir

The white crosses alter whenever I move. Row on row, they realign precisely, geometrically: perfect as close-order drill. While I look for the friend I don't find, the arms on the crosses shift, so as always to focus and open toward me. They do it by night too; faces and places I start awake from, as if hitting a trip wire. Back where the past is mined.

~

Once monsoons begin, the sky hangs dark and heavy as hides. Logs, burlap, rain. After the sixth straight 24-hours, anything wearable is sodden as bunkers and trench walls collapsing. Daytimes I choose some one patch of overcast to brighten on will power, while leather gear re-stitches itself with green mold. By week two, the only imaginable sound is rain letting up, and whenever I listen, I hear it.

~

"At ease, gentlemen. Let's keep it brief. This map gives our share of the ridge: markings in blue, our howitzers and 8-inch pieces. Lacking radios the enemy's greater numbers are noise: bugle signals, hand-sirens, even bells. We own the air. That means night attacks, with only their first two waves coming armed. Their third and fourth waves may carry scythes, hooks, farm tools, sticks. Their fifth waves carry nothing. Remind your men Eighth Army is in full support if needed. Later today my G4 will have details on the R&R we're awarding every five kills confirmed."

~

When it comes to a .50 caliber machine gun, single shots call for technique. And for tripod legs sandbagged against kick. They call for a boxed belt full of fat nails, and this flat trigger: the butterfly switch. But because any bullet that misses will crack the air overhead like a cattlewhip, my first shot could drop him from view and back under cover, leaving the eye unsure what's been hit. Here where everyone's next breath can depend on ballistics mixing with windage, my forefinger has traveled seven thousand miles by water to poise over this bit of gunmetal blue and fire at a difference in cloth. I wait till he sets down his ammo load; half standing, looking my way. Then, soft as a penis kissing an apple, my finger gives one quick, accurate tap.

∼

At Graves Registration two clerks young as I am act like old hands: "This is your first KIA, lieutenant?"

"Yes."

Whereupon, with almost a flourish, they unzipper a dark rubber bag to show a slashed head like Barnett's, the country boy who'd bragged he screwed goats. North Carolina? Possibly Georgia. It's him, but I face the remains of his face by saying inwardly, again and again, "This isn't him, he's not here. He's elsewhere." Then I sign two certifications small as cards, for sliding into the book of the dead. Outside a PFC pulls the pin on 3.2 beers we suck lather-warm from cans, talking Red Sox and Yankees under summer shreds of something once like an orchard.

∼

"Despite problems last night, mainly we held. These map-changes update our positions. Division Rear is doubling artillery. During the breakthrough, Tyler kept his head and called in fire on his own bunkers. We killed ten to their one, but their later waves picked up rifles and handguns, advancing. Temporarily, Battalion Medical will regroup back to Wonju. Stop your men shooting rats by explaining that the fever spreads when vermin desert the carcass. With perimeters fluid, be sure all squads get late changes in password. Tyler knew none of our officers has ever been captured. I'm putting his name in for a Silver Star. Now G4 has one or two changes on ammo and food."

∼

Patrolling the river by night our cover is chestnut trees. Near the south bank we snort and choke as we drink from the stream, like hogs at trough. Luhan sits back on his haunches, dark hair dripping, the butt-plate of his rifle grinding on rock in the shallows. A moon, large and low, rises through leaves as one by one other faces tilt, look toward it, blinking streamwater off lashes. Stagner lifts his eyes, forehead still streaming: "Fuck the moon!" And watches the moon go up.

∼

In Battalion HQ, from commo wire looped between tent poles, a skull swings as a joke, though nobody can say whose side it was on. Because of that gunk they soak into the army's tent canvas, daylight barely penetrates;

yet the sergeant-major and I can see well enough to feel we're growing into our jobs. He gives me a grin like the pearl handles customizing his gunmetal hip as he twists the skull round to show off its eyes, green crabapples plugged into each socket.

~

"Word on the fever seems good. Eighth Army says close to a cure. Warn units that self-inflicted wounds equal refusal to serve. And appoint someone from each crew to make sure men don't fill their canteens out of your water-cooled .30 calibers. Our flares last night lit up their dead by the hundreds along the major assault routes, though by daybreak the bodies were gone. With so much ammo showing corrosion, check boxes for date. Take names of men who pocket those leaflets offering soft terms for surrender. Remind each man that First Battalion has never abandoned its wounded. Later, possibly even today, a member of my staff will outline the new situation on water."

~

Fresh bursts. Against the night sky, more parachute flares ignite, float smoking down, oscillating like pendulums. As the stadium audience applauds like rain, rice farmers go poking along muddy ox-roads, into the usual drizzle. Far south of the MLR by now, traveling perhaps by dog.

And still on the 4th, every 4th of July, after the municipal sunset, after applause for each name on the committee, the skyrockets rise and die beautifully, the white-hot shrapnel spurts, furrows the air, each burst. Aerial salutes report to the eye as muzzle flash and sheared jaw, red teeth, clay dirt on the brains. Or maybe with one long zipper pull some corporal exactly my age throws open a dark rubber bag, there yet, in any such zipper I hear: a metallic hiss taking my breath, taking it back through tanks gutted and rusting like fire, through cratering in fields and roads, through stump forests reseeded in shoe mines that end legs at the ankle.

A stadium anthem can do it, or flag at a ballpark, its vague sidle, stirring in breeze over one or two rows of empty seats. The flag slowly dipping, lifting, over nobody there. Explaining. Trying to explain.

William Wantling

Korea 1953

Endless weeks of zero
A lurking bunker on a barren
    hill
Waiting to receive our orders
    Probe, Capture, Kill
As if one must recompense in
       limbo
For each probe which lacked
         all sense

In that strange war that was not
a war, that came to us too late
When we enjoyed sanctioned
      Murder
And sought the purge of murderous
          hate
We found a certain inner logic to
         our violence
A game in which each player and
    his mate
        understood all rules
(each sensing his brother's center)
And at expense of this—genius of
         fools
One might purge oneself
    so clean
That love would come to our dead
    winter
      for one cannot hold
       an inner void
And if one's hate is utterly
        purged
One's intuition told
    that love could enter
And we, bold, would become merged
    with our idiot other selves
And returned to time of childhood
       Grace

Yet we became
as a pack of maddened dogs that race
    caged, snarling, for the hand
        which flings
The one small piece of rancid meat
in the center of our corrupted sand
. . . And the single victor cannot eat
The prize before dying in his blood's
    slow-cooling heat

The Korean

stood stiffly pressed against
    the wall
arms folded
        staring
. . . flinched
when the bullet sang
           fell
outward into the cobblestoned
    court
one too many holes in his head
for stealing from Americans

Without Laying Claim

without laying claim
to an impossible innocence
I must tell you how
in the midst of that crowd
we calmly pulled the pins
from six grenades
mumbling an explanation
even we didn't believe
& released the spoons
a lump in our throats

I Remember

I remember the time
Black got it
incoming knocked him back
into a snowbank
     buried him
he was Missing in Action
     all winter

spring thaw & we were
back on the same hill &
the Lt. stumbled on him
cracked his shin-bone on
Black's helmet & looked
down at Black, preserved like
a fresh side of beef
     all winter

"You Sonofabitch," he said
to Black's stiff corpse

"You Sonofabitch, if you'd
been more careful I
wouldn't hafta write
all those Goddam letters"

"You Sonofabitch" & he spit

but I'd seen his eyes
watering before he looked
straight up into the sun

Pusan Liberty

the 6x6 bounces me down the
washboard roads, I see the

sun-eaten walls of Korea,
my girl-wife & child in a mud &

straw hut back in Taegu & here
I am meeting the SEAL as he

sits on his roller-skate cart
minus arms & legs but beneath

his ass a million $'s worth
of heroin—I make my buy

walk through the 10,000 cam-
era market-place, jeeps for

sale, people for sale, I'm
even for sale as I find the

porch of Cutie's suckahatchi
house & fix, sitting in the

sun on the adobe veranda, the
2 Chinese agents come around

to make their buy, 2 young
boys, they're hooked bad & I

charge them too much—we sit
there and fix, I fix again, the

so-called Enemy & I, but just
three angry boys lost in the immense

absurdity of War & State sudden
friends who have decided that

our hatred of Government exceeds
the furthest imaginable limits

of human calculation.

Sure

sure
I'd like to love
altogether & believe
absolutely in non-
violence & make
this a world
where children
no longer suffer
& die
where deer
can graze in our
backyards &
"passport" is a
forgotten anachronism
where everyone
understands Camus
& Schweitzer . . .

but
can you be a
pacifist
after you've killed
too many
& if one is too many
where do I stand
with *my* score?
what I wouldn't
give to go back, to
start all over

and you?

The Day the Dam Burst

& what if the dam should
    suddenly burst
if suddenly I should run
headlong, frothing, haphazardly
hurling shrapnel grenades
into high-noon crowds?
if suddenly tossing aside the
    dead ugly ache of it
all, I equalled the senseless
with my brute senseless act?

O My, wouldn't I
shine?   wouldn't
I shine then?
wouldn't it be *I* then who
had created God
at last?

The Awakening

I found the bee as it fumbled about the ground
Its leg mangled, its wing torn, its sting gone
I picked it up, marveled at its insistence
    to continue on, despite the dumb brute
    thing that had occurred
I considered, remembered the fatal struggle
    the agony on the face of wounded friends
    and the same dumb drive to continue
I became angry at the unfair conflict suffered
    by will and organism
I became just, I became unreasoned, I became
    extravagant
I observed the bee, there, lying in my palm
I looked and I commanded in a harsh and angry shout—
    STOP THAT!
Then it ceased to struggle, and somehow suddenly
    became marvelously whole, and it arose
    and it flew away
I stared, I was appalled, I was overwhelmed
    with responsibility, and I knew not where to
    begin.

Keith Wilson

The Captain

Und bebende Trommeln.

the captain:

Army of the United States. About 40,
small, lean. Colt .32 Auto
snug under his armpit, the kind eyes
of somebody's uncle.

His men: tall for Koreans, all
carried M-1's (because there, big men
have big rifles, it is the custom)

& what happened to his eyes
the changes when he spoke of their raids
of villages flaming, women & children
machinegunned as they ran
screaming from their huts:

> his own sense of the stillness
> (which he told of) as the Gray
> Marine engines caught & they
> drew away, leaving the bodies
> in their white clothes
> sprawled here & there, big
> & small, blood seeping into
> white, junks slipping
> smoothly away

... *ganz in Waffen*

Along the coast heavy clouds of dawn
bucked and heaved, arteries of flame pulsed
subsided

      aboard ship, signal flags
     popped in the wind

& slowly the amphibious squadron took station;
the flagship, dead center of the formation,
moved slowly, then faster

        quiet intensified.
    no one spoke, the ship scuttled
    its 11 knots across a passive sea

         Gunflashes grew vivid now
but still they heard only the engines of the ship,
the wind. A cruiser, lying off a small island
rocked, fired in heavy salvos

        then LST followed
    the breeze-whipped Flag
    straight for the beach
    & the guns . . .

He'd been watching his face,
speaking to him occasionally,
sensing the recruited strength.
The boy rarely answered.
The guns could be heard now. Low, distant.

Heavy 8" whooms! lighter 5's, auto 3's
from the cruiser. A few destroyers also
popped away when suddenly a round from the beach
burst off the bow into a
yellow flower

    the kid broke, no real danger
    but he broke. It was in
    his eyes, in terror
    he edged for the hatch

The officer stopped him with his voice. Quick, flat.
The boy looked about 10 standing there, the wind
from the open bridge tugging his hair.
Come back here, he said. The boy did.
Stand here by me, he ordered. He did, close.
They went through the action that way, & neither
was afraid.

Guerilla Camp

(Korea, 1952)

We arrived at Sok To
before dawn, caught the last
of the tide & slipped the LST's bow
high on the beach.

        he was waiting, bent
        slightly over, hiding
        his hand. he didn't
        wave.

Later, after a good breakfast
aboard, an Army captain took
us on a tour of the guerilla
camp:

        & he followed, tagged
        along like somebody's
        dog, a tall Korean,
        patient

We were shown the kitchens, & the
tent barracks, the specially built
junks with their concealed engines

        & he watched, never
        leaving us with his
        eyes

Through the hospital, saw 4
sheetcovered bodies from the
raid the night before, didn't
ask whose men they were, spoke
kindly to the wounded & gave
them cigarettes

        until he strode up,
        stuck his shattered hand
        in my face, anger & hatred
        flaming in his eyes &
        shouted & shouted & shouted

waving that hand, the
bones crumpled by a rifle slug & pushed
almost through the skin,
hardened into a glistening
knot

He was one of ours, a retired fighter,
about my age, my height. They told me
he wanted to know how a man
could farm
with a hand like that.

The Circle

—U.S.S. *Valley Forge, 1950*

Out of the stirrings of the Yellow Sea,
20 miles off from Inchon Channel
we came to—blue *leis*
thrown on the water.

Sea, glassy. No wind.
I sat atop a 5" director, the ship
steamed on, no planes in sight:
a pleasant gunwatch, little excitement,
lost in quiet.

The first I knew we
were among them, circles of men
bound in faded blue lifejackets,
lashed together

Most of the men leaned
back, heads bobbing against
kapok collars, mouths open,
tongues swollen

—hundreds of them.
We steamed by, group after group,
for all my watch. I searched for
any sign of motion, any gesture
of any hand, but soon I just
watched as

                    bobbing gently, each circle
                    undulated, moved independently;
                    once or twice a hand did flop
                    & I caught the man's face in
                    my binoculars instantly,
                    slowly let them drop

We sailed on. I suppose that's all
there is to say: wartime commitments
the necessity for being where you must
be & when

they were dead, hundreds
of them, a troopship gone down somewhere
—Korean, uncounted.

> I remember one man, remember
> him clearly. God knows why
> but his ass was up instead
> of his head; no pants left,
> his buttocks glistened
> greyish white in the clear sun.
> the only one.

& we steamed on, routine patrol,
launched planes at 1800 for night
CAP, leaving the last of the circles
rocking gently in our darkening wake.

> *. . . seid stolz: Ich trage die Fahne,*
> *seid ohne Sorge: Ich trage die Fahne,*
> *habt mich lieb: Ich trage die Fahne—*
>
> ~
>
> *. . . und die reglose Fahne hat unruhige*
> *Schatten. Sie träumt.*

The Girl

"Bist Du die Nacht?"

the girl,

in an Inchon officers club,
small breasts, thin indirect face
but with a silk gown, marks of rank
about her

& how easily she came
later, in the dark, the lips parted
Korean words in passion in light
not understood

the crinkle of paper,
passing hands

Waterfront Bars

& how they look—from the sea
the neon glitter softens, grows
warm

       —a man can almost smell
beer, women

From Beppu, on the Inland Sea,
the giant "Asahi" beersign stood
steady as any navigational light

                drew, caught
attention: we, sailing by
returned to seadamp bunks
strong coffee

3 months on service duty ahead
north of the bombline &
then back we came, wondering

      —lights of Yokusuka, Sasebo
Yokohama. We sailed to them
each in turn. Worlds brushed,
passed

        each in turn.

—leaving the darkness of
watches, silver turning of screws,
wake piled high behind
the blackened ship: little pieces
of a man, left here, there.

December, 1952

Back to the combat zone.

Ships, exactly stationed, at darkness
their wakes catch white fire, long graceful lines
blue stacksmoke, fading to night

red battle lamps, men walking
ghosts in the chain lockers
old chanties sung in the small watches
of morning

Nelson, battle signals snapping,
coming about, broadside ready

Farragut, headed in . . .
the shores blazing with light
exploding shells a terror,
the calm voice on the bridge

Skeleton crews, prize ships,
returning to Ur of the Chaldees, swords raised
gleaming before the dying sun

A blue United Nations patch on the arm, a new
dream. One World. One
Nation.

Peace.

The old bangles, dangled
once more, always working,
buying allegiances

                    stabbing
            tracers hit a village,
            the screams of women, children
            men die

It is when the bodies are counted
man sees the cost of lies, tricks
that blind the eyes of the young. *Freedom.*
Death. *A life safe for.* The Dead.

Casualties are statistics
for a rising New York Stock Market—
its ticker tapes hail the darkeyed
survivors, and cash registers
click, all over the nation, these men
deceive themselves. War is for. The Dead.

Commentary

After the raid, the bodies
are lined on the beach. We can
see them across the way, the living,
standing beside them in their white
robes, the wind hitting in gusts
across the separating bay

that these men died
that our guerillas shot them
down in a darkness
is perhaps not so important.

God kills, they say
justifying man's ways
to those patterns they
see surround them

deaths. lists of victims
in a language the uncle
back home couldn't read
if he saw it, whose enemies
are always faceless, numbers
in a paper blowing in the
Stateside wind.

How many bodies would
fill a room
living room with TV, soft
chairs & the hiss
of opened beer?

We have killed more.
The children's bodies alone
would suffice.

The women, their admittedly
brown faces frozen in the agony
of steel buried in their stomachs,
they too would be enough

but aren't, are
finally not piled high enough

the cost of war must be paid, bullets
made for firing, fired. O,
do not dream of peace while such bodies
line the beaches & dead men float
the seas, waving, their hands
beckoning
                   rot, white bones
           settle on yellow bottom mud.

The Ex-Officer, Navy

the man, in whose eyes gunfire
is a memory, a restless dream
of stuttering mouths, bright flame

a man, who no matter how long the days
faces still the combat, the long night's terror—

       beyond the shoreline, grey muzzles train,
       the destroyer's bow breaks cleanly, all mounts
       at ready, general quarters: racing feet
       grunting rasping horn. tight stomach.
       knotted muscles in the shoulder, neck.

on white bare feet, with flaring eyes he greets
the morning, peace-advancing age. the dead faces once
again firm, smiling, ready for battle fade
grey smoke against a city's sun.

Memory of a Victory

Off the Korean Coast, beyond Wonsan
waiting for invasion soft winds blew
the scent of squid drying in the sun,
homely smells of rice paddies, cooking fires.

It was a picture world with low hills
much like New Mexico, except for water,
the strange smells. Little plumes of smoke.
Here & there, the glint of steel.

Under the waiting guns lay peachblossoms.
I could see them with my binoculars.
The planes still had not come, all eternity
waited beneath the sweep second hand.

Then the crackling radio commanded
"Fire!" and a distant world I could have loved
went up in shattering bursts, in greyblack explosions,
the strange trees that suddenly grew on the hillside.

They fired their rifles, light howitzers
back. After a while we sent boats into the silence.

Works for Further Study

James R. Kerin, Jr., Philip K. Jason, and W. D. Ehrhart

Novels of the The Korean War

Anderson, Thomas. *Your Own Beloved Sons.* New York: Random House, 1956.
Excellent battle scenes and a range of perspectives across various military ranks distinguish this well-received novel. Essentially a "coming-of-age" ordeal for young Richard Avery, the novel portrays a volunteer patrol on a hazardous mission through territory held by the enemy. By rotating the narrator's omniscience through the six members of the patrol, Anderson provides an encompassing drama. This novel is also a fine exploration of evolving teamwork and, in the character of Sergeant Stanley, leadership.

Condon, Richard. *The Manchurian Candidate.* New York: McGraw-Hill, 1959.
While the action of this novel occurs in the several years that follow the Korean War, that conflict provides the basis for a plot that imaginatively explores the possibilities surrounding the brainwashing that Communist captors allegedly inflicted upon American prisoners of war. Condon's rather gripping story suggests the mood and politics of a particular moment in American history through the depiction of an international conspiracy in which the Soviets pull some sinister Pavlovian strings. This book is a reminder that one must not disregard the relationship of the Korean War to its larger Cold War context.

Coon, Gene L. *Meanwhile, Back at the Front.* New York: Crown, 1961.
This humorous novel is notable for its parodic view of the (in)famous Marine Corps propaganda machine. Coon manages to poke fun at the mythologized dimension of the Marines without suggesting that they are anything in the final analysis but the proud and effective fighting force that they claim to be. Another victim of the author's barbed touch is the overblown and cliché-ridden prose written by combat correspondents of the day.

Flood, Charles Bracelen. *More Lives Than One.* Boston: Houghton Mifflin, 1967.
The central figure of this novel is prisoner of war Harry Purdick, whose family and fiancée at home believe him to be dead. Flood succeeds in depicting the stark contrasts between the miseries of those imprisoned in Korea and the more or less business-as-usual existence of those back home in a country relatively unaffected by this foreign war. Another of the author's concerns is American naiveté, if not downright ignorance, concerning Asia and its peoples.

Frank, Pat. *Hold Back the Night.* Philadelphia: Lippincott, 1952.
This novel memorializes the Marines' legendary winter withdrawal from the Chosin Reservoir at the end of 1950. The book's central character is Captain Sam Mackenzie, a World War II veteran who represents the best qualities of the career Marine. Both he and his battalion commander are admirable figures who help to make survival of the Chosin ordeal an ultimate success. On the other hand, flag-rank officers (generals and admirals) are depicted as pompous fools who are out of touch with the real war and dare not risk being wrong.

Franklin, Edward. *It's Cold in Pongo-ni.* New York: Vanguard, 1965.
Largely through the employment of dark humor, this novel depicts the essential futility of warfare—particularly in a war such as that in Korea. The protagonist, a lieutenant named only "Richard," assesses bitterly but accurately the ultimately pointless ebb and flow of patrols and limited attacks into the mid-century version of no man's land. Not surprisingly, Franklin's portrayal of those senior in rank to the lieutenant is hardly flattering.

Hickey, James. *Chrysanthemum in the Snow: The Novel of the Korean War.* New York: Crown, 1990.
One of the more recent Korean War novels, this book clearly aspires to the role of memorialization; its interesting subtitle says as much. The central character, an Army lieutenant named Donald Robertson, spends nearly the entire novel seeking expiation for an atrocity he committed early in the war. His search for atonement illuminates a central thematic concern of this narrative: the cultural gulf between East and West, specifically the denigrating view of Asians all too often evinced by Americans in this war (and others).

Kim, Richard E. *The Martyred.* New York: George Braziller, 1964.
This novel presents American readers with a Korean perspective. Set after the United Nations capture of Pyongyang, the capital of North Korea, it is narrated by a South Korean intelligence officer, Captain Lee, who is assigned there. The story hinges on the mysteries—of fact and faith—surrounding the deaths of fourteen Christian ministers. Kim's sophisticated philosophical orientation has been praised by many critics, as has his portrait of the psychological and public opinion dimensions of war. His portrait of Lee's efficient yet perplexing commander, Colonel Chang, is particularly skillful.

Lynch, Michael. *An American Soldier.* Boston: Little, Brown, 1969.
A remarkable and compelling portrait of the terrors of waiting, this stylistically innovative novel treats the later stages of the war. Ed Conduit becomes obsessed with death as the Panmunjom peace talks go on endlessly. He questions his earlier, naïve sense of duty. Lynch examines the demoralizing effects of "limited war," unsteady objectives, and a seemingly unreliable ally. A well-drawn cast of minor characters aids Lynch's portrait of the psychological strains of combat and the maintenance of combat readiness.

Michener, James. *The Bridges at Toko-ri.* New York: Random House, 1953.
This short novel tells the story of a recalled reservist, naval aviator Lieutenant Harry Brubaker, whose discontent is only exacerbated by the lack of interest in and commitment to the war by those on the home front. Michener contrasts the non-professional who is drawn back into service with the career officer under whose command he flies, but the development of the story indicates clearly that they are brothers under the skin where duty is concerned. This text is valuable also for its glimpse of combat life aboard an aircraft carrier.

Pollini, Francis. *Night.* Boston: Houghton Mifflin, 1961.
POW narratives are a major subdivision of Korean War fiction. In *Night*, Pollini examines the power of Communist brainwashing techniques after Marty Landi and his company are captured and confined to a Chinese POW camp. Marty is manipulated into acts of betrayal and commits suicide following repatriation. Because of its unpleasant portraits of Americans breaking under pressure, this book had difficulty finding an American publisher and was first released by the Olympia Press in Paris.

Salter, James. *The Hunters.* New York: Harper, 1956. Revised edition, Washington, D.C.: Counterpoint, 1997.
Written by a Korean War fighter pilot who has since achieved some renown as a writer, this novel portrays the Air Force war in Korea through the person of Captain Cleve Saville, a dedicated, competent, and thoughtful officer who embodies the virtue of teamwork over glory-seeking in a world where egos can loom large. The title suggests the nature of the jet air war in Korean skies, a vestigial form of single combat. An interesting subplot concerns Saville's love for a young Japanese woman named Eico. The film version (1958), directed by Dick Powell, stars Robert Mitchum and Robert Wagner.

Sidney, George. *For the Love of Dying.* New York: William Morrow, 1969.
This novel follows the several surviving members of a Marine Corps rifle company that landed at Inchon in the amphibious operation of September 1950. The setting is approximately one year later as rotation time approaches for those who remain. The various fates of the book's principal figures suggest the additional layer of mortality—or at least vulnerability—that seems to develop when a kind of artificial limit is applied to the already-perilous business of combat. Sidney has created some very eccentric, and not always admirable, U.S. Marines.

Styron, William. *The Long March.* New York: Random House, 1952.
This novelette records the plight of the recalled Marine Corps reservist in the Korean War period. Although the setting for this story is a stateside training base, the influence of the war is palpable; the primary conflict in the book is that between a regular Marine and one of those called up precisely because of the Korean situation. The title reflects the physical manifestation of an intense battle of wills between the training battalion commander, a quintessential career Marine, and a company commander who would rather be back in Brooklyn minding his radio store.

Walker, Wilbert L. *Stalemate at Panmunjon.* Baltimore: Heritage Press, 1980.
This book is important for its delineation of the integration of US fighting forces. Charlie Brooks, a black junior officer, finds his way through the racial tensions and military challenges that test him as a platoon leader. He is ready to call the integration experiment a success until a senior officer affronts him with racial slurs. Brooks's attempt to vindicate himself for drawing a pistol on this officer takes up the latter stages of this novel. The chapters are headed by newspaper headlines outlining the slow progress of the truce talks; thus, the novel parallels the pursuit of peace on military, racial, and psychological levels.

See also Axelsson, Arne. *Restrained Response: American Novels of the Cold War and Korea, 1945–1962.* New York: Greenwood Press, 1990.

Histories and Personal Narratives of the Korean War

Berry, Henry. *Hey, Mac, Where Ya Been? Living Memories of the U.S. Marines in the Korean War.* New York: St. Martin's Press, 1988.
This oral history, a compilation of relatively brief anecdotes and vignettes from numerous sources, sheds light on various aspects of the war in Korea. A recorder of "living memories" from several wars, Berry characteristically demonstrates the distinctive (and often vulgar or profane) rhetoric of the veteran, and his respondents comment on both the dark and lighter sides of wartime experience.

Blair, Clay. *The Forgotten War: America in Korea 1950–1953.* New York: Times Books, 1987.
Comprehensive and well-documented, this general history focuses primarily on US Army ground operations—with some attention paid in particular to the role of West Point graduates and the combat performance of African-American troops. Numerous photographs complement the text.

Brady, James. *The Coldest War: A Memoir of Korea.* New York: Orion Books, 1990.
Reflecting upon the author's wartime tour of duty nearly four decades after it happened, this memoir is notable for Brady's ability to place his personal expe-

rience into historical context and to look back upon his younger self with some helpful detachment. The result is a nicely written narrative rich in description and feeling, a book that reflects a callow Marine lieutenant's journey from innocence to experience. Among other things, this memoir paints a vividly detailed picture of life in the stalemated second year of the war.

Duncan, David Douglas. *This Is War! A Photo-Narrative in Three Parts.* New York: Harper, 1951.

This is arguably the best of several books published by photojournalists on the subject of the Korean War. Based on the author's work for *Life* magazine, it contains some of the more enduring photographs from Korea: pictures from Marine Corps operations in the Pusan Perimeter, in the occupation of Seoul, and in the fighting withdrawal from the Chosin Reservoir. Duncan's accompanying narrative is largely a prose paean to the Marine Corps (in which he had previously served).

Fehrenbach, T.R. *This Kind of War: A Study in Unpreparedness.* New York: Macmillan, 1963. Reissued as *This Kind of War: The Classic Korean War History.* Washington, D.C.: Brassey's, 1994.

While the main focus of this book is on ground combat operations, it is nevertheless an excellent general history of the Korean War—very readable and informative—that has not been significantly surpassed or superceded by any account published subsequently. That the book is highly reflective of the Cold War in the midst of which it was written makes it a primary historical document in its own right, and all the more fascinating because of that. Though we don't recommend reading only one history of the Korean War, this would be the one we'd recommend if we did.

Halliday, John and Bruce Cumings. *Korea: The Unknown War.* London: Viking, 1988; Penguin, 1990.

This "illustrated history" is derived in part from the Thames Television series of the same name. Superior maps, accessible facts, and hundreds of carefully selected photographs combine in a forceful rendering of Korea's wartime experience. Given its origin, this study has a European perspective that provides a useful counterbalance to most other popular treatments.

Higgins, Marguerite. *War in Korea: The Report of a Woman Combat Correspondent.* Garden City, N.Y.: Doubleday, 1951.

Written by a feistily aggressive journalist who insisted on being in the thick of things during the war's manic first half-year in spite of official resistance and the resentment of male colleagues, this book is at once a report from the front by a combat correspondent, a kind of feminist narrative written before that adjective was a common term, and a rather polemical call to arms. Although her rendition of dialogue and her descriptions of battle scenes are somewhat problematic, this is an interesting period piece by a colorful and somewhat controversial figure.

Knox, Donald. *The Korean War—Pusan to Chosin: An Oral History* and (with Alfred Coppel) *The Korean War—Uncertain Victory: An Oral History.* San Diego: Harcourt Brace Jovanovich, 1985, 1988.

This monumental history is based on hundreds of interviews with Korean War combat veterans. It includes the words of fighting men of virtually all ranks and all campaigns. The first volume treats the first—and busiest—six months of the war. The second volume treats the following thirty months. The interviews are juxtaposed and the chapters designed with the scenario-building talents of a producer-director, which Donald Knox was. Coppel, himself a novelist and military expert, finished the project according to Knox's design.

Marshall, S.L.A. *Pork Chop Hill: The American Fighting Man in Action in Korea, Spring 1953.* New York: William Morrow; 1956; rpt. Nashville: Battery Press, 1986, and New York: Jove, 1986.

Marshall's task, as an infantry operations analyst, was to evaluate tactics and recommend corrections. In the process, he produced the classic and definitive account of the kind of fighting that occurred during the last two years of the war when great numbers of lives were lost in battles over small pieces of real estate along otherwise fixed lines (see also "Films").

Paschall, Rod. *Witness to War: Korea.* New York: Perigee, 1995.

An extremely lively and engaging treatment that blends documentary and narrative material into a well-shaped overview of the war. Paschall's bridging commentaries are succinct and lucid. Well-chosen photographs and maps help convey the conduct of the war. A commendable, compact collage, this book would be a handy supplement in a course focused on the literature of the war.

Ridgway, Matthew B. *The Korean War.* Garden City, N.Y.: Doubleday, 1967.

This book is a history of the war that doubles as memoir, written by the officer who succeeded Douglas MacArthur in the Far East and United Nations Commands after MacArthur's controversial relief by President Harry Truman. A significant aspect of Ridgway's narrative is his frank assessment of his five-star predecessor, including commentary on the latter's rather self-serving own reminiscences about the conflict in Korea.

Russ, Martin. *The Last Parallel: A Marine's War Journal.* New York: Rinehart, 1957.

One of the best-known Korean War narratives, this is a particularly well-crafted account that amply demonstrates its author's wit and sense of humor, rare elements in the often dreary and sometimes dull world of war memoirs. Based on his combat-zone diary, this is a literate memoir by a well-educated young Marine caught in the most egalitarian of circumstances and a valuable contemporaneous account of the nature of warfare in the trench-based latter phase of the Korean War.

Toland, John. *In Mortal Combat: Korea, 1950–1953*. New York: William Morrow, 1991.

Though not as reader-friendly a work as one might expect from the author of the Pulitzer Prize-winning *The Rising Sun*, this study is among the most comprehensive one-volume treatments of the war. The book is geared more toward presenting the facts than interpreting them. It is not always easy to connect materials found in the text with the notes found at the end, but everything most readers need to know is here.

Tomedi, Rudy. *No Bugles, No Drums: An Oral History of the Korean War*. New York: John Wiley, 1993.

Written after a number of conventional Korean War histories had been published, this oral history specifically sets out to personalize the war through the recollections of selected veterans. Structured chronologically with an attempt to be inclusive in kinds of wartime experience, it is significant for its demonstration of the very limited perspective of the frontline soldier and for the way in which many of its voices serve as interesting correctives to standard accounts or received impressions.

Zellers, Larry. *In Enemy Hands: A Prisoner in North Korea*. Lexington: University Press of Kentucky, 1991.

Writing nearly forty years after the war, the author reflects upon his experience as a captured Methodist missionary who was working in Korea at the beginning of the conflict. Since chronological distance enables at least some amount of emotional detachment, the tone of this narrative is more analytical and dispassionate than earlier prisoner accounts. Still, he communicates the nature and degree of the pain and suffering experienced by the eclectic group of international civilian POWs of which he was a part—and the extreme cruelty exhibited by their captors.

Films of the Korean War

All the Young Men. Dir. Hall Bartlett. Columbia, 1960.

The Korean War saw the end of institutionalized racial segregation in the American military, and this film reflects that development as it addresses the contemporaneously controversial issue of the performance of African-Americans in combat. Sidney Poitier's character updates by his presence the war-film staple of the culturally variegated small unit, and the movie's cast seems even more eclectic than the squad itself. Joining hard-boiled actor Alan Ladd as the oft-busted lifer are comedian Mort Sahl (the urban Jew), singer and teenage heartthrob James Darren ("the kid"), and former heavyweight boxing champion Ingemar Johansson (a transplanted Swede—a United Nations touch?).

The Bridges at Toko-ri. Dir. Mark Robson. Paramount, 1954.

Though very much a product of its time, this faithful and accomplished adaptation of James Michener's novel wears rather well. William Holden's stolid carrier pilot Lieutenant Brubaker exemplifies the frustrations of those called back to duty for service in Korea. He flies combat missions under the command of Fredric March as Admiral Tarrant, the quintessential military professional. Mickey Rooney's performance as the eccentric helicopter pilot Mike Forney is memorable, and Grace Kelly is the all-American waiting wife. The production reflects the benefits of full military cooperation in its detail and authenticity, and John P. Fulton's superb special-effects work earned the film an Academy Award.

The Manchurian Candidate. Dir. John Frankenheimer. United Artists, 1962. This excellent adaptation of the Richard Condon novel (see "Novels") features fine performances by Laurence Harvey as the hopelessly manipulated Raymond Shaw, Angela Lansbury as his evilly manipulative mother, and Frank Sinatra as the weary but dedicated Major Marco.

M*A*S*H. Dir. Robert Altman. Twentieth Century-Fox, 1970.
Based on Richard Hooker's 1968 novel and subsequently the inspiration for an enormously successful television series, this film firmly occupies its own place as an American comedy classic. Made during the Vietnam era and doubtless a comment on that later war, the film is nonetheless clearly set in Korea and has something to say about that conflict to those who will listen. Though the film is hilarious, with humor both slapstick and subtle in nature, there are moments that effectively reflect the grim daily business of the Mobile Army Surgical Hospital—a Korean War development. Donald Sutherland as Hawkeye Pierce and Elliot Gould as Trapper John are first among equals in an excellent acting ensemble.

Men in War. Dir. Anthony Mann. United Artists, 1957.
Centered on the struggle for power between a lieutenant (Robert Ryan) and his sergeant (Aldo Ray) during the formulaic retrograde movement of a small unit early in the war, this film effectively makes the point that combat is fundamentally a nasty and forbidding business of attrition and survival. Skillfully employing both somber mood music and, at times, the sound of silence, the movie depicts in a film noir style the essence of the infantryman's life: constant movement into lethal threats that vary only in kind—from mortars to mines to entrenched enemy troops. The film's introductory title card says it all: "Tell me the story of the foot soldier and I will tell you the story of all wars."

Pork Chop Hill. Dir. Lewis Milestone. United Artists, 1959.
Some will argue that this is the best Korean War film. Based on S.L.A. Marshall's classic study of combat in Korea, this film is distinguished by superior cinematography and acting, attention to military detail, and a screenplay that avoids the lapses into cliché that characterize all too many war films. This movie strikingly illustrates the similarity between the latter part of the war in Korea and the trench-based fighting of the First World War—even as it now almost necessarily brings to mind the waste of life and similarly frustrating negotiations that would characterize another war in Asia nearly two decades later.

Gregory Peck is memorable as Lieutenant Joe Clemons while Woody Strode and James Edwards both play a role in a relatively rare cinematic consideration of the black soldier's situation in a newly integrated American military.

The Rack. Dir. Arnold Laven. Metro-Goldwyn-Mayer, 1956.
This film, based on a teleplay by Rod Serling, stars Paul Newman as a repatriated Korean War POW. Its merit resides largely in its fairly sophisticated approach to a particularly problematic aspect of the three-year conflict: the collaboration of U.S. prisoners of war with their North Korean or Chinese captors. The chief dramatic interest of the fim lies in the court-martial of Newman's Captain Ed Hall: an infantryman with a splendid combat record prior to his capture who is also the son of a retired career officer and the older brother of a Korean War KIA.

The Steel Helmet. Dir. Samuel Fuller. Lippert, 1951.
This Samuel Fuller movie is the first Korean War combat film. Made in October 1950 in less than two weeks on a very small budget, this film enjoys something of a cult status, and considering the limitations of its production parameters, it is actually rather good. The rough-hewn lifer Sergeant Zack, played by Gene Evans, is the central figure in a picture that considers several relevant themes and issues: the nature of war in general; the nature of this war in particular; the conflicts between military professionals and others, between the individual and the group, and between people of different racial backgrounds; and the contrast between innocence and experience.

Time Limit. Dir. Karl Malden. United Artists, 1957.
Adapted by Henry Denker from a Broadway play that he co-authored with Ralph Berkey, this film (like *The Rack*) concerns the POW collaboration issue. In this case, the plot concerns a preliminary investigation to the court-martial of Major Harry Cargill, an artillery officer with an otherwise fine record who freely confesses his guilt but offers no explanation. Richard Basehart is Cargill while Richard Widmark plays Lieutenant Colonel Edwards, the officer charged with the investigation—and urged, in fact, to make it an open-and-shut case. Edwards suspects—correctly, of course—that there's more to the story. *Time Limit* and *The Rack* share an approach to their subject that refrains from either simple condemnation or easy acceptance of collaborative behavior by prisoners of war.

War Hunt. Dir. Denis Sanders. United Artists, 1962.
Set late in the Korean War, this film depicts the conflict as a matter of violence and desolation that could be embraced only by a psychopath who loves to kill for killing's sake. There is such a figure in the film: a veteran loner named Raymond Endore (John Saxon), who makes personal raids across the line at night to kill the enemy one at a time. Endore's foil is Private Roy Loomis, played by Robert Redford in his first movie role. Loomis is a newcomer to the war who attempts to learn the ropes just to survive; indeed, his journey from innocence to experience begins with this unsettling greeting from a Korean woman:

"Welcome to Korea. I hope you don't die." The screenplay is by Stanford Whitmore, whose story "Lost Soldier" appears in this anthology.

See also Edwards, Paul M. *A Guide to Films on the Korean War*. Westport, Conn.: Greenwood Press, 1997.

Poetry of the Korean War

Ehrhart, W. D., ed. *I Remember: Soldier-Poets of the Korean War*, vol. 9, no. 2 of *War, Literature & the Arts*, Fall/Winter 1997.

This special issue of a humanities journal published by the English Department of the US Air Force Academy includes a lengthy historical and literary essay on Korean War poetry by the editor, extensive biographical and bibliographical information on the six Korean War veteran-poets in *Retrieving Bones*, and a large selection of their poetry, including the full text of Rolando Hinojosa's *Korean Love Songs*. Most of the publications in which these poems originally appeared are all but unavailable. Any further exploration of Korean War poetry should begin with this journal issue.

Chronology

1945

February: As the Philippines are liberated from Japan, Robert O. Bowen is released from POW camp and discharged from Navy. He had served since 1937.

August 9: Declaring war on Japan and belatedly entering the Pacific theatre of World War II, Soviet forces invade Manchuria and advance toward northern Korea.

August 15: Japan surrenders, ending both World War II and 40 years of Japanese colonial rule in Korea. Agreement divides Korea into US and Soviet occupation zones along the 38th parallel.

September 8: US occupation forces land at Inchon and occupy southern Korea.

September: Vern Sneider, after serving in the Army (1941–1944) and with the US Military Government on Okinawa, is transferred to South Korea as administrator of welfare and education functions of Kyonggi province (which includes the capital city of Seoul).

1946

Eugene Burdick, Stanford Whitmore, and William Chamberlain end military service. Each saw active duty during World War II, Burdick and Whitmore in the Pacific.

March to May: US–USSR Joint Commission on reunifiying the northern and southern occupation zones of Korea meets in Seoul. Discussions deadlocked.

November 23: French navy shells Hai Phong, Vietnam; start of French Indochina War or First Indochina War.

1947

Henry Steiner leaves South Korea, where he had worked as a civil engineer.

1948

August 15: US Military Government turns over power to the Republic of Korea (ROK) under President Syngman Rhee.

September 9: Democratic People's Republic of Korea (DPRK) inaugurated in Pyongyang; Kim Il Sung proclaimed premier.

December 25: Soviet army withdraws from North Korea. Advisers remain.

1949

June 29–30: Last US troops withdrawn from South Korea. Advisers remain.

August: Sporadic fighting between ROK and DPRK armed forces across 38th parallel intensifies.

October: Communist forces under Mao Tse-tung defeat Chiang Kai-shek's Nationalist army and establish the Democratic People's Republic of China.

1950

January 1: US formally recognizes ROK; appoints John J. Muccio ambassador.

January 12: Secretary of State Dean Acheson states that the Western defense perimeter of the United States stops short of South Korea.

June 25: North Korean People's Army [NKPA] invades South Korea.

June 27: United Nations asks member countries to aid the Republic of Korea. President Truman announces US intervention.

June 28–29: Seoul captured by NKPA.

July: Keith Wilson arrives in Korean waters, newly commissioned from United States Naval Academy, to begin the first of three naval tours.

July 1: First US troops begin arriving in Korea.

July 3: Rolando Hinojosa arrives in Korea. Serves as tank crewman.

July 5: Task Force Smith (commanded by Lieutenant Colonel Charles B. Smith) makes first contact with NKPA near Osan. US forces take heavy casualties and retreat.

July 7: UN creates United Nations Command under General Douglas MacArthur, who already commands all US forces in the Far East and is military governor of occupied Japan.

July 20: Major General William F. Dean captured by North Koreans. Highest ranking US POW of the Korean War. US/ROK forces still retreating.

August 1–4: US/ROK forces under Lieutenant General Walton Walker establish Pusan Perimeter in southeastern Korea. NKPA holds 90% of South Korea. Heavy fighting over next six weeks as NKPA strives for complete victory.

September 15: US Marines and soldiers land at Inchon (MacArthur's daring offensive) just west of Seoul and well behind NKPA lines.

September 16: US/ROK troops begin breakout from Pusan Perimeter; North Korean troops retreat north.

September 28–29: Seoul retaken by US/ROK troops.

September 30: ROK troops cross 38th parallel.

October: John Deck begins four-year Navy enlistment. Serves as crewman on anti-submarine patrol aircraft off the Korean coast.

October 7: US troops invade North Korea; UN sanctions US/ROK attempt to reunify country. Early story of the Korean War, John H. Holland's "Commuter's War," published in *Collier's*.

October 19: US forces take North Korean capital (Pyongyang).

October 26: ROK troops reach Chinese border (Yalu River).

November 1: Communist Chinese Forces (CCF) ambush and maul US forces at Unsan, then disengage as quickly as they appeared. US intelligence badly underestimates both the presence and the size of CCF in North Korea.

November 15: James Magner arrives in Korea.

November 24: MacArthur initiates "Home by Christmas" offensive, but advance almost immediately becomes retreat in the face of massive and unanticipated CCF counteroffensive. US suffers defeats at the Chongchon River and Chosin Reservoir (more appropriately referred to as Changjin Reservoir, its Korean name).

November 25: William Chamberlain publishes "The Enemy Beach," his first of several *Saturday Evening Post* stories of the Korean War.

December 5: US forces abandon Pyongyang.

December 15: US/ ROK armies withdraw below 38th parallel.

December 23: General Walker killed in jeep accident. Lieutenant General Matthew Ridgway succeeds him as commander of Eighth Army.

December 24: Last US/ROK forces evacuate North Korea via port of Hungnam.

December 30: US Air Force planes encounter Communist Chinese MiG-15 fighters near Yalu River.

1951

Marguerite Higgins's *War in Korea: The Report of a Woman Combat Correspondent* published.

January 3–4: Seoul recaptured by CCF/NKPA.

January 14: US/ROK retreat halts at 37th parallel.

February 1: UN abandons goal of reuniting Korea by force of arms; votes to end fighting by "peaceful means."

February 15: James Magner wounded in action and evacuated.

March 18: Seoul retaken by US/ROK forces.

March 24: Eugene Burdick's "Cold Day, Cold Fear" published in *Collier's*.

April 11: MacArthur relieved as Supreme Commander. Ridgway appointed.

April 14: General James Van Fleet takes over command of Eighth Army.

April–June: battle lines shift alternately north and south as CCF/NKPA and US/ROK forces press offensives and counteroffensives; Seoul remains in US/ROK hands.

June 13: US/ROK forces once again established at 38th parallel.

June 23: Soviet UN delegate Jacob Malik proposes truce.

July 10: Truce negotiations open at Kaesong.

August: Pat Frank's novel *Hold Back the Night* published. Most important early novel of the Korean War.

August–October: US forces launch a series of limited attacks to consolidate lines: Punchbowl, Bloody Ridge, Heartbreak Ridge.

August 22: Truce talks suspended.

September: Henry Steiner's "Rice" published in *Antioch Review*.

September 2: Rolando Hinojosa leaves Korea.

October 25: Truce talks resume, this time at Panmunjom.

November–April 1952: Stalemate continues along 38th Parallel.

1952

James Drought begins two-year hitch with 82nd Airborne Division at Fort Bragg, N.C. Serves as paratrooper and public relations writer.

US now paying two-thirds cost of French war in Vietnam.

January: Donald R. Depew arrives in Korea to serve as sergeant in Quartermaster Corps.

April: Reg Saner arrives in Korea.

May 7: Brigadier General Francis Dodd, commander of the US/ROK-run prisoner compound on Koje-do, an island off the South Korean coast, captured by Communist POWs and held hostage until May 11.

May 12: General Ridgway assumes command of NATO; General Mark Clark replaces Ridgway.

June–October: Continuing stalemate along battlefront; truce talks deadlocked, largely over issue of POW repatriation. Communist China and North Korea insist that all POWs must be repatriated. US refuses to forcibly repatriate POWs who do not want to be returned.

September: William Childress arrives in Korea; Donald R. Depew leaves

October 8: Truce talks recessed; complete deadlock.

November: Republican candidate and former General of the Army Dwight D. Eisenhower defeats Democratic candidate Adlai E. Stevenson for the presidency of the US (Truman having chosen not to run for re-election); will take office in January 1953. William Wantling arrives in Korea.

December 2–5: Eisenhower visits Korea, keeping a campaign promise.

1953

Stanford Whitmore's "Lost Soldier" published in Winter issue of *Accent*.

January: Reg Saner leaves Korea.

January 3: William Chamberlain's "The Trapped Battalion" published in *Saturday Evening Post*.

February 11: General Maxwell D. Taylor replaces General Van Fleet at Eighth Army.

March: Donald R. Depew's "Indigenous Girls" published in *Harper's Monthly*.

March 5: With the death of Joseph Stalin, new Soviet Premier Georgi Malenkov talks of peaceful coexistence.

March–June: Bloody hill battles; heavy fighting all along front as NKPA/CCF and US/ROK forces each try to achieve most favorable final truce line.

March 30: Truce talks resume at Panmunjom.

April: Keith Wilson leaves Korean waters, concluding the third of three naval tours.

April 16–18: Battle for Pork Chop Hill.

April 20–26: Exchange of sick and wounded POWs.

June: James Michener's *The Bridges at Toko-Ri* published.

June 25: Rhee balks at final truce terms, which all but guarantee a divided Korea for generations to come; finally agrees on July 7 only after great pressure from US

July 27: Cease-fire signed at Panmunjom.

August: William Childress leaves Korea.

1954

Robert O. Bowen's "A Matter of Price" published in *Prairie Schooner*. US suppling 80% of French war expenditures in Vietnam.

May 7: French defeated by Viet Minh at Dien Bien Phu, effectively ending the First Indochina War.

July: Vietnam split at 17th parallel as part of Geneva Accords; like the division of Korea in 1945, this too is supposed to be only a temporary division.

1956

South Vietnamese President Ngo Dinh Diem, with full backing of the US, refuses to hold reunification elections. US assumes full responsibility for training South Vietnamese Army.

Published: Sneider's collection *A Long Way from Home and Other Stories*, James Salter's *The Hunters*, Thomas Anderson's *Your Own Beloved Sons*, S. L. A. Marshall's *Pork Chop Hill*. Eugene Burdick and William J. Lederer publish *The Ugly American*, a novel about Vietnam.

1957

Mark Power serves in Korea from late 1957 to early 1959. Martin Russ's *The Last Parallel* published. Film *China Gate* links American involvements in Korea and Vietnam.

1958

Last Communist Chinese troops leave North Korea. US troops remain, a deployment which continues into the present.

1960

Protests and student demonstrations drive Syngman Rhee into exile in Hawaii. He is replaced by a succession of military and quasi-military governments. Truly democratic elections are not held until December 1997.

1961

John F. Kennedy becomes president. Sends US Army Green Berets to Vietnam.

1962

Albert B. Tibbets's *Courage in Korea* and William Chamberlain's *Combat Stories of World War II and Korea* published.

1965

March: President Lyndon B. Johnson orders systematic bombing of North Vietnam and sends first US combat troops into South Vietnam.

1966–1967

DMZ War in which US /ROK troops fight North Korean line-crossers in a test of US resolve as commitment in Vietnam accelerates. Several hundred US/ROK troops killed.

1968

January: US electronic spy ship *Pueblo* seized by North Korea. Communist Tet Offensive in South Vietnam begins.

Richard Hooker's M*A*S*H published.

1969

Keith Wilson's *Graves Registry and Other Poems* published.

April: US electronic spy plane shot down by North Korea.

1975

April 30: North Vietnamese and Viet Cong forces triumph in Vietnam, defeating US-backed South Vietnamese forces. The following year, North and South Vietnam are reunited politically to become the Socialist Republic of Vietnam.

1976

While pruning a tree in the Demilitarized Zone near Panmunjom, a US/ROK work party is attacked by North Korean soldiers; two American soldiers are killed, and four Americans and five South Koreans are wounded.

1978

Rolando Hinojosa's *Korean Love Songs* published.

1982

Vietnam Veterans Memorial completed and dedicated in Washington, DC.

1994

July: DPRK premier Kim Il Sung dies; succeeded by his son Kim Jong Il.

1995

Korean War Memorial completed and dedicated in Washington, DC.

1997

July 16: North and South Korean troops exchange mortar and machine-gun fire along the DMZ, another small episode in a continuous series of incidents since the truce was signed in July 1953.

Copyrights and Permissions

About the Editors

W. D. Ehrhart is a former Marine sergeant and veteran of the Vietnam War. He is author of numerous books of poetry and prose and editor of three previous anthologies. He has been a visiting professor at the William Joiner Center for the Study of War and Social Consequences, University of Massachusetts at Boston, and is currently a research fellow of the American Studies Department, University of Wales, Swansea, United Kingdom. He lives in Philadelphia, Pennsylvania, with his wife Anne and daughter Leela.

Philip K. Jason is professor of English at the United States Naval Academy in Annapolis. He has written several reference volumes and critical studies, three collections of poetry, and co-authored a creative writing text. Also, he has prepared two anthologies of poetry as well as collections of criticism on Anaïs Nin and on the literature of the Vietnam War. Editor of the journal *Poet Lore* since 1979, Jason and his wife Ruth divide their time between Annapolis, Maryland, and Naples, Florida.

~

The editors wish to thank the United States Naval Academy Research Council and the American Studies Department of the University of Wales at Swansea for their generous support of this project.